The Pacific States

TIME
LIFE
BOOKS ®

TIME-LIFE LIBRARY OF AMERICA
LIFE SCIENCE LIBRARY
LIFE NATURE LIBRARY
LIFE WORLD LIBRARY
GREAT AGES OF MAN
THE LIFE HISTORY OF THE UNITED STATES
TIME-LIFE LIBRARY OF ART
TIME READING PROGRAM
INTERNATIONAL BOOK SOCIETY

LIFE Pictorial Atlas of the World
The Epic of Man
The Wonders of Life on Earth
The World We Live In
The World's Great Religions
The LIFE Book of Christmas
LIFE'S Picture History of Western Man
The LIFE Treasury of American Folklore
America's Arts and Skills
300 Years of American Painting
The Second World War
LIFE'S Picture History of World War II
Picture Cook Book
LIFE Guide to Paris

TIME-LIFE Library of America

The Pacific
States

California Oregon Washington

By Neil Morgan
and the Editors of
TIME-LIFE BOOKS

Time Incorporated, New York

The Author: Neil Morgan, a North Carolinian by birth, became familiar with the West Coast during service with the Navy in World War II and moved there after the war. Now a daily columnist on San Diego affairs for the San Diego *Evening Tribune*, Mr. Morgan also writes a weekly column on Western matters, "Assignment West," which is syndicated to about 40 newspapers. A resident of La Jolla, he is the author of *Westward Tilt*, a study of 11 Western states, of which three are the subject of this volume in the TIME-LIFE Library of America.

The Consulting Editor: Oscar Handlin, Winthrop Professor of History at Harvard University and chairman of the university's Charles Warren Center for Studies in American History, is one of America's foremost social historians. His work on U.S. immigrants, *The Uprooted*, won the Pulitzer Prize in 1952.

Pacific States Consultant: Earl Pomeroy, Beekman Professor of History at the University of Oregon, is the author of *The Pacific Slope*, a history of the West.

The Cover: Gleaming in its spectacular Bay Area setting, San Francisco rises majestically beyond the graceful sweep of the Golden Gate Bridge.

TIME-LIFE BOOKS

Editor
Maitland A. Edey

Text Director   **Art Director**
Jerry Korn   Sheldon Cotler

Chief of Research
Beatrice T. Dobie

Assistant Text Directors:
Harold C. Field, Ogden Tanner

Assistant Chiefs of Research:
Monica O. Horne, Martha Turner

Publisher
Rhett Austell
General Manager: Joseph C. Hazen Jr.
Circulation Director: Joan D. Manley
Marketing Director: Carter Smith
Business Manager: John D. McSweeney
Publishing Board: Nicholas Benton,
Louis Bronzo, James Wendell Forbes

TIME-LIFE Library of America

Series Editor: Oliver E. Allen
Editorial Staff for *The Pacific States:*
Assistant Editors: Jay Brennan, David S. Thomson
Picture Editor: Grace M. Brynolson
Designer: Ben Schultz
Assistant Designer: John Newcomb
Staff Writers: Simon Johnson, Jonathan Kastner
Chief Researcher: Clara E. Nicolai
Text Research: Ruth Silva, Don Nelson,
Louise Samuels, Sondra Albert
Picture Research: Ellen Youngblood,
Sandra Van Doren, Diane Wynne

Editorial Production

Color Director: Robert L. Young
Assistant: James J. Cox
Copy Staff: Marian Gordon Goldman,
Patricia Miller, Dolores A. Littles
Picture Bureau: Margaret K. Goldsmith, Joan Lynch
Traffic: Douglas B. Graham
Art Assistant: Carol Iselin

The text for the chapters of this book was written by Neil Morgan, the picture essays by Simon Johnson and Jonathan Kastner. Valuable help was provided by these individuals and departments of Time Inc.: Chief of the LIFE Picture Library, Doris O'Neil; Chief of the Bureau of Editorial Reference, Peter Draz; Chief of the TIME-LIFE News Service, Richard M. Clurman; Correspondents Jane Estes (Seattle), Martha Green (San Francisco), Mayo Mohs and Carole Magnuson (Los Angeles), Robert Stein (Portland) and Tom Arden (Sacramento).

Contents

Introduction

At 16 I first came to the West, hitchhiking, riding freights and blind baggage on the Great Northern, the Northern Pacific, the Milwaukee Road. I worked the harvest out of Spokane, picked fruit near Wenatchee, got a job as a cook's helper on a ranch near Pendleton. The next summer I went back, and every summer after until I was 20. Mostly I worked for the Forest Service as a patrolman, or as cook and horse wrangler for trail crews and pack outfits in the spring drive or fall gathering. I have traveled on horseback with a pack mule loaded with pamphlets on healthful diet, razor-strop ointment, miracle can openers, mend-all glue and vegetable graters, high pitching by kerosene flares on windy corners in faraway cow towns.

All that was a lifetime ago. I was lucky to have been precocious enough to have caught the last of the Old West. But there is always a "last of the Old West." There are still vast tracks of country where the transistor and gasoline have not made all that much difference. There are still bits and tatters of the frontier surviving. Today the frontier has been internalized. From Seattle to San Diego, as Neil Morgan indicates in this volume, new kinds of life, new forms of human relationships are developing, not uniformly over the whole Pacific slope, but differently in the different regions.

There is an indisputable uniformity, however, behind the differences. Once I was flying from Flagstaff down to Phoenix to connect with a plane to San Francisco and the captain announced the temperature at Phoenix: 72° Fahrenheit (it was in the early autumn). Then he said, "Listen to this: Anchorage 72, Vancouver 72, Seattle 72, Portland 72, San Francisco 72, Los Angeles 72, San Diego 72." That does not happen very often, but it is highly unlikely to occur at all in any other part of the world over so immense a sweep of latitude. The inhabitants of the Pacific States are always talking about the climate, especially with Easterners, and it is true that there are more important things in life than climate. But the special conditions of the Pacific Coast have gone to help form a special quality of life.

It is a life free of many of the severe pressures that have operated in other environments, an outdoor life, and a well-fed one. Philosophers of history have questioned whether this is a good thing. Arnold Toynbee believes that civilizations develop in response to hard conditions. The Indians of the Pacific Coast states lived in the midst of so great a primitive abundance that they lost many of the talents they had brought with them when they came. A whole family could live well on the acorns from a small oak grove, the fish in the streams, the shellfish along the shore, and rabbits that they killed with sticks.

It will take a century or more to show whether modern civilization will thrive or decline in such an environment. Right now it thrives. Of course, already many people do not like it. A friend of mine once commented, flying into Los Angeles with me one evening above the millions of sparkling lights, "As Katherine Mansfield said of James Joyce's *Ulysses*, 'This is the future, and I'm glad I've got tuberculosis!'" Maybe. But what is certain is that although the old external frontier has largely passed away, a new internal frontier has opened out, into a new kind of life, and the possibility at least of profound changes in the quality of that life.

Many of the contradictions that beset and bedevil the communities of the West Coast are due to the conflict between these two ways of life: the spirit of the extractive industries—mining, oil, and once lumber, "get yours and get out"—and a new economy based on settled communities engaged in the work of the technological age, of jets and rockets and computers and automation. There is not only conflict, however; there is blending. Old and new share the sense of freedom and of unlimited possibilities, just as they share the natural background of mountains and sea, abundant food and sunshine.

Many students of population believe that the demands of the technological age and the welfare state are such that the centers of civilization will shift back once more to the Mediterranean—but a worldwide Mediterranean that includes Australia, New Zealand, Chile and the Pacific Coast of North America. So in all the West Coast communities the old Puritan ethic, shaped in conflict with an environment of storms and violent changes of weather, of struggle with nature, seems to be withering away, to be replaced, in widely varying degree, by the old "*vie Méditerranée*" of interpersonal laissez faire and *dolce far niente*, of wide tolerance and easy manners. This is disturbed by the tremendous population explosion and an unparalleled prosperity.

The West Coast is now undergoing a time of stress and strain, but the stresses and strains are absorbed and buffered by a new resilience in the society. This does not mean the West Coast cities and states are all alike. Seattle is marked by the Alaska Gold Rush, and largely settled by people from the northern Plains and Midwest states. Oregon was colonized by the overland migration of groups, many of them under religious leadership, and it shares with Maine, Indiana and Kansas a strong lingering flavor of the past that we think of as "typically American"—Puritan, Populist, progressive. Los Angeles is a special phenomenon, a City of the Future, with hardly a past and with a chaotic present. Most urbanists consider it a horrible example of how not to be a city, but the public thinks differently. More people have migrated to Southern California since the last war than took part in all the Great Migrations at the end of the Roman Empire.

San Francisco, too, is a special case. It is the only city in the Northern U.S. untouched by the overland spread of the New England Puritan tradition. It was first settled mostly by sea, and by rascals. The Gold Rush drew the adventurers and hippies of 1849 to San Francisco and drove the squares north to Oregon. The city has never lost the character it acquired in those days. Far more than Barcelona or Marseilles or Naples, San Francisco is today the true home of *la vie Méditerranée*. From postwar San Francisco have come ways of dressing, styles of painting, new kinds of poetry and music—jazz or electronic—and, more fundamentally, a new attitude toward life, which taken all together make up a worldwide cultural revolution.

I am writing this in Munich. In the café on the corner are paintings by a San Francisco artist. In the record shop next door, records by John Handy,

the revolutionary young jazz musician who lives down the street from me at home, are on display—along with records by several San Francisco rock groups, and even some by me, Lawrence Ferlinghetti and Kenneth Patchen. Young people with long hair, beards and bare feet, carrying guitars, speak to me in the English Garden—they sing Peter, Paul and Mary or Bob Dylan with no trace of accent—and then I discover that they speak less English than I do German, and have never been out of Munich in their lives. But they know all about the Haight-Ashbury District and the Fillmore Auditorium. *Gammlers? Reds? Beatniks?* Maybe. But the people in expensive imitations of the mode Carnaby Street–Haight-Ashbury are hardly beatniks.

What both types actually represent are the ever-increasing secession from the old industrial society of the exploitation of human labor power as the source of all economic life. They are people who have moved into the new technological society, the electronic age, without asking anybody's permission. This is the real secret of the difference in the culture of the West Coast and the rest of America, and the explanation of the role that San Francisco plays in the continuous orientation and stimulation of new elements of that culture. The inhabitants of the Pacific Coast are in the front rank of a world revolution that will make a far greater difference in human life than either the French or the Russian Revolutions, or both of them together.

Of course it is fun to ski and swim all year round, to eat in San Francisco's unsurpassed restaurants, to catch trout in the Sierras and skin dive for abalones at Big Sur, to have friends whose poetry, painting, music or dance is making a difference all over the world, but what is most important is, first, effectiveness and respect (San Francisco is the only city on earth in which poetry is an important social force) and second, the exciting sense that we are part of a still more important force— a revolution in ever-increasing self-determination, and a responsibility which continuously grows more aware of what it is doing, something the participants in the revolutions of the past have notoriously not been. To reverse the epigram of Marx—we are changing history, but we are also beginning to understand it. By "we" I do not mean beatniks and throwers of bombs, but poets and physicists, painters and engineers, playwrights and even an amazing number of businessmen, who together are creating a new, unique, West Coast civilization.

—Kenneth Rexroth,
Poet and critic

1

The

Restless Edge

As the wagon trains moved westward across America a century ago, small bands of pioneers in Oregon and California were urging that the Pacific Coast be declared an independent republic. They sensed something unique about this rugged shoreland of blue and green and gold, set apart by mountains higher and deserts drier than those encountered by any other American settlers. They already suspected that it was an abundant land, rich in resources, that could become self-sufficient. They had found it, and some of them, perhaps touched by greed, proposed to keep it. But the independence movement won little support. It became quickly evident that this coast was to provide the setting for a lusty and ebullient phase in the national history of the United States. It still does.

The waves crash against the land, a jagged outthrust arc from Canada to Mexico, as they have for centuries. It is a sudden land; cliffs surge up out of the sea to flat-topped mesas and valleys and hills, where the cities are built, and then, always present like a backdrop to the stage, the mountains rise.

Beyond may lie fertile valleys or desert crags, but from the widest valley or the driest waste, you look up toward mountains. Ski slopes soar above desert swimming pools; new housing tracts tear into serene mountainsides. In the cities the senses are assaulted by images of newness and motion.

Peopled by Americans from other states in a massive, continuing migration, the West Coast has become the epitome of changing America. It has never been let alone long enough to grow static. In the minds of many of the millions who have moved to California, Oregon and Washington, the Coast is like a large country that has come into being within the last generation or two. Settlement and growth have been so rapid that to some of the newcomers the region appears to have been born full-grown—but with complications. The citizen of the West Coast still seeks to wrest the land from nature. Full of hope and industry, he dreams of building a better world in this still-fresh and malleable region. The exuberance of his dream affects all who come to the West Coast; the drama of the Western setting makes the realization of the dream seem a possibility.

Along the Pacific Coast, America does not slope down so gradually from mountains to sea as it does along the Atlantic seaboard. Anyone who sails

Bathers splash through the surf at Malibu, one of the many fine stretches of sand in the Los Angeles area. In all, the West Coast has more than 2,700 miles of shoreline, made up of sandy beaches, rocky cliffs and quiet coves, where nearby residents can play.

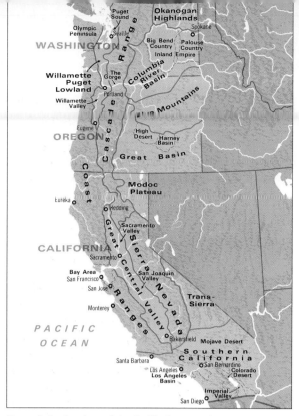

The varied subregions of the Pacific States and geographic areas within them are shown above. Many subregions—like the Cascade Range—are named for natural features. Other names—like that of Southern California, which occupies only about half of the southern part of the state—are the result of local custom.

from Puget Sound to San Diego Harbor will sense the wonder that has excited explorers and spurred settlers. Near the start there are snug, wooded islands off Seattle, followed by great forests reaching into the clouds atop the Olympic Peninsula, by the lonely Washington coast, and then by the churning mouth of the mighty Columbia, the waterway of the Northwest, which here forms the border between Washington and Oregon. The Oregon coast is wild, rocky and solitary, battered by giant waves and winds carrying the force of their 4,500-mile sweep across the Pacific. The cities of the Northwest do not lie beside the sea. One sees little evidence that man has conquered this coast; it is still a place for Indians and, in the summer, for those who seek a quiet retreat. Only rarely from offshore can the coastal highway be seen at the edge of the forests. The receding mountains are carpeted green by the fir and spruce and then the redwood. As the coastline reaches out at Cape Mendocino to its apogee and begins its eastward retreat, it has already become California. Rivers named Klamath, Mad and Eel find their turbulent way down to the surf. The forests thicken and grow darker as the redwoods grow taller. This is the land of brown trout and black-tailed deer, of mountain and rain forest, of buckthorn and fog-hung cliffs.

The Golden Gate looms as a stunning surprise, the urbane skyline of San Francisco interrupting more than a thousand miles of coastline along which the largest settlements have been slow-paced towns, most of them concerned with lumber or pulp, cheese or fishing. Once south of San Francisco the towns present familiar names. Where the sea pushes back the land in a great, sweeping indentation lies Monterey, the first capital of California. Its peninsula is gilded now with the homes of the well-to-do—some of them third- or fourth-generation descendants of those who heeded the call of Western gold and silver, some of them refugees from the first families of the East. Just to the south, where the Santa Lucia Mountains leap suddenly from the sea, the scattered houses of the community of Big Sur crouch on sheer, awesome cliffs that rise 800 feet above the water; behind great slabs of plate glass, Big Sur residents look down on crashing surf and barking sea lions. In these waters are the seething crosscurrents of converging tides that often make the central California coast hazardous for small craft. Along this coast, paralleling the unseen Great Central Valley that lies inland, one passes range country—both cattle and missile.

The coast veers due east at Point Conception. The mountains that swell up from the sea become the Tehachapi, and Southern California is at hand. To the south lies the placid harbor of Santa Barbara, and off to the west is San Miguel, the first of the dry, mostly barren offshore islands that seem magnified and elevated against the setting sun. Seagoing traffic grows thicker, and the voyager more frequently observes the glint of sunlight reflected by automobiles moving on coastal highways, by homes clinging to cliffsides or by glass-walled office towers. Los Angeles goes on seemingly forever but in due course merges imperceptibly into neighboring Long Beach. Then the chain of coastal towns continues until the boat rounds Point Loma to finish its voyage in the sheltered natural harbor of San Diego, where the first Spanish settlement in California was established in 1769.

The view from the sea gives little hint of the contrasts that lie inland. Seldom is the land dull or tiring to the eye. California alone offers almost as much physical diversity as the other 49 states, and examples of nearly all the geologic processes that shaped the earth. The heralded California climate is the sunny subtropical one of the southern coastal area, but in fact there are many climates. In the deserts along the eastern border summer temperatures are frequently the highest in the nation;

winter minimums in the Sierra Nevada or on the northeastern plateau are close to the coldest. The eastern deserts are brutally dry; the forests of northwestern California, like those of western Oregon and of the Olympic Peninsula of Washington, are among the wettest regions of the North American continent. From north to south, California ranges across nearly 10 degrees of latitude (about the same span as that from Cape Cod to Savannah on the opposite coast) and encompasses within its borders the highest (except for Alaska) and the lowest points of the United States: 14,495-foot Mount Whitney, and Death Valley, which drops to 282 feet below sea level.

To best see the hand of man, one must travel by car. A coastal highway hugs cliffs and bores through forests; an eastern route holds to the high desert. The fastest and most heavily traveled is a central freeway system that links the highly urbanized areas of the Pacific States. From the little harbor town of Blaine, where the stolid Peace Arch marks the border between Washington and the Canadian province of British Columbia, it is more than 1,400 miles by this route to the somnolent village of San Ysidro and the dry Tijuana River bed, which marks the end of California and the start of Mexican Baja California.

Driving south from Canada through the towns that face the majestic San Juan Islands, the first metropolis the traveler encounters is Seattle, a city of hills and lakes set on Puget Sound between the mountainous Olympic Peninsula and snow-crested Mount Rainier. Its smaller neighbor to the south is Tacoma, a city of electrochemical and forest industries, garnished with stately homes. Then the freeway unwinds through rolling farmlands to the Columbia River and across to Portland. Less spectacular than Seattle, it is another hill city, an inland river port.

Portland lies in the rich Willamette Valley, the historic center of Oregon settlement and agriculture. Oregon pioneers came mainly from the Midwest and from the Middle Atlantic States, but many of them had begun their move in New England. They brought with them the Eastern place names that are often seen here in the Willamette: Portland, Salem, Albany, Springfield. Between the towns are neat fields of strawberries and beans or groves of filberts and walnuts. The valley, its people proclaim, is capable of feeding 12 million people. Its feel of rurality is heightened by trim white farmhouses, church spires and the brilliant hues of flower beds. But Oregon is the leading state in forest products, and as the highway climbs into the

Cascade Range in southwestern Oregon, the pastoral valley falls behind; the traveler now sees lumber trucks, bare mountainsides and tree farms.

It is still forestland as California highway builders take over the roadway and bring the traveler past the glacial cone of Mount Shasta, past the 602-foot-high Shasta Dam, and finally to the northern floor of the Great Central Valley, which runs like a trough for 450 miles down California between the coastal mountains and the higher Sierra Nevada inland. The valley makes up one sixth of the land area of California. Within it are no scenic majesties; the land is flat, the fields are immense, the towns and cities are repetitive. But from this highly mechanized farming area comes more than one third of the nation's fruits and vegetables—the heart of an annual farm crop, valued in excess of two billion dollars, that makes California the nation's leading agricultural state. The upper half of the Great Central Valley follows the path of the Sacramento River, whose waters are diverted by the vast Central Valley Project to irrigate the drier San Joaquin River Valley of the southern region.

At its southern end the valley is closed off by the Tehachapi Range; beyond is Southern California. The Los Angeles megalopolis, which some visionaries believe will eventually become a continuous urban area extending along the coast from Santa Barbara through Los Angeles to San Diego, lies within this tip. To enter it the freeway traveler winds over the Tehachapi at Tejon Pass and down into the San Fernando Valley. If he is attentive to freeway signs, he can speed without a stop for an hour or two through the core of the megalopolis and emerge on a scenic coastal highway where once again he will find open space. In the southwestern corner of California and the nation looms San Diego, placid and shining on the hills and mesas overlooking the sea and its glittering natural harbor. San Diego has become the third-largest Pacific Coast city (after Los Angeles and San Francisco) without the traditional catalysts of growth. Its mountains impede transcontinental commerce. It is not rich in natural resources. It is only lightly industrialized; it is oriented more toward its longtime role as a naval bastion, and toward tourism and research and educational complexes. No other American city owes its growth so much to superb climate.

Yet despite the sprawl of the cities of California and the size of the state's agricultural output, only 14 per cent of the land is urbanized or cultivated. Forestry is the major economic pursuit in nearly 20 per cent of the state and grazing in another 30

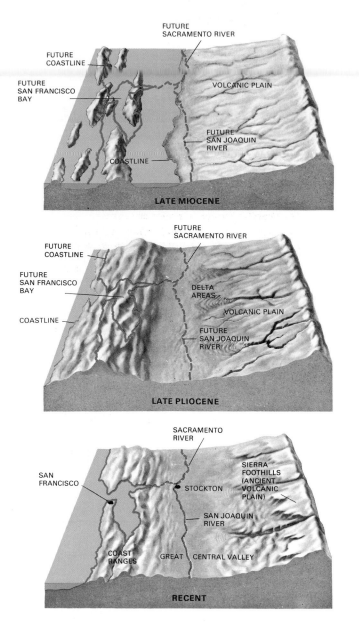

FUTURE
SACRAMENTO RIVER

FUTURE
COASTLINE

FUTURE
SAN FRANCISCO
BAY

VOLCANIC PLAIN

FUTURE
SAN JOAQUIN
RIVER

COASTLINE

LATE MIOCENE

FUTURE
SACRAMENTO RIVER

FUTURE
COASTLINE

FUTURE
SAN FRANCISCO
BAY

DELTA
AREAS

VOLCANIC PLAIN

COASTLINE

FUTURE
SAN JOAQUIN
RIVER

LATE PLIOCENE

SACRAMENTO
RIVER

SAN
FRANCISCO

SIERRA
FOOTHILLS
(ANCIENT
VOLCANIC
PLAIN)

STOCKTON

SAN JOAQUIN
RIVER

COAST
RANGES

GREAT CENTRAL VALLEY

RECENT

How part of California was formed

The geologic evolution of central California is shown in
the cross sections above. Toward the end of the Miocene
epoch, about 13 million years ago *(top)*, the coastline lay
far inland, perhaps near what are now the beds of the
Sacramento and San Joaquin Rivers. What is now the
eastern section of the Great Central Valley was a gentle
plain covered with volcanic debris from the Sierra
Nevada. The future Coast Ranges were a group of
offshore islands, remnants of once much higher
mountains. During the late Pliocene epoch *(middle)*, the
coastal mountains rose again, blocking the sea from the
plain. At the same time, the Sierra Nevada was being
eroded by streams that carried rich sediment into the
future Great Central Valley, forming a base for the valley's
fertile farmland. Over the centuries the ancient volcanic
plain has been eroded, bringing into existence the
present Sierra foothills. The coastal mountains, after
being eroded in the next geologic epoch, rose once more.
The mountains are still being eroded, a process creating
the familiar outlines of today's landscape *(bottom)*.

per cent. Even when the visitor has seen the Pacific
Coast from the sea and from its central freeways,
he has only begun to sense the vastness of California and the Northwest. There remain the great backbone of mountains, the ethereal high plateaus and
scorching low deserts to the east.

From San Diego another highway strikes out
northward toward the sheer east face of the Sierra Nevada, across the Mojave Desert, up between
Mount Whitney and Death Valley, through for-
saken regions where tiny towns cater to fishermen
and to hunters and hikers seeking out the wild side
of California. After passing alkali lakes and dry
lake beds, beneath the uptilted eastern rim of the
Sequoia, Kings Canyon and Yosemite National
Parks, the highway skirts Lake Tahoe, the favored
lake resort of Northern Californians. It then moves
northwestward to the isolated northeastern California plateau, an inhospitable lava country whose
few inhabitants vie for the sparse water supply and
limited cultivable land. Farther on, in eastern Oregon, one can drive for almost 40 miles through high
desert without sight of human or animal life. The
highway winds beside alkali-ridden Lake Abert and
by an escarpment whose rim rises 2,000 feet above
the desert, its lava cap ending in a sulfurous preci-
pice. The next town is Wagontire, and it is only a
house and a filling station.

Eastern Washington is more populous. The highway passes the Hanford plutonium works and moves
northeast through wheat country to Spokane, the
second-largest city of Washington. In rolling pine
forests close to the Idaho border, Spokane is a natural market and distribution center for the Inland
Empire, a region including the Idaho panhandle,
western Montana and northeastern Oregon, areas
isolated by mountains from the larger cities of their
own states.

From the air, finally, the moods and images of
the Pacific States blend into perspective. On a clear
day the northbound airline passenger can see California from the cobalt Pacific across green-blue
mountains to the beige desert. The offshore islands
are brown warts in the sea. Freight trains push
slowly up desert grades, looking like fallen bobby
pins on a drab carpet. Los Angeles fills its vast sau-
cer and spills over the San Gabriel Mountains and
the Hollywood Hills to the desert valleys. The Great
Central Valley is harassed by dust layers and fog
patches while nearby snow clouds truncate the
higher peaks of the Sierra Nevada and whiten the
granite domes of Yosemite. To the northwest the
graceful, wooded ridgeback of the San Francisco

Peninsula ends in the tiny thumb that is the city of San Francisco, a citadel of hill-borne towers beside the Golden Gate. Then come the darkening green of the Northern California forests, the plumes of smoke from lumber mills, the log rafts of the rivers and coastal waters. To the right rears the white peak of Mount Shasta, and ahead nestles the gleaming sapphire that is Crater Lake; beyond sprawls the wide, rich, graceful Willamette Valley. Mount Hood crowns the city of Portland, and then the widening Columbia River comes into view on the horizon, the Bonneville Dam upriver to the east. Western Washington valleys appear, surrounded by their family of peaks: Adams, Saint Helens and, stately above them all, the almost flawlessly formed Rainier. Over the tall mountains to the east are the white dot of Grand Coulee Dam and the green carpeting of the rich, irrigated farmland of Moses Lake Basin.

If one flies southward again after dark, the lights of Western cities and highways will outline the pattern of settlement and of transportation. In the central mountains and eastern deserts scattered grids of lights reveal the widely separated towns; not enough night traffic appears in these regions to delineate the highways. But near San Francisco and southward, seen from jet altitudes on clear evenings, the coastal and central freeways are ribbons of headlights. The large towns of the Great Central Valley —spaced at almost regular intervals—appear as swollen sunbursts along the freeway route. After a San Francisco takeoff a jetliner scarcely attains its cruising altitude before a glow appears in the distant southern sky: the airborne traveler is looking at the Southern California megalopolis beyond the dark curtain of the Tehachapi. To thousands of California air commuters the sight of those faraway lights is as familiar as home; no air route in the world is more traveled than that between San Francisco and Los Angeles.

More and more persons are becoming acquainted with such scenes. To this extravagantly varied coast, Americans are moving in numbers that dwarf the migrations of the California Gold Rush or the subsequent hectic movements along the Oregon Trail. The urge to wester has been inherent in the American temperament; to many the contemporary attractions of the Pacific States are as compelling as were those of free farmland and gold nuggets a century or more ago. The continuing migration to California since World War II has been the largest displacement of Americans in the national history; Oregon and Washington have shared in this movement, although to a lesser extent. Generally, these

The Pacific Ocean's shaky shores

The Pacific is girdled by a "ring of fire," a band of volcanic activity where earthquakes frequently occur *(above)*. The U.S. West Coast is subject to both types of disturbance *(below)*. Oregon and Washington are dotted with volcanoes, and California has been plagued by earthquakes. A weakness in the earth's crust called the San Andreas Fault, plus its possible extensions *(dotted lines)* and neighboring faults, has caused many tremors, including the San Francisco quake of 1906 (whose center was actually northwest of the city). Land on the west side of the fault strains northward, while land east of it presses southward. When tensions reach a sufficient level, there is movement—and earthquake.

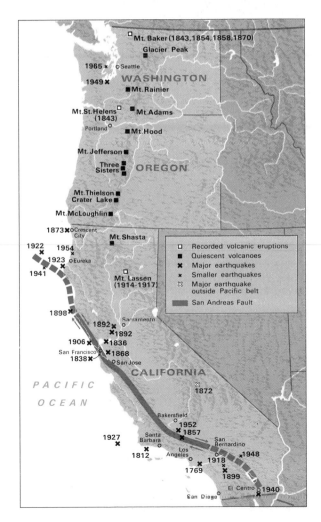

A variety of land types

The drawings on these pages show the five major land types—each with its own pattern of vegetation, animal life, terrain and climate—that are found in the Pacific States. In general, the land in the northwestern section of the region is wet, cool and mountainous; the southeastern section is dry, hot and low. Local variations in terrain or weather cause exceptions, but the greatest exceptions are brought about by man. In the hostile southeast, for instance, irrigation has turned desert areas into verdant oases. Economic and social activities also of course vary with the different sections.

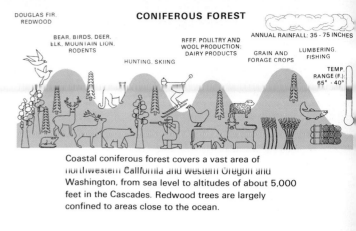

CONIFEROUS FOREST

DOUGLAS FIR, REDWOOD

BEAR, BIRDS, DEER, ELK, MOUNTAIN LION, RODENTS

BEEF, POULTRY AND WOOL PRODUCTION: DAIRY PRODUCTS

GRAIN AND FORAGE CROPS

LUMBERING, FISHING

HUNTING, SKIING

ANNUAL RAINFALL: 35 - 75 INCHES

TEMP. RANGE (F.): 65° - 40°

Coastal coniferous forest covers a vast area of northwestern California and western Oregon and Washington, from sea level to altitudes of about 5,000 feet in the Cascades. Redwood trees are largely confined to areas close to the ocean.

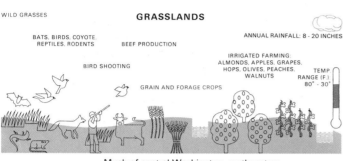

GRASSLANDS

WILD GRASSES

BATS, BIRDS, COYOTE, REPTILES, RODENTS

BEEF PRODUCTION

BIRD SHOOTING

IRRIGATED FARMING: ALMONDS, APPLES, GRAPES, HOPS, OLIVES, PEACHES, WALNUTS

GRAIN AND FORAGE CROPS

ANNUAL RAINFALL: 8 - 20 INCHES

TEMP. RANGE (F.): 80° - 30°

Much of central Washington, northeastern Oregon and the Great Central Valley is grassland. In these areas cultivated grasses like wheat and barley often grow successfully without irrigation. Irrigation is, however, necessary for most other crops.

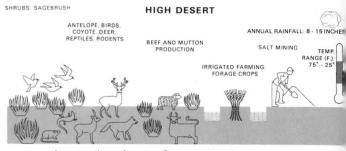

HIGH DESERT

SHRUBS: SAGEBRUSH

ANTELOPE, BIRDS, COYOTE, DEER, REPTILES, RODENTS

BEEF AND MUTTON PRODUCTION

SALT MINING

IRRIGATED FARMING: FORAGE CROPS

ANNUAL RAINFALL: 8 - 15 INCHES

TEMP. RANGE (F.): 75° - 25°

Large sections of eastern Oregon and northeastern California consist of cold, high desert, a land type found at altitudes of 4,000 to 7,500 feet and characterized by frosts and scant rainfall. These conditions deter most farming, but the sagebrush cover supports grazing.

---

new Westerners match or exceed the national median in economic status and schooling and are slightly older than the national median age. Although many of them bring old habits and seek to re-establish much of their former pattern of living, a basic implication of their migration from other parts of the nation is their readiness to accept new ways of life.

In their restless pushing, their striving for an infinite variety of things, the people of the Pacific States are more akin to one another than are the people of the East Coast of America to one another. They often share the same origins and mores and the same broad goal: the dream of some new and better society in which their individual economic status can be improved. There are few conventionally regional traits: no distinguishing dialect, dress or folklore. Most of the migrants have been Americans with a generation or more of heritage within the United States. They came to the Pacific States only recently, for even the earliest American settlement began only at the mid-point of the 19th Century; until then few knew this region but Indians, fur trappers and Mexican *vaqueros*. Moreover, while many settlers came to the West Coast in the late 19th and early 20th Centuries, the peak of migration was not reached until after World War II,

a century after California had achieved statehood. The perilous work of pioneering was done; the golden era of economic opportunity was at hand, and there was space for millions of Americans to share in it. The freshness of the West is a fact of history. The United States was on the verge of civil war when California and Oregon became states, and that war was long past when Washington achieved statehood. Yet these states have rapidly acquired characteristics that give them uniqueness on the national scene.

In a recently published study of the Pacific States the University of Oregon scholar Earl Pomeroy found the people to be more prosperous and more urban than the nation as a whole, more literate and more criminal. Pomeroy reported that the region "reads more, drinks more, goes to church less, and has more automobiles and smaller families. It is more in favor of birth control and also of foreign cars. Its people move more, travel more, camp out more. . . . It has more space, more wilderness, and also more suburbs and more new suburbanites and newcomers generally. . . . It produces more doctors than its share in the natural sciences and in education, slightly less than its share in the humanities, social sciences and arts, but has fewer . . . chemists, economists and historians. . . . It receives aca-

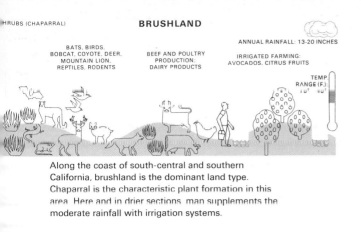

BRUSHLAND

HRUBS (CHAPARRAL)

ANNUAL RAINFALL: 13-20 INCHES

BATS, BIRDS,
BOBCAT, COYOTE, DEER,
MOUNTAIN LION,
REPTILES, RODENTS

BEEF AND POULTRY
PRODUCTION;
DAIRY PRODUCTS

IRRIGATED FARMING:
AVOCADOS, CITRUS FRUITS

TEMP.
RANGE (F.):
10° - 40°

Along the coast of south-central and southern
California, brushland is the dominant land type.
Chaparral is the characteristic plant formation in this
area. Here and in drier sections, man supplements the
moderate rainfall with irrigation systems.

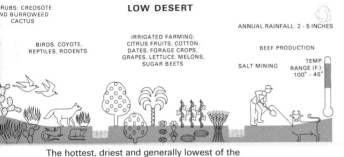

LOW DESERT

RUBS: CREOSOTE
ND BURROWEED
CACTUS

ANNUAL RAINFALL: 2 - 5 INCHES

BIRDS, COYOTE,
REPTILES, RODENTS

IRRIGATED FARMING:
CITRUS FRUITS, COTTON,
DATES, FORAGE CROPS,
GRAPES, LETTUCE, MELONS,
SUGAR BEETS

BEEF PRODUCTION

SALT MINING

TEMP.
RANGE (F.):
100° - 45°

The hottest, driest and generally lowest of the
five major land types, the low desert extends over most
of southeastern California. In the south, rich
soil from the old Colorado River delta provides
excellent land for irrigated farming.

demic honors much more than the rest of the nation."

The author Wallace Stegner, an adopted Californian, made similar observations in 1959. "In a prosperous country," he wrote, "we are more prosperous than most; in an urban country more urban than most; in a gadget-happy country, more addicted to gadgets; in a mobile country, more mobile; in a tasteless country, more tasteless; in a creative country, more energetically creative; in an optimistic society, more optimistic; in an anxious society, more anxious. Contribute regionally to the national culture? We *are* the national culture, at its most energetic end." Six years later he added: "What was true then is more true now. Population explosion, growth, suburban sprawl, air and water pollution, literary despair, the boldest scientific and technological adventurousness, increased leisure, the sexual revolution, the guilt and fear of the Bomb, widespread agnosticism, last-ditch religiosity, Birchite reaction—these are tunes that do not change when you cross the border into California. Only the volume goes up, the tape spins faster, the tempo accelerates toward a hysterical twittering."

This intense distillation of national characteristics is inherent in the westward march. It is a result both of transplanted mores and of adaptation. Since the people of California, Oregon and

Washington have come from every part of the United States, they have made the region an all-American melting pot. What the East Coast was for many years to Europeans, the West Coast is becoming to Americans: a place to escape—not famine or persecution, but clogged cities and stifling tradition; a place to begin again, where hopes and ambitions are not foredoomed by the ponderous social structures, lethargies or cluttered environments of older, more rigid communities.

For a century Western writers have insisted that the migrants to the Pacific Coast have constituted not a cross section of Americans but a selection of them. A corollary theme has been that this quasi-elite migration has spawned a society that is quintessentially American: the tides of American life first reach fruition, rejection or extremity in the West. Californians believe that their state is the cutting edge of America, the patron of change for fads and fashions and, in a broader sense, for economic, political and cultural evolution. Such a role is possible, they argue, because Californians are able to utilize the longer experience of the rest of the nation as a basis on which to build their society without the impediment of entrenched and possibly deteriorating power structures. In the East, where many remain mistrustful of the sudden size and strength of California, the state is sometimes dismissed as the breeding ground of kook and extremist, a barbecue culture held shakily in place by ribbons of freeways.

Something of both attitudes is valid. California's is still a young society. The urban Westerner appraises his acquaintances in terms of present and future interests, not family heritage or social position. Two Western strangers meeting for the first time will question each other unabashedly on matters like these: What brought you out here? Where do you come from? What do you do? Notably absent will be the probing, however subtle, that is familiar in more established regions on such matters as family, schooling or friends. The new Westerner senses more likelihood of an equal start with the next newcomer at his side, creating what the sociologist Carle C. Zimmerman has called communities of strangers. Having broken old ties in moving West, the migrant is often slow in making new ones. He is not likely to be deeply involved with his neighbors. In Los Angeles, after seeing a client almost daily in his offices for six years, a stockbroker asked for his home address in order to deliver some documents for signing. It was only mildly startling to the two men to discover that, for all those six years of business acquaintanceship,

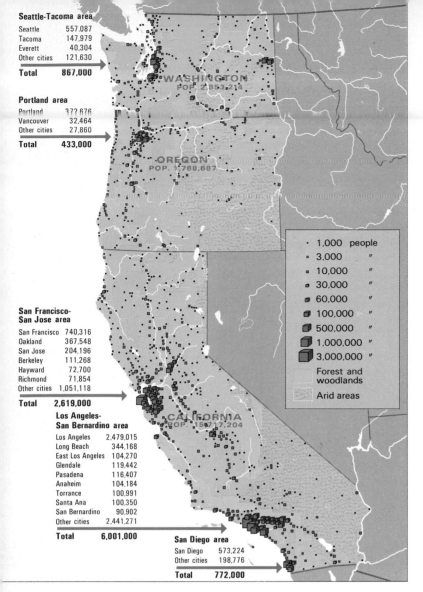

Seattle-Tacoma area

Seattle	557,087
Tacoma	147,979
Everett	40,304
Other cities	121,630
Total	**867,000**

Portland area

Portland	372,676
Vancouver	32,464
Other cities	27,860
Total	**433,000**

WASHINGTON POP. 2,853,214

OREGON POP. 1,768,687

San Francisco-San Jose area

San Francisco	740,316
Oakland	367,548
San Jose	204,196
Berkeley	111,268
Hayward	72,700
Richmond	71,854
Other cities	1,051,118
Total	**2,619,000**

Los Angeles-San Bernardino area

Los Angeles	2,479,015
Long Beach	344,168
East Los Angeles	104,270
Glendale	119,442
Pasadena	116,407
Anaheim	104,184
Torrance	100,991
Santa Ana	100,350
San Bernardino	90,902
Other cities	2,441,271
Total	**6,001,000**

CALIFORNIA POP. 15,717,204

San Diego area

San Diego	573,224
Other cities	198,776
Total	**772,000**

Legend:

- 1,000 people
- 3,000 "
- 10,000 "
- 30,000 "
- 60,000 "
- 100,000 "
- 500,000 "
- 1,000,000 "
- 3,000,000 "

Forest and woodlands

Arid areas

Urban growth in a rural setting

Where the people of the West Coast live is shown in the map above, based on 1960 census figures. In all three states most of the people are clustered in a few densely populated areas near the coast or in productive farm country, leaving forest and arid areas relatively uninhabited. California, which in 1964 became the most populous state in the U.S., ranks second among all states in percentage of people in urban areas, but because of its impressive size ranks only 13th in population density. Not only has it grown faster in recent years than Washington and Oregon (*below*) but more than twice as fast as any other state.

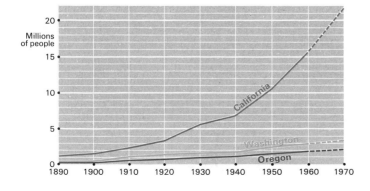

they had lived directly across a quiet residential street from each other.

Often such neighbors have come West and settled tentatively, expecting to stay in motion in their search. A sociological term—"anomie"—has found massive application in West Coast cities. Anomie is a condition of society, as Webster's puts it, "in which normative standards of conduct and belief have weakened or disappeared"; in the individual it is "characterized by personal disorientation, anxiety, and social isolation."

In such matters it seems reasonable to regard the Californian apart from the Northwesterner, if only because the Californian—insistently, though somewhat vaguely—is forever proclaiming his difference from everyone. The resident of Oregon or Washington is quick to concede the point; he will even imply gratefulness at being set apart from the Californian, who then, imbued with his feelings of destiny, ignores the Northwesterner's slur as though it were some jealous off-stage whisper.

Anomie is not so measurable in the Northwest as it is in California; this is because the phenomenon is a by-product of migration. Between 1940 and 1960 Oregon grew by about 700,000 people and Washington by slightly more than a million, but California expanded by nearly nine million. "One says 'West Coast'; one means, at least for the present, California," writes Wallace Stegner. "For comparatively the Pacific Northwest is still in the state of innocence." There are about four times as many persons living in California as in Oregon and Washington combined, and the specter of the south is an overshadowing one. Nothing unites the people of the Northwest more quickly than involvement in a regional dispute with California. The Northwest regards California with awe, resentment and despair. It fears being overwhelmed by California. Californians lead the parade of vacationers escaping to the quiet, green Northwest, and form a major market for Northwest forest products and fruit, but the Northwest is troubled by the fact that these same Californians talk of piping Columbia River water southward to support their growth; already, Northwesterners note, the Californians are funneling off Northwest electric power through an interstate grid.

The people of the Northwest seem more deeply rooted, less prone to extremes. They crave stability and are more skeptical of change than Californians. They look with alarm at the more capricious behavior of their less inhibited neighbors to the south.

Anthony Netboy, a professor of English at Portland State College, saw the region on another plane

How West Coast people differ

The bar graphs below illustrate ways in which people living on the West Coast differ from the national average. California has the greatest influence on the figures. However, except for the fact that Oregon lags in incomes over $10,000, the trends in the three states are similar.

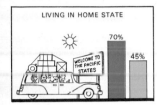

LIVING IN HOME STATE

70% 45%

Most Americans live in the state they were born in, but on the West Coast more than half do not.

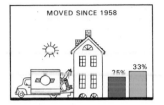

MOVED SINCE 1958

25% 33%

Even after arriving on the Coast, people continue to move more often than people elsewhere.

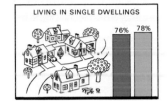

LIVING IN SINGLE DWELLINGS

76% 78%

A slightly higher percentage of people on the Pacific Coast live in single-family dwellings.

MEDIAN FAMILY INCOME

$5,660 $6,580

West Coast families tend to have larger incomes than the average for the nation as a whole.

INCOMES $10,000 OR ABOVE

15% 20%

A larger percentage of families on the Coast have incomes of $10,000 or more a year.

INCOMES UNDER $3,000

21% 16%

Fewer families living on the West Coast have incomes of less than $3,000 a year.

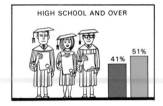

HIGH SCHOOL AND OVER

41% 51%

People growing up on the West Coast, or moving to it, tend to complete more years of schooling.

USE OF PUBLIC TRANSPORT

12% 7%

Workers on the West Coast are less likely to use public transportation than other workers.

---

in a foreword to a volume examining the temper, environment and atmosphere of the Pacific Northwest published not long ago: "People attracted there seem to share the same penchant for natural beauty, for responding to challenge, for being resourcefully independent and yet conservative. . . ." The furor over the preservation of Northwest forests and rivers suggests an intense pride in the land. In Portland and Seattle the arguments for conservation make it clear that these people feel a deep kinship with their environment.

Portland and Seattle, the two urban centers of the Northwest, are not alike. Seattle is an intriguing blend of aggressive growth patterns and leisurely, open-armed living. It is stable but lively, its people deeply conscious of esthetics; to many the setting of Seattle is more beautiful than that of San Francisco. The city came to raucous life with the Alaska gold booms, and it has not lost the naughty twinkle in its eyes. It is a rugged but naïve place, expectant, overwhelmingly friendly. There is considerable rivalry with Portland; Seattleites enjoy pointing out that Oregon's Mount Hood is not so high as Washington's Rainier, nor Portland so large as Seattle. As with San Francisco and Los Angeles, the rivalries are long-standing. Portland was an established city when Seattle was a camp. Portland

is demure, conservative, eager to identify with its Rose Festival and the glories of Mount Hood—although during much of the year cold, rain or snow renders both roses and mountains invisible. The Portland economy has had wide swings between wartime shipbuilding booms and postwar lumber recessions; the city has grown when it did not expect to and stood still when it thought itself growing, and its civic ego has sometimes been battered into lethargy. It has made impressive civic advances, but many members of its old guard retain a nostalgic leaning that has impeded cohesive civic action and fended off sophistication as inherently suspect.

Despite such traits a new mobility has seeped into urban life in Portland and Seattle. It bespeaks change. One in three families now changes residence each year, compared with a national average of one in five. The ratio approaches that of California cities, which have the most extreme mobility in America. Such residential movement is closely related to the driftlessness of anomie. In the San Francisco Bay area two out of five families move each year, twice the national level; in Southern California one in two families moves each year. Californians tend to buy and sell their homes like cars. Since they are living in a community of strangers, with the family often regarded as the ultimate social unit, there is less reluctance to change residence than there is in more established communities.

Californians move when they change jobs, when new freeways open, or when new tracts offer houses with more gadgetry or lower down payments. As a family grows larger or smaller, it is less inclined than an Eastern family to add a room or close off a wing. Moving-van firms regard Southern California as their richest market. Half a million residents even live in homes with wheels. Here the trailer has graduated into something called the mobile home —a mammoth unit that expands to twice its normal width on arrival at its destination. One fifth of all mobile-home parks in America are found in California.

The apex of California mobility has perhaps been reached east of Los Angeles in San Bernardino County, the largest county in the nation. There, an Air Force captain who had moved his family 12 times in 32 months said: "It doesn't seem to matter much. We go from one tract house to another and they're all about the same. You get used to the next one after a week or so. There's always a good new school not too far away, and a shopping center where my wife can pick up the same kind of specials."

Since so many Californians have come from other states, breaking old roots as they left, it is understandable that they keep moving in California. They drive longer distances as freeway commuters. They take more business trips and more pleasure trips. The people of California cities are found in great numbers on transcontinental jet flights. Their perpetual motion reflects their high level of prosperity and leisure, their vigor and their ready adaptability to restless contemporary trends.

A symptom of anomie that is more difficult for the Californian to rationalize is his involvement with his automobile. "The national flower in this country today is the 'cloverleaf,'" the author and critic Lewis Mumford has remarked. Nowhere is that flower in such abundant bloom as in California. Gasoline taxes and a powerful hierarchy in the California Division of Highways have led to the most intricate multilane highway system ever constructed. The automobile has become the symbol of Southern California living—a factor in, and a response to, the horizontal sprawl of cities lacking rapid-transit systems.

No other city so large as Los Angeles is so young; soon after it became a metropolis it began to place unusual reliance on the automobile—so great that interurban rail lines have lapsed into oblivion. By the early 1980s three adjacent Southern California counties—Los Angeles, Orange and Ventura— alone will have been slashed by a network of 1,535 miles of freeway to be built at a cost of $5.2 billion, more than one third of it is already in existence. By 1980 there will be an estimated 17 million motor vehicles on California highways. The inevitable result of such numbers is another California superlative: even today the state boasts the nation's greatest highway carnage, more than 4,000 deaths each year. The mayhem does not discourage movement. In San Diego not long ago, a newspaper reader telephoned from a community 20 miles distant to ask for late reports on a Caribbean hurricane. As an editor sought the information, the caller hung up, only to appear in the city room 30 minutes later to repeat his question. "You took so long I had to hang up," he explained. "After all, that was a long-distance call."

There is a seeming parallel between such extreme mobility and the woes of West Coast society: indifference to metropolitan planning, high divorce and suicide rates, uneven participation in community and cultural affairs, and soaring crime rates. The sense of community responsibility is blurred in so fluid a society. Yet this Western rootlessness may be merely an acceleration of a national trend. Indeed, the Californian is convinced that his state is setting a pattern for the country as a whole. More than one third of the people of the three Pacific States live in the narrow coastal strip of Southern California; for the sociologist the region might someday serve as a laboratory for the study of national trends.

It is undeniable that the West Coast has become a center of innovation, an unorthodox land that attracts those of high energy and adventurous spirit. Gargantuan California is often called a subnation. The Northwest is rich in the few resources California lacks, notably water and power. Few regions are as well endowed to stand alone as the Pacific States. In that sense the Pacific Coast nation proposed by early settlers was not an absurd idea.

Much of the lure of this new land is nebulous, some of it simply the pull of a fresh world. Perhaps no other regional literature abandons itself so recklessly to excesses of description as that of the Far West. Even so, the newcomers show little feeling that the region has failed to live up to its notices. They tend instead to accept the West as their own. Like the pioneers, they believe that the West offers a chance for a better life, and they intend to be part of it. The West has become the most dynamic region of America. It is the restless edge of the American society.

Dramatic variety and sudden change

As though intended as a model for the whole world, the Pacific States are endowed with nearly every geographical and climatic condition the earth can boast. Everywhere is a sense of dramatic confrontation—of crashing breakers and sheer cliffs, of fertile valleys and sere wasteland, of junglelike rain forests and snowy peaks. As one spectacular scene gives way to another, one climate dissolves into another just as quickly—the arctic cold of the mountaintops gives way to the Mediterranean balminess of the south coast or to the Saharan heat of the desert. In this near-paradise man has raised cities, sown fields and built factories, joining them all with white ribbons of superhighway. Speed and mobility are his watchwords: wherever he is, he is never more than a short drive from the sudden beauty of another kind of land.

Squeezed between mountains and an arm of the sea lies the Washington city of Bellingham. Though canneries and shipyards lie where virgin forest stood less than a century ago, the land has lost little of its beauty, and stately Mount Baker is unchanged.

19

Puget Sound, a basin rimmed by prosperous cities

Presided over by lofty, glistening Mount Rainier (*left background*), the southern half of Puget Sound and its surrounding cities bask in the midday sun. The area's chief metropolis, Seattle, first boomed in 1898 shortly after gold was discovered in the Klondike—selling the miners their supplies proved a profitable business. More important in the long run to Seattle and to the other communities such as Tacoma and Olympia that ring the sound (*see diagram at right*) have been agriculture, lumbering and, in recent decades, the aircraft industry.

Puget Sound itself has also been vital to the region's growth. A salt-water arm of the Pacific, it is navigable throughout its length. Seattle and several neighboring cities have become busy seaports, although they are more than 100 miles from the open ocean. Today the area is becoming rapidly urbanized as the cities expand to meet one another. But the beautiful sound remains for the people to sail on, and its hundreds of bays and inlets provide a total of no less than 1,800 miles of shoreline, many sections of it still tree-lined and unspoiled.

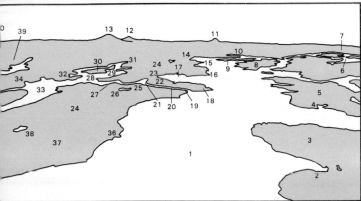

Places of interest in the Puget Sound area can be identified by reference to the diagram at left: Puget Sound (1); Kingston (2); Port Madison Indian Reservation (3); Port Madison (4); Bainbridge Island (5); Carr Inlet (6); Olympia (7); Vashon Island (8); Maury Island (9); Tacoma (10); Mount Saint Helens (11); Mount Adams (12); Mount Rainier (13); Seattle-Tacoma airport (14); Three Tree Point (15); Alki Point (16); Elliott Bay (17); Fort Lawton (18); Chittenden Locks (19) on Lake Washington Canal (20); Lake Union (21); Seattle Center, the site of the 1962 World's Fair (22); downtown Seattle (23); Seattle city limits (24); Woodland Park (25); Green Lake (26); University of Washington (27); Evergreen Point and Lake Washington Floating Bridges (28) and (29); Mercer Island (30); Renton (31); Bellevue (32); Lake Washington (33); Kirkland (34); Sheridan Beach (35); Richmond Beach (36); Edmonds (37); Lake Ballinger (38); Lake Sammamish (39); Snoqualmie (40).

Backed against a mountain, a rain cloud fills a valley on the
Olympic Peninsula, in northwestern Washington. With an average
annual rainfall of more than 100 inches, the rain forest of the
southwestern part of the peninsula is the wettest area in the U.S.

The many climates
of the Pacific Northwest

Slicing both Washington and Oregon from north to south is a series of craggy, snow-topped peaks called the Cascade Range. Thrusting high against the sky, the range does more than provide scenery; it divides the Northwest into sharply differentiated sections. On the far-western side of the chain lies the rain-soaked Olympic Peninsula and the industrialized Puget Sound area of Washington. Southward is the fertile Willamette Valley of Oregon, a highly diversified farming area. Across the Cascade Range the scene changes abruptly. The dry, eastern portion of Oregon is dotted with cattle ranches. Eastern Washington, where the rainfall is slightly heavier, is covered with wheat farms and orchards.

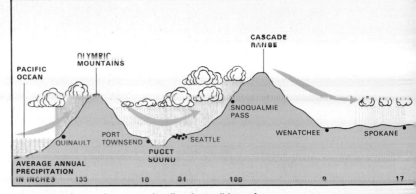

Meteorologic factors that create the climatic conditions of Washington are illustrated by the cross section above. Water vapor in winds blowing in from the Pacific condenses as the winds rise to cross the Olympic Mountains and drops as heavy rain upon the Olympic Peninsula. Rain also falls heavily east of Puget Sound as the winds rise again to surmount the Cascades. Only a little of the moisture remains to fall on eastern Washington.

Spraying insecticide, a crop duster flies low over the Palouse Hills of eastern Washington. With about 15 inches of rainfall a year, this area is excellent grain country. Its output enables Washington to rank as the nation's fifth-largest wheat producer.

The San Francisco Bay Area: a gracious city's noble setting

Sparkling in the afternoon sun, the Pacific rolls into the broad, magnificent mouth of the Golden Gate *(right foreground)*, entrance to the deepwater harbor that awed explorers and helped San Francisco become the region's leading city during the first years of West Coast settlement. From its birthplace near the present-day financial district *(see diagram below)*, San Francisco spread southward. In 1936 the city, previously accessible from the north and east only by water, was linked to Oakland by the Bay Bridge *(upper left)*. The following year the Golden Gate Bridge *(left center)* was completed. With the city as their center, suburbs multiplied—Pacifica, San Mateo, Palo Alto and a score of others that now stretch 40 miles south to San Jose and from the Pacific to Oakland and beyond, forming the megalopolis called the San Francisco Bay Area.

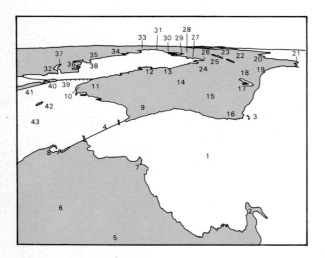

Places of importance in the Bay Area can be identified by reference to the numbers on the diagram above: the Golden Gate (1), bounded by Point Bonita (2), Seal Rocks (3) and the Golden Gate Bridge (4); Marin Peninsula (5); Fort Barry Military Reservation (6); Point Diablo (7); Horseshoe Bay (8); the Presidio (9); the Port of San Francisco (10); the Financial District (11); the Naval Shipyard (12); Candlestick Park (13); Twin Peaks (14); Golden Gate Park (15); Lincoln Park (16); Lake Merced (17); Daly City (18); Pacifica (19); Montara Mountain (20); Moss Beach (21); San Andreas Lake (22); Crystal Springs Reservoir (23); San Bruno Mountain (24); the city of South San Francisco (25); San Francisco Airport (26); the suburbs of Burlingame (27), San Mateo (28), Redwood City (29) and Palo Alto (30); San Jose (31), a food-processing center; the port of Oakland (32) and its suburbs Fremont (33), Hayward (34), San Leandro (35) and Alameda (36); Oakland Inner Harbor (37); Oakland Airport (38); the San Francisco-Oakland Bay Bridge (39); Yerba Buena Island (40); Treasure Island (41); Alcatraz Island (42); San Francisco Bay (43).

A fogbound coast and a valley of lush farms

From Santa Barbara to the border of Oregon the coastal mountain ranges of California rise steeply from the sea. Only once is this wall breached at sea level, and that is by the body of water named the Golden Gate. Through this gap flow a variety of weather conditions. In San Francisco a one-block walk can mean the difference between sun and fog. While the Golden Gate area is wrapped in a wet 50-degree chill, the people of the inland suburbs may be basking in a balmy 70 degrees and farmers in the Great Central Valley sweltering in 100-degree temperatures. But the farmers love their lengthy growing season, and San Franciscans long ago decided to take pride in the vagaries of their foggy coast.

Slashing diagonally through neat, rectangular fields in the San Joaquin Valley, the 153-mile-long Friant-Kern Canal carries water to growing areas. Before such canals were dug, the valley's sparse rainfall forced farmers who did not live near a river or other water source to grow only hardy crops like wheat. With irrigation the valley now also produces immense quantities of cotton and fruits.

Fog rolls into San Francisco Bay, almost blotting out the 746-foot north tower of the Golden Gate Bridge. As a fog bank steals up the bay, its arrival is trumpeted throughout the city by foghorns. At its thickest, a San Francisco fog blankets everything—bridges, cars, ships and buildings—and advances inland carrying, in the form of vapor, as much as one million gallons of water an hour.

If one word can describe San Francisco's weather, that word is "fog."
As the top diagram at right indicates, fogs from the Pacific roll
into the Golden Gate, blanketing San Francisco and its neighboring
cities. These fogs originate over the ocean: during the spring and
summer damp winds are propelled eastward by a large high-pressure
area called the Pacific High; when these winds cross the cold waters
of the California Current, their moisture condenses. The resulting
fog builds up offshore, then floods through the Golden Gate, still
pushed by the Pacific High but now also pulled by the low-pressure
area created by the hot, rising air mass over the Great Central Valley.
In winter (lower diagram) the situation is reversed. Then the
so-called tule fog (named for a species of rush that once grew in the
deltas of the Sacramento and San Joaquin Rivers) begins to form in
the Great Central Valley. Following heavy rains, a thick, low-lying fog
builds up, often covering the valley floor to a depth of 10 feet. When
this fog becomes even heavier, it sometimes moves westward
through a pass in the Diablo Range called the Carquinez Strait. From
there it flows down into the San Francisco area and across the bay,
where it finally dissipates.

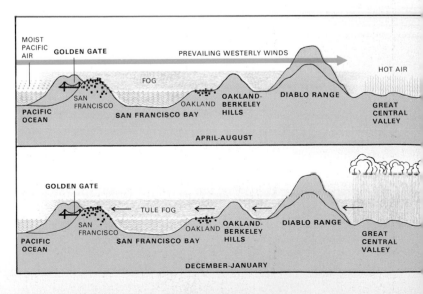

The many cities
of sprawling Los Angeles

Like dancers executing a fantastic Virginia reel, cars converge from all directions, whirl around an interchange in downtown Los Angeles, and speed outward along the Santa Monica and Harbor Freeways (*see diagram*), part of the city's far-reaching network of superhighways. The embodiment of urban sprawl, the megalopolis or supercity that is the Los Angeles Metropolitan Area is made up of 89 cities covering 1,800 square miles. This aerial view,

looking northeast from a point approximately at the center of the city proper, shows less than half of the great urban complex; another half is behind the camera. Bordered on the north by the San Gabriel Mountains (*top left*), the metropolitan area reaches south to Newport Beach; from the Puente Hills in the east (*far right*) it spreads 35 miles westward to the Pacific shore. Los Angeles was still a hamlet at the beginning of the 19th Century. Not until the 1880s, after the railroads arrived, did it begin to grow. With almost three million people today, Los Angeles is the West Coast's largest city.

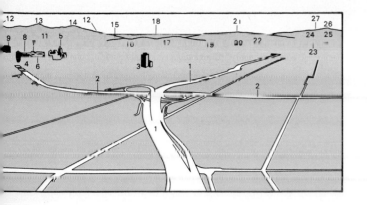

Places of importance in the Los Angeles area can be identified by referring to the diagram at the left: Santa Monica Freeway (1); Harbor Freeway (2); Occidental Center, one of the city's tallest buildings (3); Bunker Hill, site of extensive urban renewal (4); City Hall (5), County Courthouse (6), County Administration Building (7), Music Center (8), and Department of Water and Power Building (9), all part of the Los Angeles Civic Center; Pasadena, a manufacturing and residential city (10); Arcadia (11); San Gabriel Mountains (12); Mount San Antonio (13); Cucamonga Peak (14); Alhambra (15); East Los Angeles (16); Monterey Park (17); San Bernardino Mountains (18); Montebello, a growing industrial area (19); Pico Rivera (20); Puente Hills (21); Whittier (22); Los Angeles River (23); Fullerton, a food-processing center (24); Anaheim, home of Disneyland (25); Santiago Peak (26); Santa Ana Mountains (27).

A blanket of smog hanging over Los Angeles is clearly visible in this view from the northern rim of the bowl in which the city sits. Smog sometimes hampers the work of astronomers at Mount Wilson Observatory *(lower left)*, but generally the mountain air is clear.

A smoggy "Riviera" and man-made oases

Like the coast of Southern France, the 3,000-square-mile Los Angeles Basin has a benign climate the year round. Ironically, the same conditions that produce the climate are partly responsible for Los Angeles' smog, which covers the city almost 200 days a year. Poisonous wastes of cars and factories become trapped in the basin, causing the people to gasp and wheeze. When this man-made miasma lifts, however, the area can be a paradise of sun and gentle breezes. Curiously, Angelenos appear to be dissatisfied with having only one paradise; they are spreading inland over the San Gabriel and San Bernardino Mountains and, with considerable effort, making Edenic artificial oases in the hot, dry desert.

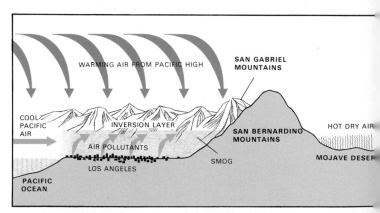

The Los Angeles smog is caused by a process called inversion, as shown above. Cool Pacific air becomes trapped by the mountains and by a descending mass of warm air. An inversion layer forms where the warm and cool air meet, creating a lid that traps auto exhausts and other wastes. Sunshine triggers a photochemical reaction, converting the pollutants into potentially harmful gases.

A splash of green on the desert, the golf resort area of Borrego Springs lies at the foot of the parched slopes of the San Ysidro Mountains. Borrego Springs, like other desert towns such as Salton City and Palm Springs, taps underground sources for its water, and the golf course is well kept and green. Not far from Borrego Springs, 6,000 acres that once were wasteland are under cultivation, producing grapes, melons, tomatoes and grain in a continuous growing season that permits three or four harvests a year.

2

The
Westering Urge

On the Overland Trail in 1862 migrants pause during their
2,000-mile, five-month trip from Independence, Missouri, to the
Coast. An ordeal for early travelers, the trail had by this date
become a well-marked road for which guidebooks were available.

The West Coast has progressed through history on surging waves of migration. The motivations of the migrants have not been the traditional ones of refuge. Never before have great numbers of people been affluent enough and mobile enough, as have Americans by the millions, to leave what they regard as a good life to search for one they hope will be better. Since the Gold Rush of 1849 those who have moved west have generally had something extra. They have been slightly more prosperous, somewhat better schooled, perhaps even a trace more adventurous than the American norm. They have westered with such velocity that their shock waves have shaken the world. Yet, as history goes, it has all happened quite recently. For three centuries before the forty-niners came, California had spawned legend, but little else.

The white man had named California before he saw it. In 1535, far to the south of what later became California, the Spanish conquistador Hernan Cortés visited a rugged peninsula that he thought was an island. It was the tip of what is now called Baja California, a part of Mexico. The coastline evoked images of a fictional Indies island described in a popular Spanish novel of the time as "one of the most rugged in the world, with bold rocks and crags." Ruled by a black Amazon named Calafia, the legendary island possessed only one metal: gold. By the time Juan Rodríguez Cabrillo stepped ashore for Spain in San Diego Bay on September 28, 1542, to become the first European on California soil, the land had derived its name from that of the island of the black Queen Calafia.

Cabrillo found no hint of riches. At San Diego he visited with friendly Indians and rode out a three-day storm. Then he sailed north, perhaps to what is now the Oregon border. But he grew ill, and the discoverer of California became the first European known to have been buried in its earth. The news of its existence had to be brought back by his second-in-command, Bartolomé Ferrelo.

That zealous Englishman Sir Francis Drake anchored his *Golden Hind* north of San Francisco Bay in 1579, but only to await good weather for a Pacific crossing. Another Spaniard, the merchant

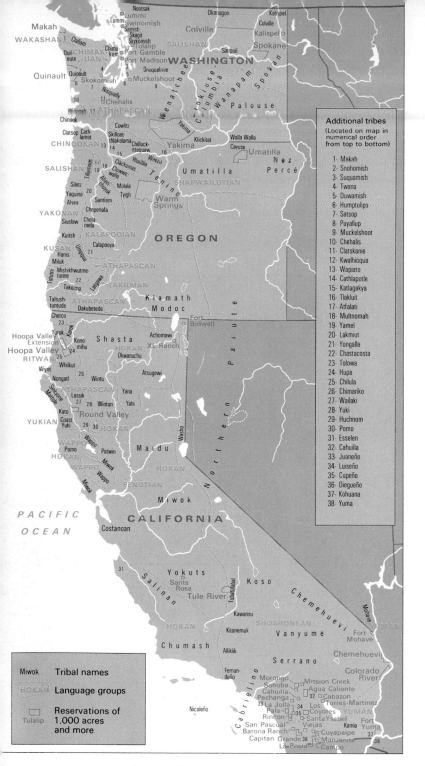

Additional tribes
(Located on map in numerical order from top to bottom)

1. Makah
2. Snohomish
3. Suquamish
4. Twana
5. Duwamish
6. Humptulips
7. Satsop
8. Puyallup
9. Muckelshoot
10. Chehalis
11. Clatskanie
12. Kwalhioqua
13. Wapiato
14. Cathlapotle
15. Katlagakya
16. Tlakluit
17. Atfalati
18. Multnomah
19. Yamel
20. Lakmiut
21. Yongalla
22. Chastacosta
23. Tolowa
24. Hupa
25. Chilula
26. Chimariko
27. Wailaki
28. Yuki
29. Huchnom
30. Pomo
31. Esselen
32. Cahuilla
33. Juaneño
34. Luiseño
35. Cupeño
36. Diegueño
37. Kohuana
38. Yuma

Miwok — Tribal names
HOKAN — Language groups
Tulalip — Reservations of 1,000 acres and more

Indians yesterday and today

Where Indians lived on the West Coast shortly after the Europeans arrived and the location of large present-day reservations can be seen on this map. The estimated 225,000 Indians in the region in 1650 belonged to some 140 tribes. In some areas the tribes were so closely clustered that not all of their names can be shown on the map; the habitat of such tribes can be found by reference to the numbers in the box at the right. By 1900 disease, exploitation, and systematic extermination by troops and settlers had reduced the Indians' numbers to about 30,400. Today they have increased to more than 80,000, of whom some 23,000 live on 87 reservations totaling 3.6 million acres.

Sebastián Vizcaíno, followed Cabrillo's course in 1602, naming San Diego, Santa Monica, Santa Barbara and Monterey, which he cited as an ideal port of call for Spanish galleons en route home from trading in the Far East. Yet 168 years were to pass before Spain occupied Monterey, for Spanish officialdom did not suspect the aptness of naming the region for a fictional island of gold.

Almost nothing of the Northwest coast was seen by these early explorers. Near the Oregon border Drake discovered "most vile, thicke and stinking fogges," and turned south. But the prized pelts of Northwest sea otters eventually lured sea traders. Russians began moving down the Pacific Coast from Alaska in the early 19th Century. The British were close behind. Anticipating these moves, the Spaniards had dispatched land and sea expeditions north from Baja California as early as 1769. The settlement of California was led by a lame and aging Franciscan friar, Junípero Serra. He went by mule up the long and formidable Baja California peninsula to San Diego and there founded the first California mission. In 1770 the military commander Gaspar de Portolá advanced the Spanish frontier to Monterey by establishing there a presidio, or military post.

California was, however, remote from the power of the Spanish viceroy in Mexico City. For lack of supplies, San Diego was almost abandoned within a year. Colonization of Monterey could not begin until after 1773, when Juan Bautista de Anza, an Indian fighter, daringly opened an overland supply line across the searing Southwest deserts from Mexico. Junípero Serra and his successors slowly moved northward, eventually establishing a chain of 21 Indian missions.

There were about 130,000 Indians in California when the Spaniards arrived, and there were soon to be far fewer of them. They were more primitive than most tribes of the Southwest and Northwest; they did little farming or hunting and lived in rudimentary huts of thatch or brush. They were not warlike, and only a few southern California tribes united against the invaders. To many of the Spanish soldiers, and to the Americans who came later, the Indians represented only a problem in extermination. "The savages were in the way," the California historian Hubert Howe Bancroft wrote in the 19th Century. "The miners and settlers were arrogant and impatient; there were no missionaries or others present with even the poor pretense of soul-saving or civilizing. It was one of the last human hunts of civilization, and the basest and most brutal of them all."

The Indians of the Northwest had no recorded contact with the white man until 1774, when the Spanish captain Juan Pérez anchored at Vancouver Island. In the next year Don Bruno Hezeta and Juan de la Bodega went ashore on the Olympic Peninsula near Point Grenville and claimed the land for Spain. But it was the painstaking English captain James Cook, in search of the Northwest Passage in 1778, who first traded with the Northwest Indians and encountered such lyrically named tribes as the Tlingit, Haida, Salish, Bellacoola, Chinook, Kwakiutl and Chimmesyan. Knowing little of farming or of minerals, these peoples had adapted to an oceanfront existence, even rowing out of sight of land to kill whales. They were skilled trappers, and it was their sea-otter skins that lured the Russian and British traders into the region.

The settlement of California was a strain upon the resources of the Spanish outposts, and the Spaniards did not attempt to colonize the Northwest until the spring of 1789. They were too late. When members of an expedition sailed from Mexico to Nootka Sound at Vancouver Island that year, they were greeted in English. Five trading ships had been based at Nootka by John Meares, a former lieutenant in the Royal Navy. Also in port was a U.S. vessel under the command of Robert Gray, who, aboard the brig *Columbia*, later named the Columbia River after exploring its mouth. The Spaniards and the Englishmen clashed at Nootka Sound in an incident that later resulted in acrimonious exchanges between London and Madrid. The Americans were not yet a major force; they were bystanders to the hostility at Nootka Sound. But Washington was watching intently. Spain's empire was crumbling, and Spain withdrew its claims to the Northwest in 1793. Then began a long contest for the region between the United States and Britain.

The momentum of history lay with the Americans. In 1803 the United States negotiated the Louisiana Purchase, pushing its borders westward across the plains. Then the expeditions of the U.S. Army officers Meriwether Lewis and William Clark sketched enough details of the uncharted void beyond the plains for the West to become, as the American historian Bernard DeVoto later wrote, "something the mind could deal with."

Despite the active fur trading of the British-owned North West Company and the venerable Hudson's Bay Company of Canada, which sought without success to head off the influx of Americans, Yankee settlers — fur traders, missionaries and farmers — began pushing into the Northwest. The

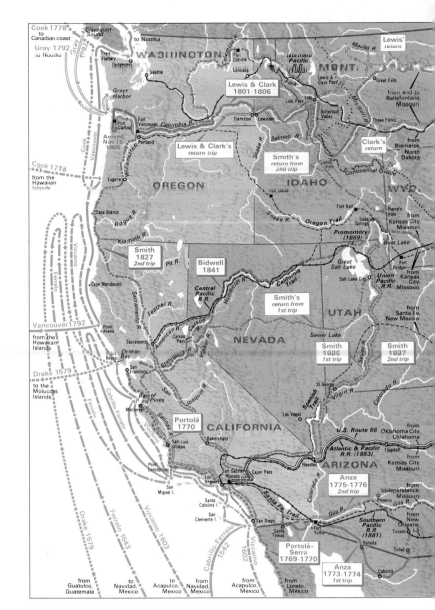

Routes for searchers and settlers

The major routes taken by explorers and settlers of the West Coast are shown above. Like Bartolomé Ferrelo of Spain and Juan Rodríguez Cabrillo of Portugal — who became, in 1542, the first Europeans to visit California — early explorers such as Francis Drake, James Cook and George Vancouver of England and Sebastián Vizcaíno of Spain came by sea. Gaspar de Portolá and the missionary Junípero Serra marched overland from Mexico in 1769, to be followed in 1773 by Juan Bautista de Anza. Soon traders began coming by sea, while trappers like Jedediah Smith traveled over the mountains. John Bidwell led the first American wagon train in 1841, and later settlers arrived over the Santa Fe, Spanish and California Trails after gold was discovered in 1848. Others came over the Oregon Trail into the country first explored by Lewis and Clark. Later settlers traveled by rail after the linkup of the Union Pacific and the Central Pacific at Promontory, Utah, in 1869. Still another wave of migrants arrived during and after the U.S. Depression of the 1930s, many via auto on U.S. Route 66.

A possible relic of Sir Francis Drake's 1579 visit, the five-by-eight-inch brass plate shown above was found lying on a California hillside in 1936. It matches —even to the irregularly shaped hole at the lower right, which once held a 16th Century sixpence—a plate reportedly left by Drake. It was described in *The World Encompassed by Sir Francis Drake,* an account compiled in 1628 (32 years after Drake's death) from the notes of one of his companions. Some authorities were skeptical, but seven months of exhaustive scientific tests indicate the plate is genuine.

Despite the sacrifice and devotion of a heroic few, the colonizing effort of the Spaniards in California left pathetically little trace. When Mexico gained its independence Spanish officials withdrew from California. The power and opulence of the missions quickly diminished; in 1833 Mexico ordered the friars to confine their activities to religious functions. Indians drifted away from the missions, many to die in epidemics of white man's diseases. The final outcome of the missionaries' work was assessed by the Harvard scholar Josiah Royce as "simply nothing. . . . For, with their power, nearly every trace of their labors vanished from the world."

After the secularization of mission lands the Mexican government made several hundred generous land grants, typically to retired soldiers from northwestern Mexico. These lands became the ranchos of a much-romanticized period in California history. The brief era of Mexican rule in California between 1821 and 1846 was flamboyant and inept, and American traders took economic command. The Mexican Californians began to mortgage their land for Yankee goods. The writer Richard Henry Dana, visiting California in 1835 on the voyage that resulted in his classic, *Two Years Before the Mast,* reported that two thirds of all goods imported into California from around Cape Horn in the preceding six years had been shipped through the Boston firm of which he was then an employee.

Published reports of Western life like those of the soldier-explorer John C. Frémont stirred curiosity in the East. Horace Greeley, editor of the New York *Tribune,* counseled young men: "If you have no family or friends to aid you, and no prospect opened to you there [in a father's workshop or his farm], turn your face to the great West, and there build up a home and fortune." Yet the Far West was still formidably remote. A seaman shipping from Boston could expect to be absent for two to three years. Overland, the Pacific Coast was almost 2,000 miles beyond the Midwest frontier. Until the completion of the first transcontinental railroad, the Coast was closer in travel time to the Orient or to South America than to the Mississippi. But the stage was being cleared. Russians at Fort Ross, an outpost on the Northern California coast, sold out in 1841 to an entrepreneur named John A. Sutter.

In that same year, when non-Mexican residents in California still numbered fewer than 400, the first wagon train moved overland from near Independence, Missouri. The newcomers were mostly Midwestern farmers. Some moved north to the farmlands of the Northwest; not all of them stayed in the West. The move was hard; the migration was

Northwest was more alluring to Americans than was California in these years, in part because the United States had laid claim to the region and because California had come under Mexican rule when Mexico won its independence from Spain in 1821. Early migrants to California often deemed it wise to seek Mexican citizenship. California had unsavory aspects as well. The pueblo of Los Angeles had been founded by imperial Spain in 1781, its illiterate colonists recruited from the most poverty-stricken classes in Mexican Sinaloa. In the California missions, Father Serra and his associates had baptized more than 6,000 Indians and taught them much about farming and making adobe. But the life of the Indians was seldom improved. Visiting the Monterey mission area in 1786, the Frenchman Jean François Gallup de Lapérouse described the Indian straw huts as "the most miserable that one could find anywhere. . . ."

The San Francisco area was no more impressive, in the opinion of early visitors. George Vancouver of the British Navy compared the local presidio in 1792 to "a pound for cattle," and went on: "If we except its natural pastures, the flocks of sheep and herds of cattle, there is not an object to indicate the most remote connection with any European, or other civilized nation."

only a trickle. Four years later the American colony in California had grown to only 700 persons.

Then came the fateful year of 1846. With startling suddenness the shape of the Far West was cast. Between 1843 and 1845 some 4,000 Americans had toiled across the Oregon Trail. The ruts they and their followers gouged became so deep that the marks can still be seen in many parts of the West. In 1846 the Northwest became a part of the United States when British and American diplomats arranged the division of the region at the 49th parallel, the present boundary between Canada and the United States. Even as that took place, a group of American settlers at Sonoma in Northern California defied Mexican authority and proclaimed an independent California Republic under the Flag of the Bear. The incident was minor in contrast to the dispute between the United States and Mexico over Texas. Nonetheless, American interest in the acquisition of California was a factor in the declaration of war against Mexico that came on May 11, 1846.

The California phase of the Mexican War had moments of high comedy and pathos; its battles were Lilliputian in scale. For several years there had been widespread apprehension over British intentions in California. The impotence of Mexico in California seemed to invite seizure by some other government, and emissaries from Washington operating in Mexico City had been unsuccessful in attempts to purchase California outright. In 1842, acting on a false report that war had been declared between the U.S. and Mexico, Commodore Thomas Catesby Jones of the United States Navy sailed into Monterey, found it "quiet, peaceful, and normally dilapidated," and raised the American flag before the eyes of the astonished Mexicans. Two days later, seeing no signs of military activity, Jones concluded that he had perhaps acted hastily, hauled down the flag, made formal apologies to the Mexicans and sailed south to pay his respects to the Mexican Governor in Los Angeles. The Governor, who had been describing himself as "a thunderbolt to fly and annihilate the invaders," gave Jones a formal ball.

There also had been one small and almost bloodless battle before word came of the declaration of the Mexican War. In July 1846 the United States flag was raised at Monterey by Commodore John D. Sloat, and this time it remained. There was only minor Mexican resistance. Troops of the Bear Flag Republic dissolved their new government and joined the American forces. Mexican forces rallied in Southern California and won a victory over General Stephen W. Kearny and 100 soldiers at San

Shape and functions of a mission

The mission of San Juan Capistrano, founded in 1776, is shown below much as it looked at its greatest extent, around 1811. Life at Capistrano centered around the patio, where Indians learned agricultural and other skills as well as the fundamentals of Roman Catholicism. They also did the heavy construction work, which continued from about 1776 to 1812, when an earthquake destroyed the large stone church. Later, other sections fell into disrepair. Some buildings were restored after 1812, and there were a few minor additions (orange), but the church was never rebuilt. Today the mission is occupied by clergy of the Los Angeles diocese. Where the use of the original buildings has changed, the new function is given in parentheses.

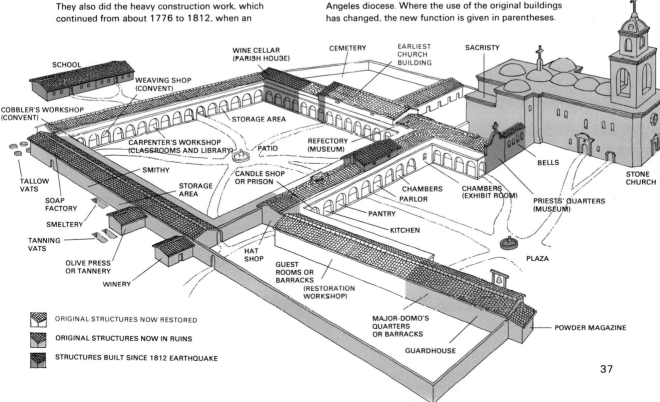

SCHOOL — WEAVING SHOP (CONVENT) — WINE CELLAR (PARISH HOUSE) — CEMETERY — EARLIEST CHURCH BUILDING — SACRISTY — COBBLER'S WORKSHOP (CONVENT) — STORAGE AREA — CARPENTER'S WORKSHOP (CLASSROOMS AND LIBRARY) — PATIO — REFECTORY (MUSEUM) — BELLS — STONE CHURCH — SMITHY — CANDLE SHOP OR PRISON — TALLOW VATS — STORAGE AREA — CHAMBERS PARLOR — CHAMBERS (EXHIBIT ROOM) — PRIESTS' QUARTERS (MUSEUM) — SOAP FACTORY — PANTRY — SMELTERY — KITCHEN — TANNING VATS — HAT SHOP — OLIVE PRESS OR TANNERY — GUEST ROOMS OR BARRACKS (RESTORATION WORKSHOP) — WINERY — PLAZA — MAJOR-DOMO'S QUARTERS OR BARRACKS — POWDER MAGAZINE — GUARDHOUSE

ORIGINAL STRUCTURES NOW RESTORED

ORIGINAL STRUCTURES NOW IN RUINS

STRUCTURES BUILT SINCE 1812 EARTHQUAKE

37

To combat gangs of outlaws, who were not kept in check by police in San Francisco in the early 1850s, respectable citizens formed groups to enforce the law. One of these, the 1851 Vigilance Committee, is shown in the contemporary print above, hanging a confessed murderer named James Stuart from a makeshift gallows erected on the Market Street wharf.

Pasqual, north of San Diego. But after other confrontations, with almost no casualties, the Mexican Californians surrendered to U.S. troops under John C. Frémont near Los Angeles on January 13, 1847, and the following year Mexico officially ceded California to the United States. There had been gallantry and dignity at the end, with no talk of imprisonment or punishment for the vanquished. Before the onslaught of the westering Yankee the Mexican bowed, but with a sense of injury. Facing the loss of California, the last Mexican Governor, Pío Pico, had indicated some of that feeling in a poignant and prophetic letter: "We find ourselves suddenly threatened by hordes of Yankee immigrants . . . whose progress we cannot arrest. They are cultivating farms, establishing vineyards, erecting mills, sawing up lumber, building workshops, and doing a thousand other things which seem natural to them."

As 1846 ended, San Francisco was a village named Yerba Buena. Early in 1848 a sawmill boss, James Marshall, picked four or five bits of gold out of the American River at the small northern settlement of Sutter's Mill and set off the California Gold Rush. Thereafter far more than the name of Yerba Buena changed. In four years the population of California increased sixfold. The shouts of gold in the streets triggered the settlement of California that imperial Spain had failed to achieve in three centuries. In its deeper sense the California Gold Rush has never ended. The historian John Caughey later wrote: "California appears to be the only place where a rush for gold was made to serve as the base for an ever-widening superstructure of attainment."

The moment was honed sharp for history. Americans had a foothold on their new coast. With the Mexican War over, veterans were looking for work; a shipload of 950 young, single New York soldiers had recently arrived in San Francisco. Subsidized steamship service was about to begin between New York and San Francisco, utilizing the narrow Isthmus of Panama as a transshipment point for passengers. It is no wonder that Americans began to associate the Far West with the manifest destiny of the nation: the gold had been discovered nine days before Mexico signed away California in the 1848 Treaty of Guadalupe Hidalgo. The following year 549 vessels arrived at San Francisco. Half came from the Atlantic seaboard, others from Europe and the Orient. Ships were diverted to California service, 71 from whaling alone. Almost 40,000 forty-niners came by sea. Now suddenly the overland trails seemed less formidable. Guidebooks were hurriedly marketed. Emigrant parties pitched camp along the trails in sight of one another's campfires. It looked, one migrant wrote in his journal, "as if a mighty army was on its march." Except on the southern trails, Indians were not the major menace; death came more often through cholera or from impetuous exploration of shortcuts across deserts and mountains.

The Gold Rush set a pattern for subsequent migrations to California. The forty-niners were typically young, male and single; they did not intend to put down roots in California. More than half of all Californians in 1850 were in their twenties, and they were by and large well educated. The forty-niners accelerated the change from Mexican to American culture, ended the isolation of California and set in tide a migration that has seldom ebbed. The Gold Rush made California famous and released human energies more valuable than any metal. It launched California into statehood, which came in 1850, with unprecedented speed and put the state ahead of others in the West. Within 20 years San Francisco regarded itself as a cultural rival of Boston and a U.S. financial center second only to New York.

All this was not merely the result of the wealth gained from gold. In 30 years of mining, more than $1.2 billion was taken from the earth, almost all of it from land in the public domain extending over an area about 300 miles in length and from 40 to 100 miles in width. But as early as 1854 the diggings were in decline. Although considerable mining went on for years in some of the Sierra Nevada gold lodes, and sporadic mining continues to this day, the Gold Rush itself was over in five years; even before that, the wisest of the forty-niners had become merchants, bankers or farmers, and many of them amassed far greater wealth than did men who went on searching for gold. San Francisco became the mining capital for other rushes in the Northwest and Nevada, notably for the Comstock Lode silver rush of 1859, in the sense that the city supplied the mines and the miners, as Portland did to a lesser extent when gold and silver strikes were later made in Oregon and Idaho. Most fortunes did not come directly from the mines. Merchants like Charles Crocker, Mark Hopkins, Collis P. Huntington and Leland Stanford accumulated sufficient capital to put up $15,000 each to build the Central Pacific Railroad; they grew enormously wealthy on the profits from that investment. Oregonians shared in the bonanza; ships from the Northwest brought grain and lumber to San Francisco.

The impact of the Gold Rush was felt only remotely at first in the cattle-raising counties of Southern California. Then, responding to the miners' demand for meat, cattle prices began to soar, and Southern California began to share in the boom. The Census Bureau moved into California for the first time in 1850 and found the county of Los Angeles to have 1,610 inhabitants, mostly Mexicans and Indians. Its people were already aiming high. The county then comprised 34,000 square miles and extended from San Diego to Santa Barbara.

The forty-niners took their places quite unexpectedly as citizens of the new state. Some returned home, but many others came west to replace them. The population almost quadrupled between 1850 and 1860. As time went on, moreover, the migration grew increasingly diverse. There were a few hundred Chinese in the state in 1850; by 1852 one in 10 Californians was Chinese. Most of the Chinese were men who had been imported to do menial labor while white men searched the hills for gold. Many Irishmen came west to build the railroads. In 1870 persons born abroad totaled nearly 30 per cent of the population. San Francisco was the choice of nearly half of the Irish, French and Italian immigrants; Los Angeles lured Mexicans and Russians.

Most of the forty-niners came from New England, New York and Pennsylvania; another large group moved west from Ohio, Indiana and Illinois. Among 136 lawyers in San Francisco in 1851, 55 had come from New York, 24 from other Eastern states and 18 from the Midwest. A survey taken in San Francisco public schools in 1860 found that children born in New York and New England outnumbered those born in all other states, including California.

Writing not long after this period, the historian John S. Hittell was impressed by the cosmopolitan nature of the new Californians and their social freedoms and mobility which, he speculated, were the result of high wages, rootlessness and bachelor life. Women were accorded marked deference, largely because of their scarcity. "When a woman is oppressed by her husband in California," he wrote, "she can generally find somebody else who will not oppress her." During the Gold Rush, California divorce rates were already among the highest in the world, and the plaintiffs were almost always women. In no group was the imbalance between the sexes greater than among the foreign-born, especially those from the Orient. As late as 1940 foreign-born Chinese men outnumbered foreign-born Chinese women by 4 to 1; Filipino men outnumbered women by 9 to 1.

In the hectic years after 1850 San Francisco was

Steaming to the West Coast, Civil War widows and other Eastern women congregate on deck in 1866 on their way to new lives. About 60 women—called Mercer's Belles, after the Washington State educator Asa S. Mercer, who devised a plan to bring "women of good character" as potential wives to the woman-short Northwest—made the 97-day voyage.

the scene of riots, bank failures, and public hangings organized by vigilantes. But the city was growing. Although it was burned to the ground six times in two years, it gradually acquired hotels and mansions. Makeshift accommodations in dilapidated vessels at dockside gave way to luxury; the Lick House, first of the gilded hostelries, was completed in 1862; the colonnaded Palace Hotel, with its imposing center courtyard, was finished in 1875. With such establishments—and with the somewhat different attractions of the raucous dance halls of the Barbary Coast section—San Francisco was quick to acquire its still-standing reputation for gentility coupled with worldliness.

Portland surprised the world too. In its Newmarket Theater, opened in 1873, the world's great artists performed for crowds that laboriously traveled from places as far as 200 miles away. Portland had been born of New England lineage, and solid respectability showed through in its architecture and its unspectacular prosperity as sovereign city of the more stable Northwest.

Los Angeles did not move so swiftly. It had not left the pastoral era of the ranchos when two successive years of drought struck in 1862 and 1863. The grass died, the land hardened like stone, and the carcasses of great herds piled up beneath the unrelenting sun. With the herds went the ranchos; scores of the huge Mexican land grants were divided and sold.

Silver and gold from the West had flowed into Union coffers during the Civil War. With the end of hostilities a new wave of westward migration began. The lure of cheap land and a fresh start seemed strong to weary soldiers. Many took the southern trails and settled in Southern California, where the relative increase in population was greatest.

After completion of the first transcontinental railroad in 1869, artificial stimuli were applied to migration. The federal government subsidized railroad building by ceding land to the lines; railroad owners were prominent among the sponsors of the California Immigrant Union, an agency with offices in San Francisco and operatives in the East and in Europe. The agency offered information on California and, to promote both passenger and freight traffic, urged the purchase of railroad land. Soon the railroads were advertising lavishly, hiring writers and publishing pamphlets to eulogize the West. No railroad developed more complex machinery to induce migration than did the Southern Pacific. It offered cut-rate fares to prospective settlers and made the price of the ticket applicable to purchase of railroad land, even by installment payments.

Awaiting customers, a Chinese merchant of the 1890s stands in a newly opened shop in San Francisco's Chinatown, a jammed, 12-block ghetto. Earlier, the Chinese had been dispersed through the region, but persecution by whites gradually drove them into such enclaves in the cities and limited them to occupations like laundering, in which whites were uninterested.

Entire cars were available without extra charge to families and groups; they could save money by doing their own cooking as they traveled west at 20 or 25 miles an hour. Houses were reserved in Texas as way stations for those who needed to stop en route to earn wages. The Southern Pacific even operated an employment service for passengers; its agents arranged interviews with prospective employers. No passenger promotion focused more attention on Western railroads than the 1887 rate war between the Southern Pacific and the Atchison, Topeka and Santa Fe; for one brief period, tickets from Kansas City to Los Angeles sold for one dollar. From 1881 through 1885 more than 50,000 prospective migrants had visited California on the Southern Pacific's rails; when the Santa Fe began service two years later, the number more than doubled.

Much of this frenzied promotion was involved with land speculation, notably in Southern California. Men who had been sensible Midwest farmers became paper millionaires, queueing up to buy business sites in desert cities that have not been built to this day, then selling the plots at vast paper profits. Some speculators, standing near the head of the lines, turned down offers of $500 for their places. Brass bands played, barbecues and free lunches were offered, and the sucker spiel was brayed on every side. There was less fraud than gullibility; the California euphoria had simply run amuck. More and more migrants came to join the frenzy. In 1880 there had been 11,183 Los Angelenos; by 1887 there were six or seven times that many. Then, early in 1888, speculators hesitated; prices nosed down, then slid faster until the game was over. All of the banks survived. But for a time the trains bore more passengers away from Southern California than they brought in. Those who stayed went back to citrus grove, farm or factory and began laying the solid economic foundations that eventually helped Los Angeles gain equal footing with San Francisco. Even in defeat the land boomers were not bitter. "I wouldn't have missed it for all I have lost," one told the author T. S. Van Dyke. "It was worth living a lifetime to see."

Despite the exodus of defeated speculators, California's growth continued. By 1890, spurred by the state's burgeoning reputation for healthful climate, the population had passed the million mark. Southern California especially was heralded as a mecca for tuberculars, asthmatics and rheumatics. Doctors of the time were quick to recommend a change in climate, and the vogue was enhanced by testimonials that California sunshine had been the instrument of various cures. Most of the ailing went to established towns: Los Angeles, San Diego, Santa Barbara or San Bernardino. Other towns took form as spas: Palm Springs, Pasadena, Santa Monica. Many of the sick found light labor in vineyards and groves to provide income during their convalescence; others became apiarists, pushing the state toward first place in honey production. In 1900 these health seekers made up an estimated 10 per cent of Southern Californians.

In the meantime the tide of migration had turned northward. In 1870 fewer persons lived in Oregon (which had become a state in 1859) and Washington combined than in San Francisco. Then in 1883 a transcontinental railroad pierced the isolation of the Northwest, and within a few years two others reached the region. For a period after completion of the railroads, more than twice as many Americans chose Washington as picked California. Not admitted as a state until 1889, Washington surpassed Oregon in population the next year, in part because many Scandinavian immigrants saw similarities between it and their homelands. They turned first to logging and fishing and later to farming. German immigration was also heavy.

Oregon, on the other hand, attracted more Yankee merchants and Midwest farmers, and its more

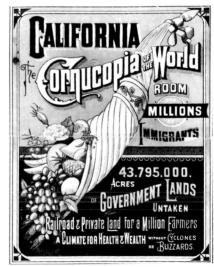

To lure customers, railroads and land speculators displayed posters and prints throughout the nation in the 1880s and 1890s touting the Coast as a paradise. Their efforts were remarkably successful. The hordes of land-hungry immigrants pouring into the region set off land booms, which soon burst but which seemed to return in cycles. In the Northwest an Illinois schoolteacher who arrived in Tacoma virtually penniless made $10,000 his first year dealing in real estate and was soon spending $5,000 a month advertising the city in Eastern papers. When that boom ended in 1893, owners of good buildings became their janitors. In Southern California one of the biggest booms came in 1887, when a railroad rate war reduced fares to the area. Lots were sold at all hours in saloons and restaurants, at curbside and in the countryside. Whole towns were laid out and networks of sidewalks were built miles out into the brush. Some of the towns never developed, but most, like Hollywood, Burbank and Escondido, survived and lived to see new booms.

gradual growth did not alter the state's stolid pattern. Oregon business and industry remained largely home-owned, while vast out-of-state investment capital followed newcomers into Washington. Rail lines and riverboats opened the rich wheat country of eastern Washington to settlers in the 1870s, yet the fastest expansion in the area took place in the cities. Seattle grew from a village of 3,533 in 1880 to a city of 42,837 in 1890. Tacoma's population went from 1,000 to 36,006 in the same decade. Although Portland also grew, the development of its northern neighbors soon ended the city's longtime regional dominance.

The Washington migration rolled on until in 1910 the state passed the million mark, almost double the population of Oregon. The continued growth was only in part the result of Washington's own attractions; again the cry of gold had arisen, this time from Alaska. In 1897 the steamer *Portland* had arrived in Seattle from Alaska with $800,000 in gold dust, and soon the city boomed as the outfitting port for the Yukon, much as San Francisco had served the Sierra Nevada in 1849. Yet along with the rougher miners, Seattle was drawing a prosperous Pullman-car migration of young, buoyant and speculative settlers. They handily weathered a depression in 1893; during a bank panic in

1907 they planned the successful Alaska-Yukon-Pacific Exposition of 1909. Seattleites were aggressive and willing to pay to improve their town. Their leaders were often transplants from Eastern seaboard cities. Portland was not stagnant, either; in 1905 it staged an exposition of its own on the 100th anniversary of the Lewis and Clark Expedition, in a prosperous decade when the railroads brought another great wave of settlers to Oregon cities, farms and forests.

Despite their contrasts the cities of the West Coast from the start displayed common characteristics that made them far more different from older American cities than from one another. To their critics, Western cities were unstable, unworkable and transitory, out of step with America. Easterners shook their heads over bonanzas that seemed to them to delay the day of reckoning for Western cities: the gold that set off booms in San Francisco, Portland and Seattle; the discovery of oil that brought prosperity to Los Angeles in the 1890s; and the United States Navy paychecks that began to sustain San Diego after World War I.

Yet as the singularities of the westward migration grew clearer, the Pacific Coast cities no longer seemed so odd. They had a significantly lower illiteracy rate than older American cities (the rate in the three states was only 4.2 per cent in 1900, when the national average was 10.7). Everywhere along the Pacific Coast the cultural level of the native American migrants was relatively high. Too, the cities were more populous in relation to the surrounding rural area; more people lived in Western cities, fewer on outlying farms. Not so many worked in factories; more were involved in service industries and the professions.

Such economic and occupational differences in the cities of the Pacific Coast evolved naturally from the distinctiveness of the migrants: the high proportion of adults, their high income and extreme mobility, and the high rate at which they imported finished goods from the East. Today prosperity and mobility continue to characterize the people of the West Coast. But age levels are dropping close to the national median now, and Western industrial growth since World War II has been so rapid that an increasing proportion of Westerners is involved in production.

Long cultivated by mission fathers, oranges became a commercial crop in the 1840s when William Wolfskill began marketing the fruit from the Los Angeles grove shown above. But the crop did not gain national popularity until after the introduction of seedless navel oranges in 1873 and the advent of refrigerator cars to keep them fresh during long trips eastward.

At the beginning of the 20th Century the tide of migration had begun to turn back toward Southern California. In 1900 only one fifth of all Californians lived south of the Tehachapi. By 1920 that proportion had swelled to two fifths, by 1940 to more than

Candy-striped tents line the Silver Strand beach leading to the fashionable Hotel del Coronado *(background)*, near San Diego, in this 1904 photograph. The Coronado, still open today, was the largest of California's early resort hotels. Its dining room seated nearly 1,000 guests, and it boasted 2,000 feet of porches. Opened in 1888, it featured electric lights and a wall safe in nearly all of its 400 guest rooms, and catered to opulent Easterners. Less affluent local residents found relief from the summer heat in the inexpensive tent city—a popular vacation idea that derived from religious camp meetings. At its height the city had about 1,000 tents; a tent for two rented for $1.25 a day. Earlier, visitors had come to the Coast for their health; they now came for recreation.

half and by 1960 to three fifths. Native-born Californians have never numbered more than about one in three in Los Angeles.

Intensive planting of citrus orchards in Southern California lured settlers from the Midwest in the first years of the new century. Another immigrant surge came from Japan, then experiencing a period of social and economic unrest. Prejudice had arisen against the Chinese, who had been the region's menial laborers; in 1882 the U.S. passed an exclusion act banning Chinese immigration. Many Chinese were forced to leave Oregon and Washington; some were lynched in California, and thousands left the state. To replace them, Japanese were encouraged to immigrate, and in 1900 alone more than 12,000 entered California. The Japanese did well as farmers, and by 1920, while constituting only 2 per cent of the California population, they controlled more than 11 per cent of the state's farmland.

The San Francisco earthquake and fire of 1906 also spurred the growth of Southern California, since many who were California-bound elected to settle in the south—which did not receive major earthquake damage until the Long Beach temblor of 1933. Despite a recession in 1907 and political and racial turbulence, Southern California attracted increasing numbers of workers to the new oil and motion-picture industries. Each decade California added about a million residents.

The floodgates opened in Southern California after World War I to admit the heaviest migration that the West had yet known. The frontier was gone and its privations had virtually disappeared from California life. Tourism expanded into a major industry, and an astonishing proportion of those who visited California came back later to live. Thousands of young Americans who first saw California in World War I training camps made the same decision. The growth of San Diego is an example. The earliest settlement in California, San Diego had languished for lack of a railroad over its mountains to the east. It began to share substantially in the migration after visitors flocked to its 1915-1916 Panama-California Exposition, and still more when a railroad finally reached the city from the east in 1919. Between 1920 and 1930 California grew by 2.25 million people, an increase of two thirds. Lesser spurts were evident in Oregon and Washington, but the vast Northwest wartime shipyards closed by 1925, and there was a period of quiet.

All over California, newcomers found their places as the economy took new strength from agriculture and industry. But by the 1930s, hit like the rest of the nation by economic depression, Los Angeles seemed in danger of fulfilling the direst warning of its critics, that it would turn into a ghost town. "Don't take anything to L.A. that you can't bring back on the *Super Chief*" was a popular Eastern joke. In 1936 civic leaders, who long had solicited tourists and new residents, sent police to the state border to turn back migrants who might become welfare charges.

The center of despair was the Great Central Valley. It received the main brunt of the Dust Bowl migration recorded in part by John Steinbeck in *The Grapes of Wrath*. One fourth of those moving to California between 1935 and 1940 came from Texas, Arkansas, Louisiana and Oklahoma. Most of them stayed; in those five years about 95,000 people moved from Oklahoma to California, and only 5,000 from California to Oklahoma. Yet the return of prosperity made this migration a classic example of California's social integration. On California university campuses it was easy by the 1950s to find progeny of the Okies as established as any other Californians—much as the offspring of the forty-niners had become the California aristocrats of the 1880s. The Northwest received some of the Dust Bowl refugees, especially as irrigation projects continued to open farmland. Others found work as dambuilders and bridgebuilders; this was the era of the Hoover, Bonneville and Grand Coulee Dams, and of the San Francisco bridges.

The Second World War caused more permanent changes along the Pacific Coast than anywhere else in the nation. Jobs were open and wages high; workers came from all over America to aircraft plants in Seattle, Los Angeles and San Diego, and to shipyards near each major city. The industrialist Henry J. Kaiser set up labor-recruiting offices in the Midwest and East and brought workers by special trains to his West Coast shipyards. In California, employment in aircraft plants rose from less than 20,000 in 1939 to 243,000 in 1943; shipyard payrolls in the same period climbed from 4,000 to 282,000. Unsightly public and private housing projects spread swiftly to accommodate the newcomers. The population of Richmond, across the bay from San Francisco, quadrupled in three wartime years; there were other such newly swollen communities in every metropolis.

Many who had been Westerners for at least a few years eagerly awaited the departure of the hordes. But there was little exodus; the familiar postwar pattern developed and another rush of veterans sought jobs and homes. Bringing in fresh energies and skills, the veterans and their families were a major factor in lowering the median age close to the national norm.

During the 1950s the nature of the California immigrant began to change. The growing research and educational facilities of California and, to some extent, of the Northwest were drawing scientists, educators and technicians—migrants of higher intellectual attainments than earlier arrivals. Where his predecessor pushed or pulled a two-wheeled cart or jounced west by covered wagon, the migrant of today not uncommonly arrives by jet with suitcase and briefcase, ready for work, while his family drives westward and weightier belongings follow by van. Public-school systems send teacher recruiters to Midwest campuses in the harshest weeks of winter to talk about California. Not untypically of Western cities, Seattle draws one third of its teachers from outside Washington.

California's growth remains a national phenomenon. From 1940 through 1965 the state's population swelled from 5 per cent to 10 per cent of the national total. In the same period the town of Concord jumped from 1,373 to 64,000, Richmond from 23,642 to 81,900, San Diego from 203,341 to 648,200 and Los Angeles from 1.5 million to 2.7 million. As the population of California approached 20 million, that of Oregon hovered near two million and Washington near three million. The growth of the Northwest states has more nearly followed the national rate. California goes rocketing along with vast momentum, seeming to renew itself like a solar cell drawing energy from the sun.

Yet many historic differences between California and the national norm are narrowing. Standardization is occurring everywhere. Widening federal regulation combines with the effects of the national communications network and speedier transportation to rub down the rough edges of difference. The move across America no longer requires courage or dedication. As casually as one moved a few generations ago to the next county, the new Westerner may come now for better climate, higher wages or even the elusive element of social prestige that is believed to accrue from the westward trek. The move is less restricted to the out-of-the-ordinary person, and the Westerner grows more average.

The West has accommodated its massive migrations ingeniously, and often with great good luck. Because Western settlement has been almost continuous, the social structure has been less rigid. The West is still relatively wide-open; each wave of newcomers tends to jar the status quo. Migration has made the Pacific Coast a crucible in which American traits are aboil.

In 1852 California miners and a lady visitor gather around a
gold-washing device called a long tom. In that year, the peak of
the Gold Rush, 100,000 men worked the fields, finding some $81
million in gold. By 1865 a total of $768 million had been found.

Episodes in
a headlong history

A handful of nuggets discovered at John
Sutter's sawmill in Northern California in 1848
started the largest gold rush in history—a rush
that was to be the dominant factor in the early
growth of the Pacific Coast states. In 1849
alone, 80,000 men surged into the new territory.
In the timber-rich Northwest, mills sprang up to
supply lumber for mines and houses. To profit
from the demand for transport to the Coast,
astute men built railroads. But by the time of
the 1906 earthquake and fire that wrecked
San Francisco, the gold era had come to an
end. In the south the climate soon provided ideal
conditions for testing the fledgling airplane and
producing motion pictures. It all happened very
quickly and very recently—so recently that most
of the important developments on the West Coast
can be traced in contemporary photographs.

Loggers prepare to drop a giant Douglas fir in the early 1900s. Known as fallers, they wielded their axes and saws from platforms set into the tree. Once it was down, buckers sawed the tree into manageable lengths. Bull punchers then hauled the lengths out with teams of oxen over log roads—an arduous task that greasers made easier by lubricating the roads with oil from fish livers. The average Douglas fir contained $28 worth of lumber during Gold Rush days. The same size tree had almost doubled in value by 1900.

On a snow-covered grade near the summit of a Cascades peak, a gang of Chinese railroad workers clears a roadbed in 1886. Nearly 15,000 Chinese were employed in the building of the several Northwest railroads that were completed during this period.

Marking an end to frontier isolation, townsmen celebrate the arrival of the first eastbound train of the Northern Pacific in The Dalles, Oregon, in 1883, shortly after the road's completion. Northern Pacific was the first transcontinental railroad to reach the Northwest.

Preparing to float logs from the Columbia River to San Diego around 1903, rivermen gather on a seagoing raft. Such rafts consisted of 1,000-foot bundles of logs held together by 150 tons of chain. They were the biggest things afloat from 1890 to 1930.

Booming industries during early years of growth

Although gold attracted many, others tapped different sources of wealth: trees and transportation. In 1847 two sawmills were operating in Washington; by 1860 there were 32. At first loggers cut small, easily managed trees; eventually they devised methods to conquer giants. With huge rafts they solved the problem of transporting the logs over vast distances. At the same time, assisted by government grants, other men turned to the building of railroads. From 1869 to 1893 five transcontinental lines were completed to the West Coast, allowing still more thousands of migrants to reach the region.

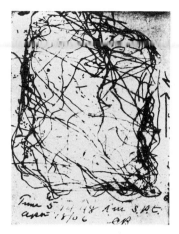

Frantic lines on a seismogram in nearby Oakland indicate the quake's severity at 5:14:48 a.m. Under normal conditions earth movements show up on seismograms as relatively straight parallel lines.

After the holocaust the shattered city lies in ruins on both sides of California Street. The Fairmont Hotel *(background, right)* withstood the quake but was gutted by one of the many fires that swept the city.

Calm residents watch a fire while others gather their belongings to flee. This particular blaze, started by sparks from a damaged flue as a woman prepared breakfast, became known as the "ham and eggs" fire.

A great city's destruction by quake and fire

Shortly after 5:12 a.m. on April 18, 1906, the first shock started in San Francisco, built in intensity, paused, then struck again with greater force. In all, the major quake that hit the city lasted less than 75 seconds, but then fires broke out, and with most water mains broken, firemen were almost helpless. Seventy-two hours later much of San Francisco was a charred ruin. Within two and a half years San Francisco was rebuilt, but for a time newcomers tended to avoid the city in favor of Southern California, foreshadowing that region's rise to eminence.

Leaning houses on Howard Street were built on unstable fill and suffered greatly. The effect of the shocks in the city depended on the type of land, not on proximity to the quake's center. Minor temblors are still a frequent occurrence in San Francisco.

San Franciscans search through the ruins for valuables after the fires had been extinguished. Owners allowed safes to cool for weeks before opening so that toasted contents would not ignite when air hit them. As a result, many valuables survived the disaster.

A wedding
of sun and stars

In search of light to finish a rained-out short entitled *The Count of Monte Cristo*, a group of Chicago moviemakers came to sunny Los Angeles in 1907. Flocks of other sun-seeking creators followed. The first permanent studio was established in 1909; by 1915 half of all American films were being shot in California. An era had been born. Stars and sets grew larger; the world marveled. The arrival of television reduced the size of both, but Hollywood still films the bulk of the national movie and TV output.

Cross-eyed Ben Turpin pleads for Polly Moran's hand in one of the Keystone comedies produced in the 1910s and 1920s by Mack Sennett, who frequently wrote the script as he filmed, hoodwinking policemen into chasing his heroes past the camera.

Delight of the feminine heart, Rudolph Valentino *(next to the stout lady)* plays an outlaw in love with Vilma Banky *(white hat)* during the filming of *The Eagle* in 1925. A star for less than six years, Valentino became as famous for his off-stage loves as for his acting.

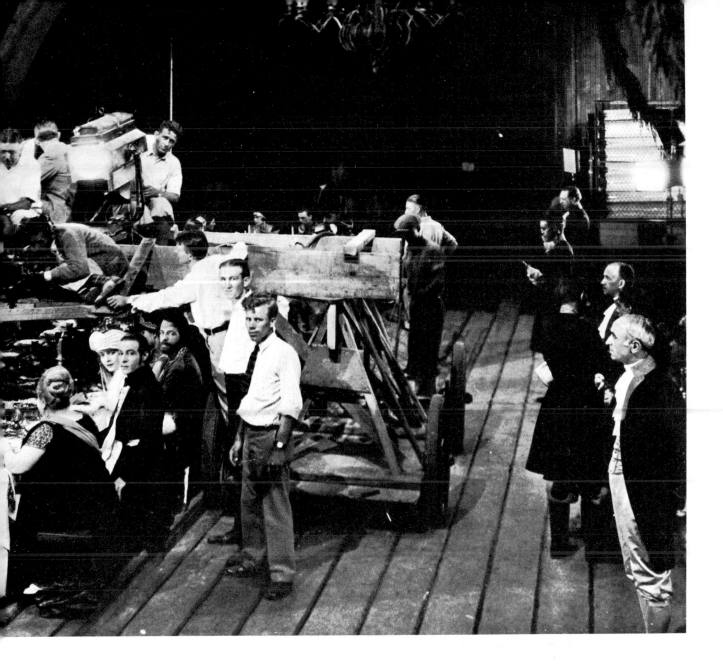

Assembling cast and crew, a previously unknown director named Cecil B. DeMille *(in light suit at center)* prepares for the first day's shooting of his first film, *The Squaw Man*, in 1913. The movie was a success, making DeMille's name a household word.

Heroine of popular serials, Ruth Roland steps into her Locomobile, one of the swankiest cars of the early 1920s. Fancy furs, huge cars, impressive pets, lavish parties and high living by the stars helped build a legend of Hollywood that lured millions to the movies.

Taking off during a U.S. Navy experiment in 1911, a test pilot named Eugene Ely flies a Curtiss biplane from a wooden platform constructed on the U.S.S. *Pennsylvania*. Ely had landed on the ship, which was moored in San Francisco Bay, an hour before, using a forerunner of modern deck arresting gear. The test helped convince the Navy of the value of the airplane. Three years later Navy pilots made military reconnaissance flights during the punitive expedition the U.S. launched against Mexico.

Developing the first successful hydroplane, Glenn Curtiss *(right)* and a mechanic work in San Diego Bay in December 1910. A major innovator in aviation, Curtiss was the first to use ailerons on airplane wings.

Passengers peer from the windows of a Ryan Airlines plane during a scheduled run between San Diego and Los Angeles in 1925. At this time other airlines concentrated on flying mail rather than passengers.

The birth
of a modern giant

"Gosh, it's aflying!" was one bystander's reaction as Glenn Curtiss took off at the first U.S. air meet, held in Los Angeles in 1910. In San Diego Curtiss later developed the original seaplanes. Other soon-to-be famous airmen like Glenn L. Martin, Donald W. Douglas and T. Claude Ryan set up aircraft-manufacturing plants in the area—and thus laid the groundwork for the mammoth aerospace industry that is today one of the bases of the West Coast economy. In 1925 Ryan started the first scheduled year-round passenger line in the nation. His factory built the *Spirit of St. Louis*, the plane that Charles A. Lindbergh flew alone across the Atlantic in 1927, ushering in the modern air age.

A former airmail pilot, Charles A. Lindbergh *(third from right)* poses with his *Spirit of St. Louis* at the Ryan plant in San Diego in 1927. Ryan's crew built the plane in 60 days. Ready for takeoff, fueled with 300 gallons of gas, it weighed only 5,000 pounds.

3

Challenge
of an Uncommon
Environment

In the West there is an eternal consciousness of the land. Nature, grandiose in scale, does not allow itself to be overlooked; it is a part of life. Few people grow blasé about the juxtaposition of mountain, sea and desert. The challenge of the uncommon physical environment has always been sensed. From the beginning the people and the place seemed almost to expect each other. "Bring me men to match my mountains" reads a line from a popular 19th Century poem inscribed on one of the state buildings in Sacramento, the capital of California. As though in answer, Westerners have moved to modify their environment spectacularly, for better and worse. Los Angeles has been built on a desert coast and is sustained by water and power transported to it from distances of hundreds of miles. Great ocean trade has developed at the city, which had no natural harbor. So that dry valleys in California and Washington may grow green, billions of dollars have been spent to move water in projects unmatched in scope. Deep canyons have been dammed and mountains have been bored through

Snaking 250 miles over dry hills and valleys, the Los Angeles Aqueduct transports 300 million gallons of water a day to help quench the city's thirst. Completed in 1913, after six years of labor, the aqueduct cost the then-fantastic sum of $25 million.

so that deserts may be irrigated, power generated, flooding controlled and recreational areas created.

While it is still possible to find the images of rurality—sheepherders' wagons on the lonely high deserts, hermits on bleak, sandy homesteads, stubborn prospectors picking over tired veins of ore—the wave of change that sweeps the landscape is urban in nature. Even the highly mechanized farms of the Great Central Valley, an area that appears rural to the eye, are controlled by men who live in San Francisco and Los Angeles; the men who operate the valley farms look to the cities for direction. Because so vast an area of the three Pacific States is so sparsely inhabited, the states do not rank high on population-density lists. California, with about 118 people to the square mile, is only about one seventh as densely settled as New Jersey or Rhode Island; Washington, with 43 to the square mile, and Oregon, with 20, are even roomier. Yet California cannot be called a rural state. More than 85 per cent of its people live in cities, three out of five of them in the Los Angeles and San Francisco metropolitan areas. About 70 per cent of the people of Washington and more than 60 per cent of Oregonians are also city residents.

So the greatest strains on the Western environment exist where the people are, in the cities and their fringes. Even though all three states are large and well endowed with resources, the impact on those resources is grave. Much of the land is sparsely vegetated and prone to erosion and slides during flash floods. The velocity of migration to the Pacific States tends to overpower the land. In California each day, more than 350 acres are bulldozed for new subdivisions, shopping centers or freeways. Often this removes from cultivation agricultural land of the highest productivity. The build-up is headlong, and urban ugliness often results, as elsewhere in the nation. The fastest-growing community in Washington is Bellevue, a maze of commuters' homes near Seattle. The University of Washington architect Victor Steinbrueck describes Bellevue as "an all-American mess." Housing developments in the San Jose area south of San Francisco, a pastoral, prune-growing valley until World War II, have sprawled so monotonously that the San Francisco columnist Herb Caen has remarked, "Los Angeles begins at San Jose." Endless tracts of houses conjure up the image of a photocopying machine that has gone berserk and cannot be cut off.

Such urban ugliness is made more offensive to many in the West because not far distant, by contrast, there is always some setting that the fallible hand of man has not reached. But the bulldozers

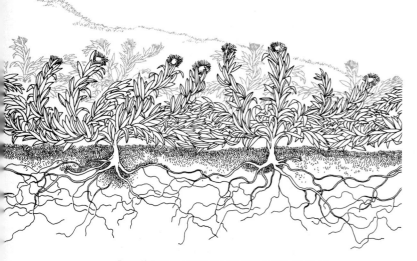

Beautifying the sandy coastal slopes and dunes of California are the lovely yellow or lavender flowers of the Hottentot fig, sometimes known as the ice plant. Originally imported from Africa, the hardy perennial serves an important purpose in the West: erosion control. The plant has a large network of sinewy roots which, as they reach outward in search of water, lock the sandy soil in place. As the plant's leaves fall to the ground, they build up a thick, water-absorbent blanket. And when the leaves decay and mix with the soil, they help form humus, thus transforming easily eroded sand into more stable earth.

are constantly on the move. The breed of restless, searching strangers who inhabit the West shows a facility for creating instant megalopolis and then escaping to an open place to do it all over again. Critics of such heedless growth insist that they are not in blind opposition to progress, but in opposition to blind progress. They are determined, in the words of the University of California biophysicist William E. Siri, that their land will not be "wrapped in power transmission lines like a giant package prepared for delivery by an idiot."

In his rush to dominate his environment the Westerner has begun to spoil it. Pollution has roiled the waters from Lake Washington in Seattle (sewage) to the rivers of the Northwest (pulp- and paper-mill discharges) to San Francisco Bay (industrial waste) and Lake Tahoe (sewage). Air pollution, long thought to be a Los Angeles monopoly, is now a problem in San Francisco and is spreading to other cities of California and the Northwest. Smog is at its worst in summer months, when, under certain atmospheric conditions, polluted air hangs over the cities like a suffocating blanket. Many experts agree that about 90 per cent of Los Angeles and San Francisco smog is caused by automobile exhaust; industrial air pollution has been largely controlled. Because the smog problem is so great, it was predictable that California would take the national lead in regulating automobile exhaust systems; in 1966 devices to control exhaust gases became mandatory on new automobiles sold in the state. Yet the problem continues, and scientists present sharply divergent proposals for solving it.

The blights of ugliness and pollution are comparatively new in the West, and public concern over them has been roused only in recent years. Public reaction has in fact arisen only since the Westerner began to win his battle with the primary threat to his survival: the aridity of much of his environment. Above all, water—or its lack—has set the pattern for settlement of the Pacific States. In the West, water dominates and controls. It is the ultimate sovereign.

An imbalance in supply renders Western water affairs contentious. Oregon and Washington usually are regarded as "have" states because of their rivers, notably the mighty Columbia; California is a "have-not." State lines, of course, were not determined by the availability of water resources; east of the Cascades in the Northwest, drought has often been as acute as in Southern California. At times, there is too much water in northwestern California, western Oregon and western Washington; floods are a frequent menace in those regions. Almost 40

per cent of California's water supply is found in the northwestern part of the state, where only 2 per cent of its people live.

Southern California, by contrast, has 60 per cent of the state's people and 2 per cent of its water. Here the problem of aridity has been greatest. The area's average annual rainfall is about 15 inches, all in the winter months—not enough in itself to support modern urban living. Spanish settlers tiled their courtyards or shuffled through dust, but the modern Southern Californian expects to keep his lawn sprinkled and his swimming pool filled, even though he lives in what is technically a desert. So the megalopolis survives only through extraordinary feats of water importation. The aqueduct is the symbol of at least temporary triumph in the contest between the Californian and his environment. But controversy and dissension have accompanied the laying of the aqueducts across the land. As Southern California has gone farther and farther away to import water, critics have risen to claim that the region has been guilty of water imperialism. Implacable bitterness has developed in localities that have been forced to yield water. For a century there have been bitter water feuds in the West. There are water specialists—attorneys and engineers —whose entire careers have been involved with the

Colorado River. The quest for water is at the heart of the California story.

Artesian wells helped Southern California to come to its first bloom. In 1900 such wells, used in conjunction with the Los Angeles River, were sufficient to supply the needs of Los Angeles, then a city of slightly more than 100,000 citizens, but they were certainly inadequate for a young metropolis anticipating a population of half a million people. A drought in 1904 enabled William Mulholland, a self-educated Irish immigrant who had worked up from a ditchdigger's job to become manager of the Los Angeles water department, to bring to fruition a long-proposed scheme to transport water to the city from the Owens River Valley, more than 200 miles north of Los Angeles. Buyers representing the city purchased 300,000 acres and the accompanying water rights in the valley without informing valley farmers of their plans. The acquisition, born in secret intrigue, bred violence. Four thousand downstream farmers and townspeople in the Owens Valley were deprived of water and the farms simply dried up. When dams were built by the Los Angeles invaders, Owens Valley farmers tried to dynamite them. In 1906 President Theodore Roosevelt, who had supported a reclamation proposal to distribute Owens River water to farmers in the valley, abandoned the

Thwarting a rampaging river, Southern Pacific Railroad cars dump earth and rocks into the path of the Colorado in 1906. Tapped for an irrigation canal by the fly-by-night California Development Company, the river had burst its banks in 1905, flowing into the Imperial Valley instead of the Gulf of California and creating a vast lake called the Salton Sea. The Salton Sea floodwaters reached depths up to 67.5 feet before the Southern Pacific, which had bought the California Development Company, could force the river back into its original channel.

plan on the principle that the needs of the citizens of Los Angeles were greater. To prevent farmers from purchasing other land in the valley to disrupt the Mulholland project—and to circumvent speculators—the federal government then classified a large, virtually treeless valley area as a part of a national forest preserve. Speculators were busy nevertheless; some of them made huge profits by buying land in the San Fernando Valley outside Los Angeles, the route of the Owens River Aqueduct. Eventually Owens River water got through to Los Angeles, in a massive supply that was the original basis of the city's spectacular growth, and that still provides more than 60 per cent of its needs.

The struggle to obtain water from the Colorado River was even more violent. The Colorado is a wild stream whose torrents slash down out of the Rocky Mountains and across the desert of the Southwest through the Grand Canyon. The Colorado drains an area of almost a quarter of a million square miles. It is brownish red with silt, carrying as much as 170 million cubic yards a year to its delta lands in Southern California and northwestern Mexico. But it has been a primary factor in California's growth.

One of the first Colorado River visionaries was a forty-niner named Oliver Meredith Wozencraft, a physician who plodded west from New Orleans across the Colorado Desert. He found a dry, silted lake bed southeast of where Palm Springs now lies, and reached the conclusion that the Colorado, whose channel was 60 miles to the east, had left its bed at some point in its millions of years of existence and created a vast lake, the lowest part of which lay 280 feet below sea level. Wozencraft proposed to open thousands of acres of rich silt deposits to cultivation by forcing the Colorado into an encore. He failed to win support, but in 1901 other private interests succeeded. Water from the Colorado was diverted into a devious series of ditches that followed the downward slope of the land into Mexico and back north again into what became known as the Imperial Valley.

Summer temperatures of 110 to 120 degrees are common in the Imperial Valley, and its average annual rainfall amounts to only three inches. But the presence of water gave the valley an incomparable potential. Today it has America's longest growing season: 300 days. In a single year its farmers can produce as many as six harvests of alfalfa. Melons and grapes ripen faster in the Imperial Valley than anywhere else in America, and a single acre may yield as much as 1,000 pounds of cotton annually, roughly twice the national average. It is no wonder that the arrival of Colorado water precipitated a boom in the valley; 10,000 people came between 1901 and 1904. The Southern Pacific built a railroad into the valley and took an active interest in the area's development. But in February of 1905 the Colorado flooded and broke out of its channels. For 16 months the river rampaged crazily over the desert, sweeping village and farmland before it. It created random channels totaling more than 40 miles with an average width of 1,000 feet. The low northwestern part of Wozencraft's dry lake bed became the 400-square-mile inland Salton Sea. For a time its level rose seven inches a day.

Underwritten by the Southern Pacific, a small army of workers tried to dam the river and turn it back into its channel. But they failed repeatedly. A last, desperate counterattack was mounted late in 1906. For 52 days Southern Pacific rail cars were conscripted from all over the Southwest to rush pilings and rock fill to the Imperial Valley. Day and night, as rapidly as the cars could be shunted on and off hastily built trestles, their loads were emptied in the path of the current—3,000 carloads in the final 15 days of the battle. The struggle was won at a cost of more than three million dollars to the Southern Pacific alone. There were other losses as well; it was estimated that the river had gouged out before it some 800 million cubic yards of soil—four times more than were later to be moved in building the Panama Canal.

Although the river had been turned back, clearly its complete control was too overwhelming a project for private enterprise to handle. The All-American Canal, which links the Colorado to the Imperial Valley, was completed in 1940. The canal was merely one part of a $400 million federal program aimed at harnessing the Colorado. Water from the canal today irrigates more than half a million acres. Its main branch is a concrete-lined river 200 feet wide, shining bright blue in the desert sun and flowing 80 miles through mountainous white sand dunes that have been the setting for countless desert movies. Even to Californians, who are accustomed to environmental incongruities, the All-American Canal is a curiosity.

The construction of the canal had been made possible by the completion in 1936 of Hoover Dam, which established control over the Colorado upstream near Las Vegas. Behind the dam, set between glistening black-and-purplish-granite canyon walls, lies its creation, Lake Mead, which is open to navigation for 115 miles upstream. Lake Mead is a reservoir so capacious that its waters would cover an area the size of New York State to the depth of one foot. Hoover was the first massive multiple-purpose dam in America, not only a water controller but a producer of hydroelectric power.

Hoover was a U.S. government project, but Westerners have not relied solely upon federal assistance for such programs. With immense foresight Southern California planners have sought out water supplies generations ahead of actual need. In 1928 Los Angeles joined 10 other Southern California cities, whose plights were potentially far more dangerous, in organizing a Metropolitan Water District, a body empowered to find new sources of supply and bring the water to the Southern California coast. In 1939 the MWD completed the Colorado River Aqueduct across a desolate, parched area of Southern California from Parker Dam, 150 miles downriver from Hoover Dam. Passing through 42 tunnels, including a 13-mile bore under the San Jacinto Mountains, the aqueduct crosses a region in which earthquakes occur frequently; where the pipes travel over the fault lines, flexible tubing is used to adjust to the tremors. Five pumping stations and huge siphons are required to lift the flow over the mountains. The Metropolitan Water District now serves 119 Southern California cities and many large unincorporated areas.

The MWD's use of Colorado River water was a

California's complex water system

The major systems of dams, reservoirs and other facilities that supply water to California are shown below. The two most complex systems are the California Water Project (*orange*) and the Central Valley Project (*green*). These systems serve several purposes. Their dams control rivers, their power stations generate electricity, and the water they pump is used both for irrigation and for city water supplies. Since 1957 all present systems, and all planned for the future, have been coordinated under The California Water Plan.

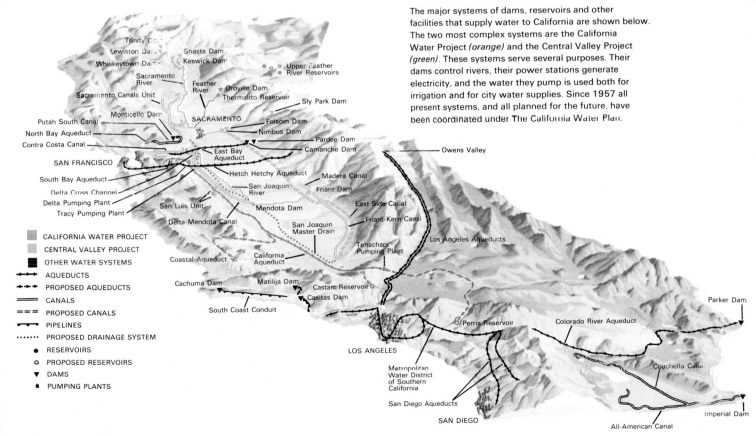

The Columbia's system of dams

Approximately a third of all the potential hydroelectric power in the United States is contained in the American part of the Columbia River and its tributaries. Of this huge potential, about one third has already been tapped by the series of dams shown below. Their present output is some 10,793,000 kilowatts a year, enough to meet the needs of virtually the entire Northwest. In addition to producing electricity, some dams store water to irrigate the farmlands of eastern Washington.

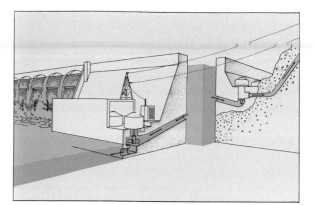

The workings of Grand Coulee Dam are shown in the simplified cutaway above. Water from the reservoir behind the dam flows through a huge pipe *(center)*, called a penstock, to turn the giant turbine that drives the generator that creates electricity *(orange)*. Overflow from the reservoir falls down the spillway *(left)*, while water for crops is pumped *(at right)* to irrigation projects.

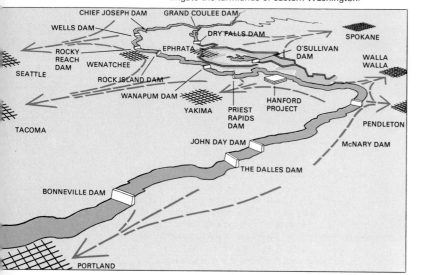

The Columbia's 11 major dams, either completed or under construction, are shown at left. These dams generate much of the electricity needed by the area's cities *(black grids)*, carried over huge power-line systems *(orange)*. The two dams not on the Columbia, the Dry Falls and O'Sullivan Dams, are used mainly to store water to irrigate nearby farmlands *(bright green)*.

major factor in several decades of court fights between California and arid Arizona, which the river passes through on its journey toward the Gulf of California. The litigation came to a climax in 1963, when the U.S. Supreme Court handed down a ruling giving Arizona a larger share of the river. The Colorado's waters are now rationed among seven states and Mexico with such thoroughness that little remains to flow into the Gulf of California.

While adequate for the present, Colorado River water will not supply all future needs in Southern California. In 1964 the Metropolitan Water District contracted with the State of California for eventual delivery of an additional 1.8 billion gallons a day from the new California Water Project. This project is designed to produce hydroelectric power and to bring surplus water from the delta of the Sacramento and San Joaquin Rivers near San Francisco to various water districts in the state as far south as the Mexican border. The project dwarfs every water-transfer system in history. The CWP keystone is the mile-wide Oroville Dam on the Feather River in Northern California, built to impound more than a trillion gallons. The project got its start in 1960 with the authorization by California voters of a $1.75 billion bond issue, the largest in the history of any state. Even that is only a part of the project's cost.

The Metropolitan Water District will bear about two thirds of the expense of building the southward-bound aqueduct system out of revenues obtained from water sales to Southern California consumers. It estimates that the expense of additions that it will be required to make to its own system to utilize project water, plus payments to the state over the 75-year life of the contract, will run close to six billion dollars. Other expenses for the entire project— estimates of its total cost run as high as $15 billion —will be borne by other benefiting water districts in the state, by the federal government and by the sale of hydroelectric power.

For a considerable time to come the entire state thus seems assured of a sufficient water supply. But planners in the California Department of Water Resources cite 2020 as the year when water shortages will become critical unless further new sources are developed. One hope for the future is the desalination of sea water. Another possibility is the dispersal of Columbia River water to the arid Southwest. A proposal advanced by the federal Bureau of Reclamation in 1949, the Columbia plan has become a tense issue in the Northwest. The flow of the Columbia is 10 times greater than that of the Colorado, and most of it now ends up in the sea. But Northwest leaders understandably do not wish to set ceilings on the expansion of their region by bargaining away water that they may eventually need. Moreover, they remember that drought is common even in much of the Northwest.

The Columbia is already vital to the Northwest, particularly to the arid regions east of the Cascades. After attempts at farming in the area had failed in the 1930s, work was begun on Grand Coulee Dam in eastern Washington. Completed in 1942, Grand Coulee is the world's most massive concrete dam. Its power capability was immediately pressed into full service for war production, notably in Northwest shipyards and aircraft plants. When the war ended, the irrigation potential of Grand Coulee was exploited by the Bureau of Reclamation with the aim of opening to agriculture a fertile million-acre region in eastern Washington. To a sprawling desert basin marked by abandoned farms, rusted windmills and dead orchards, a system of tunnels and canals began to carry the waters of the Columbia.

In the early 1950s new farm families, most of them already residents of the West, began to move into the Columbia Basin. Under the original law sponsored by the Bureau of Reclamation no farmer could receive water from a federal project if he owned more than the 160 acres that the agency then considered the ideal size for a family farm; the law has since been amended, and currently a husband and wife may receive water for as much as 320 irrigable acres. Those wishing to purchase farms today must have a net worth of at least $8,500; typically, the prospective Columbia Basin farmer now arrives with assets triple that amount. Then he plunges into production of sugar beets, potatoes, truck crops, hay or seed; peppermint and spearmint oils extracted from mint grown in the basin are shipped to chewing-gum and candy manufacturers elsewhere in the country. The landscape, once covered by dust, is today marked by neat towns and scores of recreational areas set around blue lakes.

After the Mississippi-Missouri system, the Columbia is the second river in the United States in volume of flow, with more cubic footage of water than all other Western rivers combined. The multitude of dams, storage projects and power plants up and down the Columbia gives it a greater hydroelectric development than any other American river. The Bonneville Power Administration, an arm of the Department of the Interior, markets power from more than 20 multipurpose dams on the Columbia and its tributaries through the nation's largest network of long-distance, high-voltage transmission lines. An intertie provides for the delivery of surplus power from the Northwest to the Southwest.

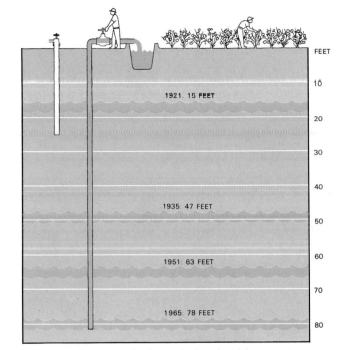

Heavy pumping has gradually reduced the amount of underground water in many areas of California, as shown by the drawing above of a section of the San Joaquin Valley. There the water table (the highest level of ground saturated with water, indicated by the green lines) dropped 63 feet from 1921 to 1965. The remaining amount is huge, but in places is being removed faster than rain and runoff can replenish it.

Other sources of power are also available in the Northwest. On the Columbia near Richland, in south-central Washington, where the Atomic Energy Commission's Hanford Project is situated, the world's largest nuclear-powered steam plant began operation in 1966; its electrical output is marketed through the Bonneville system. But as industry proliferates and the population increases, even the power-rich Northwest is ranging farther in its search for more power; a treaty with Canada ratified in 1964 opened the Upper Columbia in Canada to hydroelectric development, seemingly assuring the Northwest of abundant power for decades.

As the harnessing of the Columbia has begun to reshape the Northwest and as the Colorado has sustained Southern California, so has the Central Valley Project, an enormous, widely scattered network of dams, canals, and power and pumping plants, made the Great Central Valley the agricultural heartland of California and the most productive farming area in western America. Roughly 450 miles long and averaging 50 miles in width, the valley has stiflingly hot summers and is prone to impenetrable winter fogs. Yet its soil is rich; the bulk of irrigable California land lies in its southern part. But rainfall there is scant and evaporation greater

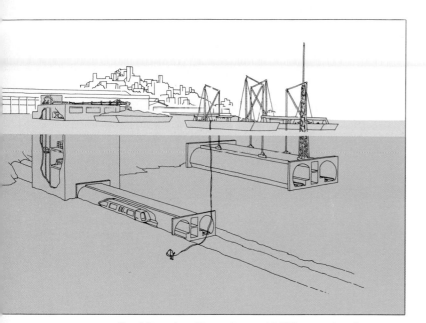

Specially equipped barges lower a 10,000-ton section of prefabricated subway tunnel into San Francisco Bay. This tunnel, which will connect San Francisco and Oakland, is part of a rapid-transit system intended to relieve the bay cities' chronic traffic congestion. Travel time from the farthest point on the line, Fremont, 30 miles from the center of San Francisco, will be an estimated 35 minutes during rush hour.

than in the north. The area is distant from the Sacramento River of Northern California, the primary source of Central Valley Project water. But because water from the Sacramento is brought to the southern section, the valley has a growing season of nine to 10 months, about four months longer than the average in the East and Midwest; three of its counties—Fresno, Kern and Tulare—lead the country in value of farm products. The Central Valley Project irrigates more than a million acres of land, and also provides power, flood and salinity control, fish and wildlife refuges, and recreational areas. The achievement is remarkable, but in the Western tradition; challenged by his environment, the Californian continues to succeed beyond his dreams.

Yet conflict rages around the Central Valley Project, notably over its control. Californians devised the plan in 1930, and in 1933 even went to the polls to authorize a $170 million bond issue to begin it. However, the bonds were never sold, for the project seemed too vast for the Depression-era state budget. In 1935 the federal government allotted funds to launch it, and its capital has continued to come from Washington. So far about one billion dollars has been invested in the project. An estimated $3.89 billion more will be spent by the end of the century; at least three million acres of irrigable land

in the valley still await water. Yet the CVP is entirely an intrastate project, and a delicate balance of administrative jurisdiction has had to be maintained between state and federal officials. The project is the first example of its type of joint action between state and federal governments, and the federal law denying irrigation water to farms larger than 320 acres in size therefore creates a problem. The Great Central Valley pattern, set long before the inception of the CVP, is one of vast absentee landholding.

Attitudes toward the uses of land and resources are undergoing change in the West. When the region was sparsely settled, those who exploited its farmland, water, timber, oil and minerals became the vested political forces. Their power is being counterbalanced today by that of the millions of prosperous, leisure-loving and restless Westerners who are as concerned about recreation areas and open space as they are about electric power and irrigation. Now sportsmen, tourists, conservationists and city dwellers anxious to preserve their water supply are beginning to exert as much political pressure as lumbermen, mineowners or cattlemen.

The trend toward citizen interest and participation in conservation matters is as evident in the West as it is elsewhere in the nation. A serious concern for the future of their environment is becoming common among Westerners. In California such concern is seen in the surge of membership in the Save-Our-Redwoods League and in the Sierra Club and the Izaak Walton League, associations dedicated to preserving recreational and wilderness areas. Northwesterners strongly support such groups as the North Cascades Conservation Council, the Columbia River Gorge Commission and the Olympic Park Associates, most of them organizations interested in maintaining clean waters or limiting land use to preserve natural beauty. There are also pressure groups like California Tomorrow, a nonprofit educational organization that concerns itself with maintaining "a beautiful and productive California." It introduced the word "slurb" to describe what one of its reports termed the "sloppy, sleazy, slovenly, slipshod semi-cities" of California.

In a confrontation that was first joined in California, many thoughtful citizens have opposed existing freeway policy, regarding it as leading to the insatiable and undiscriminating consumption of the open land that was part of the environmental heritage of the West. In the relatively uncrowded Northwest the freeway did not rapidly emerge as a villain. Nor did it in Southern California, where traffic congestion for many years has been so monumental that drastic remedies have clearly been necessary. The first major revolt against freeway development took place in San Francisco in 1959, when the California Division of Highways had completed part of the elevated Embarcadero Freeway around the downtown San Francisco waterfront. To many the new freeway was a concrete noose bifurcating the view of the Ferry Building—a symbol to San Franciscans because it survived the 1906 earthquake. City supervisors, spurred by an outraged citizenry, halted the Embarcadero Freeway after one mile of it had been completed, and prevented the Division of Highways from building seven other proposed freeways that would have crisscrossed the city. But with the highest density of automobiles of any city in the world—7,000 per square mile—San Francisco was beginning to choke on its cars, and it turned to work on an urban rapid-transit system.

Other stands have been taken elsewhere in the state against proposed freeway routing that would put roads through parks, redwood forests and historic areas. Not all have been successful, because the California Division of Highways is a formidable body. It holds a power of eminent domain superior to that of all other California agencies; its commissioners are appointed by the state governor and are not subject to recall, and its decisions are seldom reviewed by the legislature. Under a provision of the state constitution the Division of Highways receives all gasoline taxes and most motor-vehicle fees and taxes. With federal grants its annual budget is about a billion dollars.

While the moves of the Division of Highways have seemed arbitrary to some residents of the state, most Southern Californians have heartily welcomed new freeways. In Los Angeles, whose downtown area more than half a million people enter each day, about five persons commute by car to every two by bus. One third of the available downtown land is devoted to parking. There are continuing proposals to break the death lock that many believe the automobile has on Los Angeles, but as long as the elaborate freeway network continues to be enlarged and to function, most Southern Californians will undoubtedly stay with their cars. The residential pattern in sprawling Los Angeles makes rapid-transit systems of doubtful merit. Metropolitan Los Angeles has more than 5,000 people per square mile, while San Francisco has 16,500 and Manhattan 76,000. Los Angeles had a 1,200-mile interurban rail system that was the nation's lengthiest in 1930; as late as 1945 it was carrying 109 million passengers a year. But with the rapid acceptance of the automobile, usage of the system declined, and the

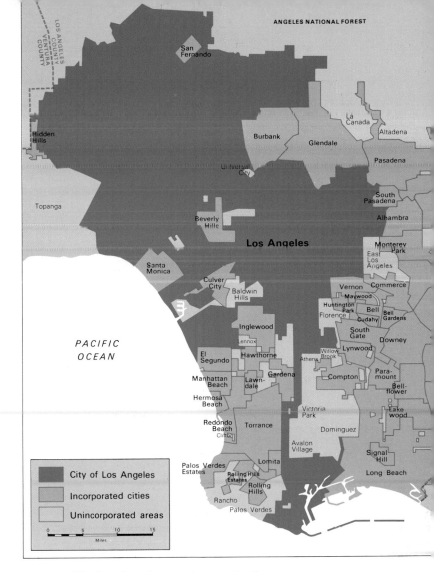

The Los Angeles area's complexity

The immediate vicinity of Los Angeles is a hodgepodge of separate cities, each with its own laws and municipal government, and of unincorporated areas controlled by the counties in which they lie (above). This confusion of separate civic units is compounded by the fact that a number of them share certain services but not others. One of the cities, for example, will provide its neighbors with school facilities but fail to cooperate in traffic regulations. However, some steps toward wider cooperation have been taken. Large districts covering many communities have been set up to cope with such problems as transportation and air pollution.

The extent of Los Angeles' Metropolitan Area and of its larger Regional Metropolitan Area are shown below.

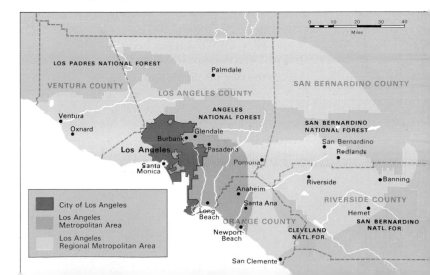

city closed it down completely in 1963. The automobile is in many ways the basis of the Southern California economy; the sprawl of the megalopolis makes the automobile, thus far, the only practical means of transportation.

The absence of a conventional urban core in Los Angeles seems to many to be the dreariest aspect of the Southern California environment. One municipal slurb blends into another; at last count there were 76 incorporated cities and towns within Los Angeles County alone and many more across the line in Orange County.

Some of these are extremely odd municipal organizations. Three were originally not cities in the traditional sense but protective societies for cows. The bizarre trio represents one innovative extreme to which Southern Californians have gone in attempting to maintain their environment against the encroachments of millions of migrants. There had been prosperous dairying areas southeast of the city for about 40 years when the residential expansion that followed World War II began to circumscribe the pastures. As a result, dairy owners began to incorporate their pastures and barns as cities rather than give up their lands and retreat from the megalopolis. A city forthrightly named Dairyland was first; its civic birth in 1955 was heralded with the motto "United to Preserve." For years it remained a small community in which cows and chickens outnumbered human residents. But in 1965 the pressure of megalopolis became too great; Dairyland changed its name to La Palma and allowed builders to begin subdividing its pastures for new housing tracts.

On the southern border of La Palma is the city of Cypress; its impetus for bursting into civic flower came from a threat by neighboring Buena Park to annex a strip of land 300 feet wide through Dutch-settled farmlands. Cypress is not all cows and chickens; from its early days it has had some residences housing nonfarmers, and a subdivider once bought 600 acres and wangled a zone variance. That set off a civic purge; one councilman resigned and two others were defeated in seeking re-election, but Cypress too may find it impossible to preserve its rural character.

Dairy Valley is the third of the cow cities. It too is being subjected to outside pressures; it lost one fight to prevent a junior college from encroaching on its pasturelands, and another to the California Division of Highways. A freeway now bisects the dairylands of Dairy Valley.

Such municipal incongruities are not typical of Los Angeles today. The city seems to be coalescing, concentrating traditional urban activities into one recognizable area. Planners talk of the emergence of a new kind of urban core—what they call their "metropolitan T." The upright of the Los Angeles "T" is the Wilshire Boulevard corridor, running 15 miles from downtown to the Pacific, an area approximating the width and length of Manhattan. Within it a vertical skyline of both commercial and residential structures has been rising. The top bar of the "T" is a five-mile section, roughly paralleling the Harbor Freeway, in which governmental, educational and cultural structures have been going up. Los Angeles is thus at last creating, its planners believe, an urban core—but one of vast dimensions.

The Los Angeles citizen seems finally to have begun caring what happens to his city. There has been enthusiastic support of recently built cultural nuclei like the Music Center and the County Art Museum, and rejuvenation of the blighted downtown is being spurred by the Bunker Hill urban-renewal project on a nearby 136-acre plot that was once a slum. Here, for the first time, tower apartments are being made available to thousands of residents in a walk-to-work location. Among the 8,000 members of California Tomorrow, Angelenos are strongly represented; they are among the leaders seeking sensible routing of freeways, more parks, fewer billboards, more zoning controls and better planning. At the University of California at Los Angeles, and elsewhere across the Los Angeles Basin, hundreds of adult citizens who are not concerned with college credits are attending seminars and lectures dealing with urban esthetics and conservation. It is no longer fashionable for an Angeleno to deprecate his city; today he yearns to improve it. His concern is part of a trend. Because his cities are growing at so fast a pace, and because he has long enjoyed so much room, the Westerner is perhaps more sensitive to crowding than are Americans living in older regions. He has therefore begun to make himself heard in the fight to prevent the suicide of his cities. No longer distracted by rigors related to the frontier, he more often employs his new-found leisure and affluence in civic affairs; the worsening plight of the physical environment is a cause of worry to many who had not previously considered such concerns within their realm. With his relatively new consciousness of the momentum that blight can achieve, the Westerner has become a most ardent conservationist. All up and down the Pacific Coast there is a marked increase of public involvement in environmental esthetics. The Westerner is now acting with a proprietary concern that reflects his pride in his new homeland.

The runaway growth of Los Angeles is dramatically shown in two pictures taken from the same spot 43 years apart. In 1922 *(left)* Wilshire Boulevard ambled among beanfields. By 1965 *(right)* it had become one of the nation's most startlingly urban thoroughfares.

Big, varied and vital cities

The major cities of the West Coast have a number of things in common. All have striking settings, all are comparatively young and all have undergone periods of explosive growth. All are big: the smallest, Portland, ranks 32nd in size among the nation's cities; the largest, Los Angeles, is third. Yet, such similarities aside, each has developed in its own distinctive way. Frenetic Los Angeles is a city forever in a hurry, furiously expanding at a pace that seems to be exceeded only by the speed of the cars hurtling along its freeways. Quiet San Diego, with a new emphasis on the aerospace industry and on urban planning, likes to consider itself a model community. Sophisticated San Francisco is at once gracious and gaudy. Seattle's dominant tone is one of vigorous hard work, while Portland resembles its conservative namesake in Maine more than it does its own neighbors.

Angelenos sun and swim at Huntington Beach State Park, part of 40 miles of beach open to the public near the city. The oil derricks mark one of the 15 major fields discovered in the area between 1917 and 1929.

Heavy traffic crowds the eight-lane Santa Monica Freeway at evening rush hour. Some 80 per cent of the workers in the Los Angeles area drive to their jobs, averaging a daily hour and 36 minutes in their cars.

Sprawling Los Angeles, where the automobile rules

Masses of people streaming into the Los Angeles area in search of good weather, good jobs or simply the good life have made the city what it is today: a prototype of the supercity of the future. The city of Los Angeles itself is enormous. Made up of what were once 64 separate communities, it covers 455 square miles. The vast metropolitan area is about four times larger. And in recent years the area's population has increased faster than that of any comparable part of the country, accounting for 10 per cent of all growth in the nation's 212 metropolitan regions. Responsible in large measure for making this uncontrolled growth possible is the automobile. Only its mobility allows Angelenos to get about their sprawling city, to drive to their jobs and to the area's numerous but far-flung beaches and other recreation areas.

Swimming pools—72 in this picture—abound in a well-to-do residential area called Hayvenhurst not far from Hollywood. The houses sell for as much as $85,000, but small down payments have enabled many families with relatively modest incomes to buy them.

Handsome mansions repose on the carefully landscaped slopes of Bel-Air, an exclusive section of Los Angeles, looking down on part of the Bel-Air Country Club golf course. Residents of the area include leaders of Los Angeles society and of the film industry.

A dedication to
comfort and easy living

Many parts of Los Angeles offer dramatic evidence of the area's affluence and of its people's determination to enjoy all the comforts and pleasures available in modern America. Middle-class housing districts display swimming pools in every other back yard, and apartment projects offer not only pools but such amenities as billiard rooms, barbecues and horseback-riding lessons. Country clubs dot the landscape, some elegant and expensive and others within the reach of even the moderately well off. The two-car—and even three-car—family has become a commonplace. Over these fortunate sections there seems to hang an optimistic glow. The people in this prosperous, growing land clearly feel that they, above all others, have discovered the good life.

Residents, most of whom are single, lounge by the pool of an apartment development called the Sunset Barrington Gardens, in the Brentwood section of Los Angeles. The management provides the residents with dances, barbecues and other festivities.

A commanding view of San Diego unfolds before diners atop the new Fifth Avenue Financial Centre. Above the city a jet glides toward Lindbergh Field, which commemorates Charles A. Lindbergh's preparations in San Diego for his epochal 1927 flight. In the distance rise buildings erected since the start in 1962 of a downtown redevelopment program. On the far right lies the $21.5 million Community Concourse, which contains a convention hall, the Civic Theatre and the city's Administration Building.

Surrounded by brilliant gardens, strollers wander through 1,400-acre Balboa Park, which borders San Diego's downtown area. The park includes one of the world's finest zoos as well as art galleries and a reconstruction of the Globe theater of Shakespeare's London.

Sunny San Diego, a model of urban planning

Sailors still stroll through San Diego looking for fun, as they have since the first Navy installation was established in 1911, but today the city is more than just a Navy town. Farsighted city planners, carefully preserving their community's charms, have attracted firms engaged in the nation's fastest-growing fields—aerospace, research, education. The money these businesses have brought in has enabled San Diego's planners to develop or modernize many parts of the city, giving it a head start on the future.

A billboard-sized painting of a destroyer looms over sailors window-shopping on Broadway, a street running toward the harbor. The Navy no longer dominates San Diego's economy, but the city remains headquarters of the 11th Naval District, the Navy's largest.

Antiquated cable cars struggle over the abrupt rolls in Powell Street, one of hilly San Francisco's many precipitous thoroughfares. San Franciscans love their cable cars, however old and inefficient they are, and refuse to let the city government retire the last of them.

Handsome, civilized and mellow San Francisco

Throughout Northern California, people refer to San Francisco simply as "The City." The tribute is justified, for San Francisco is indisputably one of the most delightful cities on earth, rivaling Paris and Rome in its beauty, New York in its sophistication and London in its amenities. Its many steep hills offer matchless views of the incomparable bay. There are excellent art galleries, a number of fine restaurants and beautiful streets lined with handsome town houses. With 20 miles of waterfront, San Francisco is also a great port and a thriving center of West Coast business and financial activity.

Rising above Telegraph Hill, the Coit Tower overlooks the bay and Alcatraz Island, brought nearer by the camera's telephoto lens.
The hill got its name in the days when it was topped by a semaphore that was used to signal the ships entering the harbor.

A few cars cross the almost deserted San Francisco-Oakland Bay Bridge at evening, while in the background lights still burn in the financial district. The lighted clock tower *(center)* rises above the Ferry Building, for many years the city's major point of entry.

San Franciscans lunch in splendor in the roofed-over courtyard of the Sheraton-Palace Hotel. Opened in 1875, it was partially destroyed in the earthquake and fire of 1906; rebuilt, it remains a fine rococo relic of San Francisco's Golden Era.

A handsome yacht floats at its mooring in the bay in view of San Francisco *(background)*. The 430 square miles of the bay offer wonderful sailing to the people living around it, and as a result some 85,000 private boats list the area's harbors as their home ports.

Industrious Seattle, prospering in the Jet Age

Seattle has long been the Northwest's most solid and progressive city, made prosperous by its fishing, lumber and other industries. In recent decades it has boomed with the success of its biggest single manufacturer, the Boeing aircraft company. World-famous for its giant jetliners, Boeing had a backlog of orders worth $3.5 billion on the company's 50th anniversary in 1966. But while the people of Seattle take pride in their city's industrial power, they are proudest of the natural beauties surrounding them —Puget Sound, dozens of crystalline lakes and the snow-capped peaks of the nearby Cascade Range.

The 600-foot-tall Space Needle, focus of Seattle's 1962 World's Fair, towers over the city's office buildings and its monorail *(lower left)*. Mount Rainier, 60 miles away, can be seen from the top of the Needle on a clear day.

A private seaplane sits on a dock outside a shorefront house on Lake Washington, which borders Seattle on the east. The shorelines of Seattle's lakes, and those of Puget Sound, give the city some 200 miles of waterfront.

Boeing jets stand by the shore of Lake Washington as logs for a lumber mill float by. Lumbering, Seattle's first big business, remains active, but is today overshadowed by Boeing. In the distance rises Mount Rainier.

Staid and stately Portland, turning toward the future

Spread out on both sides of Oregon's Willamette River, Portland is a bustling river port, as it has been for more than a century. The city nonetheless retains much of the charm of the New England villages from which its earliest settlers came. Scattered throughout Portland are small, fountain-bedecked squares and block-sized parks. Residential sections, laid out in orderly patterns, are shaded by trees and have an air of quiet calm. But the present, too, is everywhere evident. Away from the clamor of the port, skyscrapers are rising in the downtown section. Portland has also built a $30 million shopping area called Lloyd Center which, with covered walks and flowered malls, is a model of such developments. But while welcoming the new, Portland carefully preserves the old, not wishing (unlike so many other American cities) to confuse activity with progress.

Early dawn lights the sky behind Mount Hood, a long-dormant volcano, which rises east of Portland. Street lamps still burn, marking *(at left)* one of the nine highway bridges across the Willamette, the river that gives ocean ships easy access to the city.

The business section sits mainly on the west bank *(foreground)*, while the east bank remains primarily residential. But conservative Portland is changing. Hitherto cautious retailers have set up branch stores in the east-bank section and other concerns are modernizing.

4

The Western
Style

On a Sunday afternoon in the summer nobody seems to be home along the Pacific Coast. The beaches are specked with sun bathers lounging in the subtropical glare. At the foot of the southern cliffs, surfers huddle on the swells like swirls of tadpoles, their formations changing suddenly as they race to catch the waves. The freeways teem with cars, for it is the thing to be outside, whether one has a destination or not. Downtown streets are almost deserted from San Diego to Seattle. The people of the West are at their most euphoric pitch. They are outdoors, at leisure and on the move, not certain where they are going or that it matters. They will be home in time to pour a drink or two for themselves and possibly a couple of friends, and perhaps broil steaks over charcoal. But they intend to make it an early night, for tomorrow, as always, is a big day.

There is a distinctiveness about these people. A recognizable Western style has emerged from a shadowy succession of false images. Here in the Pacific Coast cities—most notably in California—

To improve their form, skiers take lessons before attempting the slopes at Snoqualmie Pass, a ski area 46 miles from Seattle where as many as 25,000 enthusiasts congregate on a busy weekend. Most come from nearby, and return home after skiing for the day.

people do indeed think differently, feel differently and act differently from the American norms. But the facts of Western differences are often quite unlike those that have been presumed. In the ballyhoo that has surrounded California since its early settlement, misinformation and myths have been widely circulated. Yet even the truth has an air of outrageousness. The unrelenting pursuit of leisure in the open air is only the most visible aspect of the Western style. A blend of buoyancy and despair, the style is based on immoderation. It has the fresh, soft feel of newness, and it encompasses a number of seeming paradoxes: rampaging crime and prejudice in a land of easy friendliness and relaxed social relationships; high suicide and divorce rates in the midst of unparalleled prosperity; little interest in formal churchgoing, but high aspiration and dedication to personal ideals. Only recently have West Coast people sensed their common ties enough to understand that there is such a thing as a Western outlook. There is. Up and down the Coast one can sense a hungry, energetic drive among the newly arrived, an effort to compensate for lost time.

Remaining neutral about this new world is almost impossible. The Western style has been created by a cosmopolitan breed of restless people

California's standing as one of the world's major wine-producing areas can be traced almost entirely to the efforts of a Hungarian immigrant named Agoston Haraszthy, who is shown at the left. When Haraszthy arrived in California in 1849, about 58,000 gallons of wine a year were being produced in the area, largely from varieties of grapes brought to the New World by the Spaniards. Haraszthy was convinced that wine making could become a profitable, larger-scale enterprise if superior varieties of European grapes were used, and in 1852 he began importing cuttings of grapes from Hungary and Spain. These did relatively well, and by 1858 Haraszthy had imported cuttings of more than 150 other European varieties. Many of these thrived at his Sonoma Valley vineyard, shown at the right, as did cuttings that Haraszthy sold to other growers. By 1869, the year of Haraszthy's death, California wine production had increased to three million gallons a year. Today the figure is up to 179 million, and some 111,000 persons are employed in the industry.

transplanted from elsewhere and possessed of motley tastes and unexpressed yearnings. The practitioners of the Western style are appraised as immoderately as they live. The Los Angeles resident is "a noble savage in a plastic jungle," wrote the Chicago journalist Nicholas von Hoffman after visiting the city. The critic Clifton Fadiman saw Californians otherwise. They are in the "vanguard of American social development," he wrote after moving to Southern California. The novelist Raymond Chandler called Los Angeles "a tired old whore," but the Shakespearean scholar Frank Baxter described it as a city where one may see three Nobel Prize winners pushing carts through a supermarket.

It is understandable that such varying interpretations of Western life exist. The West is not yet a settled society. Its parts do not equal its whole. The enlargement of contact with other people is a paramount goal for new Westerners who are escaping the anonymity of Eastern cities; others from small towns or farms hope to lose themselves in the cities of the West. Since flexibility is inherent in the Western style, newcomers can find either type of life.

To those seeking broad human contact, the West offers innovations. Social clubs of infinite variety advertise through the personal columns of daily newspapers, seeking members for groups limited to those who have been divorced, or those who are tall, or those who have migrated from specific states or regions. Bohemians and beatniks find one another in North Beach in San Francisco and across the bay in Berkeley; they can also discover compatible company along the Sunset Strip in Los Angeles and in suburban Venice. Newly arrived Scandinavians are welcomed in Washington by a network of Scandinavian-American social and church clubs.

Such Western organizations are primarily social. Others are commercial. Entrepreneurs, realizing that even the older citizens in the West seek new social patterns, have pioneered in communities designed for people past the age of 50. Scores of such communities have sprung up in California. They are known variously as retirement centers, leisure worlds and senior villages. Most of them consist of large groups of single-story dwellings set around golf courses and community centers; some of them, particularly in Seattle and Portland, take the form of high-rise apartment houses. In California there are a number of communities like Rancho Bernardo, situated in rolling hills near San Diego. It has a section called Seven Oaks set apart for older persons. Homes in Seven Oaks cost from $27,000 to $32,000; in 1966 Seven Oaks had 1,860 residents who were more than 50 years old. The amenities furnished these older citizens included a social director, a medical clinic, a community center, a golf course and a hotel for visitors.

The Northwest's high-rise apartment complexes for the elderly are often sponsored by churches offering lifetime leases ranging from $8,000 for one room to $20,000 for a double room. Other church-owned projects—some of them former resort hotels—cater to the aged person who is willing to assign a considerable portion of his estate to the church. Opulent centers for the aged include Park Shore, beside Lake Washington in Seattle, whose handsome site commands a view of Mount Rainier. Inside are facilities for the hobbyist: a darkroom, an art studio, and workshops for lapidaries, carpenters and weavers. The Park Shore admissions committee screens applicants and administers a so-called "scholarship" to aid desirable tenants for whom Park Shore may be overpriced. In Southern California, mobile-home parks for the elderly are becoming popular. But not all of these communities for older persons have proved profitable; promoters sometimes sell what individual units they can, then transfer the property to a nonprofit, nontaxable foundation operated by residents. Sometimes the residents themselves grow disenchanted with one another and with the artificialities of such communities, and there is a wave of selling.

Other real-estate promoters, tapping the housing market at the opposite end of the age spectrum, have specialized in apartment communities for unmarried young men and women, complete with swimming pools, social rooms, health clubs with sauna baths, and even riding stables. One such colony is the E'Questre Inn in Burbank, near Los Angeles. Residents are offered dancing lessons and creative-writing courses, group horseback rides and mixed billiards. A Sunday breakfast party is part of the package, and so are parties at which the apartment management provides a bartender, drink mixes and music; residents bring their own bottles of liquor.

In such residential frameworks the Westerner evinces his intention to seek new living patterns, and to be his own keeper. The older person separates himself from family dependence; the younger one does too, and additionally experiments in a kind of communal living. There are other evidences of individuality in the Western style. There is no social stigma to divorce. Many persons attach no importance to church life, charity work or other traditional gauges of responsibility. The Westerner has abandoned the deep-rooted interdependence

of older societies. There is no more sense of community in the West than one chooses to feel. Yet even in the largest Western cities, churchgoing is used to initiate social contact. Coffee hours in schools and churches bring strangers together, and neighborhood bars play a part too. Soon the newcomer finds he has fresh roots spread over a wide radius. All over the Los Angeles Basin, for instance, people of similar backgrounds tend to associate together. Friendships, club ties and church affiliations may be distributed over distances of 30 to 40 miles; in this strange, floating community, even the freeway contributes a sense of mobile interconnection. Along the entire Coast, private clubs proliferate. Only a few, notably the Pacific Union of San Francisco, are so formidably exclusive that they discourage prospective members.

In the stricter sense of the word, society—with its implications of elite and tradition—exists only in embryonic form on the West Coast. Those few persons who do aspire to social prestige, moreover, find the task of entering what society there is simpler than do newcomers to older American cities. The tendency in the Northwest and in Southern California is to place a social premium on cultural and institutional leadership rather than on subtler social status; perhaps it is a carry-over from the

Bohemian Club members congregate in 1896 during the club's annual outing. The Bohemian is one of the few exclusive clubs among the thousands of social organizations on the West Coast. It attracts some of the nation's leading businessmen and politicians to its 2,437-acre redwood grove north of San Francisco.

frontier that proved service to community is as weighty a factor in determining social rank as are genealogical and financial inheritances. "Blue books" listing socially prominent persons come and go on the West Coast. They are often boycotted by those whom the registers need most, and they fail.

In certain communities of the Pacific States a student of social status may find firm patterns taking shape; social stratification is, after all, an evolutionary process. San Francisco comes closest to having a society with a capital "S," although its society is still a self-conscious blend of affable newcomers, artistic Bohemians and third-generation Californians, all swept up in their varied images of the uniqueness of their city. The most socially acceptable addresses in California are in the Russian Hill and Pacific Heights sections of San Francisco; in the nearby suburbs of Atherton, Hillsborough and Burlingame; in Santa Barbara and La Jolla; and in the Los Angeles communities of Brentwood, Bel-Air, Beverly Hills, San Marino and Pasadena. In such communities one often finds expatriates from Eastern society serving as nuclei for cells of what will become West Coast society. In Portland and Seattle and their fashionable suburbs, society has a firmer if more provincial feel; neither café society nor the jet set ever flourished there, and the

entrenched are the descendants of Northwest families that made it in banking and trade, mining, lumbering or fishing. The people of the Northwest are more anxious than Californians to look back a generation or two before accepting credentials.

Everywhere along the Coast a forthright approach to personal contact is acceptable. Less subtlety is expected than in older societies, and overtures that might be considered gauche in the East are applauded for their ingenuity in the West. Such a case was that of a young lieutenant, about to leave the Navy and settle in Southern California, who mailed a career résumé to prospective employers. "I'm from Tennessee," it began, "but I've put on my shoes and I'm ready for work in California." His new California mailbox was filled with hearty replies, and within a week he was at work for the state Division of Highways. As he settled into his new life, everyone around him suddenly seemed his friend. The casual kindness of people is a surprise to the new Westerner; it is part of the Western style, as is a kind of small-town friendliness. In a Seattle suburb a woman planning a treasure hunt for her daughter's Girl Scout troop put a clue in her mailbox. But the mailman got there first, and the mother went out to explain. She was too late. "Lady," the mailman said, "I've looked under the

West Coast crab recipes

The Dungeness crab
A number of different kinds of edible crab are found in the waters of the Pacific Ocean, but by far the most highly esteemed by West Coast gourmets is the Dungeness, shown above. A large crab, the Dungeness frequently attains a size of seven inches across its body. It prefers to live where the ocean has a sandy bottom, but its range is wide—crab fishermen find it as far north as Alaska and as far south as the waters off the California-Mexico border. The following recipes give three of the easiest and most popular ways the Dungeness crab is prepared by the Coast's chefs.

Pacific cracked crab
This method of preparing crabs is much the same as that used everywhere to boil lobsters. Plunge live crabs into boiling salted water and continue to boil the crabs slowly for from 10 to 25 minutes, depending on their size. Remove the shells on the undersides of the crabs and discard the stomachs. Remove the claws and crack them by striking them gently with a mallet, and cut the bodies into four sections with a large knife. Place the crabs on a preheated platter and serve at once with melted butter. If a cold dinner is preferred, the crabs may be chilled and served with mayonnaise. In either case the diners should be provided with nutcrackers and picks so that they can dig out every morsel. French bread and a chilled white wine are excellent additions to the meal.

Crab Louis
Crab Louis is essentially boiled crab, cooked as described above, and served cold with a spicy dressing. This dressing is made by combining

a cup of mayonnaise, 1/4 cup each of heavy cream, chili sauce, chopped green peppers and chopped scallions, and two tablespoons of chopped green olives. The dressing is poured over the meat of one large boiled crab and the dish is garnished with the crab's legs, quartered tomatoes and quartered hard-boiled eggs. Artichoke hearts may be added if desired, plus salt and lemon juice to taste. Serves two.

Palace Court salad
Make a crab salad by adding mayonnaise and diced celery to the chilled meat of boiled crabs (see first recipe). Place portions of this salad in cups made with the edible bottoms of artichokes, which in turn rest on a bed of shredded lettuce and thick slices of ripe tomato. Garnish with chopped hard-boiled egg yolks and serve with Thousand Island dressing. This fine salad is named for the elegant dining court of the old Palace Hotel (now the Sheraton-Palace) in San Francisco, shown on pages 74-75.

tree and I've looked under the big rock, but I still haven't found your letter."

In many ways inhabitants of this region of fragile façades seek to make a virtue of the novel, the unique, the rebellious, the emerging. There is a void of authority and tradition, to which reaction ranges from violence to hasty improvisation. "I called the board of directors together for our first meeting," a young La Jolla executive recalled recently, "and established a few traditions."

In the first decades of West Coast settlement there already had been hints of contrasts in the way people would live. But it was difficult to sense any unity of outlook among the three states. It became popular to generalize: Southern Californians were small-town people, Midwestern or Southern, and Los Angeles was a collection of suburbs in search of a city; San Franciscans were people of style and grace, worldly and urbane; Oregon had a kind of woodsiness that bespoke solidity and conservatism with a hint of provinciality; Seattleites had good manners and easy pace and, as the journalist George Sessions Perry once observed, were so unsophisticated as to seem "a mite short on sin." These were the stereotypes, and they were as defensible as any.

By World War II Southern Californians stood indicted as a breed of shallow-minded lotus-eaters, the men in gaudy sports shirts and the women in tight slacks and spike heels—an image augmented by the fantasies of Eastern editors who assigned writing that fit convenient stereotypes about the West. There were other stereotypes as well. Hollywood was bawdy and bacchanalian. San Francisco remained an oasis of amenities. Oregon had not yet emerged from the smoldering haze of burning waste lumber in its sawmills. Seattle was smarting from a remark by Sir Thomas Beecham; after a season conducting the Seattle Symphony Orchestra, he commented that the city was sometimes regarded as an esthetic dustbin.

While there was a modicum of truth in these stereotypes, the facts of the emerging Western style were otherwise. The war diminished regional contrasts everywhere on the West Coast. As freeways and airlines brought the people of the West Coast into more frequent contact with one another, sociologists noted common traits from Seattle to San Diego. Energy and self-confidence, those precursors of change, seemed to surge with postwar growth. It became possible to bracket the people of California, Oregon and Washington in terms of their prosperity and leisure.

Berries for pies and jams
The crossbred berries shown below, much used in pies and jams, are most widely grown on the West Coast. The oldest is the loganberry, a tart fruit first grown in 1881 in the Santa Cruz garden of Judge J. H. Logan, an early California jurist and horticulturist, from an accidental crossing of a native wild blackberry and a European red raspberry. The youngberry was developed about 1905 in Louisiana by a plant breeder named Byron M. Young, from a crossing of a dewberry and a berry related to the loganberry. The newest of the three is the boysenberry, developed in the 1920s on the Napa, California, farm of Rudolph Boysen, probably from a crossing of loganberry, raspberry and blackberry. Because it grows larger, yields more fruit per acre and is more disease-resistant, the boysenberry is threatening to replace its earlier cousins.

INCHES
1
½

LOGANBERRY   YOUNGBERRY   BOYSENBERRY

In the 1960s they were earning 14 per cent more than the national average and they were purchasing much more than their share in the national market. They were spending about 15 per cent more than the national rate on automobiles and automobile equipment, building more than twice as many homes and acquiring 50 per cent more passports. West Coast people were buying more frozen foods and household appliances, and drinking more bourbon, rum, vodka and wine, but less gin, blended whiskey and Scotch. West Coast families were larger and Westerners had spent more years in school. The population was becoming younger; with the postwar surge in births, the percentage of Westerners over 65 years of age dropped below the national level.

Some other facts about them are grimmer. The Western style is seen in different perspective when one examines suicide and divorce rates, race relations and crime. There are pockmarks in this adolescent Western society. In suicide rates four Western metropolitan areas—San Francisco-Oakland, Los Angeles-Long Beach, Seattle and Sacramento—have ranked consistently (after St. Petersburg-Tampa) as the highest four U.S. cities of more than 500,000 population. In church membership

Oregon and Washington ranked in the mid-1960s as the lowest states, both with only about one third of the population affiliated, less than half of Californians were church members, compared with the estimated national average of 60 per cent. Crime rates were rising and racial problems were proliferating all along the Coast.

In crime, as in so much else, California heads many lists. Oregon and Washington, growing more slowly, have been less troubled. Criminals have joined the migration to California in disproportionate numbers; many others have been bred in the state. One result is that Los Angeles' assault rate is 65 per cent greater than New York's; its rape rate is almost triple. Law enforcement in Los Angeles is complicated by the proximity of two underworld havens: Las Vegas, in neighboring Nevada, and Tijuana, just across the Mexican border. Crimes involving narcotics are abundant; Tijuana is a portal through which vast amounts of narcotics are smuggled into the United States.

Crime in Los Angeles has been dramatized in the novels and screenplays of James M. Cain and Raymond Chandler, but nothing illuminated the city's explosive problems more vividly than the outbreak of the Negro riots in the Watts district of Los Angeles in 1965. Until then most Westerners had blithely considered the region free of serious racial friction. It had been a pleasant illusion, a significant one in terms of the Western euphoria, but one not founded in history. Until World War II, Negroes did not constitute a sizable minority in the West; before then, racial prejudices had been concentrated against Orientals and Mexicans.

The Chinese began encountering outbreaks of prejudice almost immediately after their arrival in the 1850s and 1860s. In Los Angeles in 1871, twenty-two Chinese were lynched; Chinese laundries in San Francisco were sacked in 1877. Under the California constitution of 1879 the Chinese-born were excluded from the suffrage; the Oregon Bill of Rights of 1857 had contained a similar provision. More violent action was taken in Washington in 1886, when the Seattle Chinatown was raided and most of its residents were shipped back to the Orient on the steamer *Queen of the Pacific*.

Antipathy toward Orientals was seen again after the turn of the century, when Japanese immigrants began to arrive. Japanese school pupils were segregated in San Francisco starting in 1906. By 1913 the prospering Japanese farmers had so offended Californians that an Alien Land Law was enacted barring ownership of land by Orientals; while the Japanese found means of circumventing the law, it

stood for four decades before the California supreme court found it unconstitutional in 1952.

In Washington the overwhelmingly white population enacted discriminatory laws against the Japanese in the 1920s. Oregon passed discriminatory laws in 1923 after a period of Ku Klux Klan activity, and in later years moved slowly in the area of civil rights. California passed a public accommodations law forbidding discrimination on the basis of race, religion or origin in 1905, and Washington enacted a similar law in 1909. Oregon failed to pass such legislation until 1949, when it finally wiped the books clean of discriminatory laws, including one requiring a census of the sanitary and thrift habits of Orientals.

The first major influx of Negroes to the West Coast came with World War II. At the start of the war there were only about 5,000 Negroes in San Francisco; by 1964 there were an estimated 90,000. Next to New York, California showed the greatest gain in Negro population between 1950 and 1960. One of every four Negroes who left the South in those years went to California. The West offered an atmosphere of less overt discrimination toward the Negro than did other areas of the country; although far from a utopia, it provided better job opportunities. Many smaller Western cities, where the Negro population grew less rapidly, offered the best chance for Negroes—but relatively few Negroes took advantage of that fact. In 1960 Seattle and San Diego ranked 15th and 16th in Negro population among the 18 U.S. cities of comparable size. By 1964 only about 18,000 Negroes lived in Oregon, most of them in the relatively untroubled Albina district of Portland.

There has been rapidly increasing social intermingling between white and Negro in San Francisco, where the Negro migration has been accepted more smoothly than it has in Los Angeles. The greatest resentment toward Negroes comes from whites who have previously lived in economically underprivileged areas, not necessarily those in the South. More persons fall into this category in Los Angeles than in San Francisco; it was the Southern California vote that helped a discriminatory housing amendment to be made a part of the state constitution in 1964, a piece of legislation later ruled unconstitutional by the state supreme court. Yet Los Angeles, whose population is about 15 per cent Negro, lacks slums of the type familiar in older cities. The Watts district, for example, is a community made up in large part of single-family dwellings. It has relatively good schools. Its population density is about 25 persons per acre, compared with more than 100 in central Harlem in New York. But Watts in the mid-1950s became the informal port of entry for about 1,000 Negroes each month. Many of them were poorly schooled and lacked job training. Their unemployment rate reached 30 per cent, and their crime rate became the highest in the city.

The many thousands of these Los Angeles Negroes will not be rescued from their plight by any of the civic task forces and sociological studies that are now proliferating. Schooling and job training are the long-range antidotes for the Negroes' poverty and hostilities, along with the increasing willingness in Southern California to give Negroes equal job opportunities. Discounting peak crises caused by the heavy influx of the untrained and undereducated poor, long-range prospects for the California Negro are bright. Some labor unions are beginning to give him equal opportunities with white men. In the state's vast governmental structures the Negro jobholder is moving up rapidly. Negro women do not find it difficult to obtain jobs as secretaries and stenographers in business offices. The Negro vote has become a potent political factor in Los Angeles. Negro families find decreasing difficulty in buying homes in non-Negro districts. Although de facto school segregation remains an issue, massive efforts are being made to boost Negro status through the schools.

The arrival of the Negro in the West simply added new complexities to an already intricate ethnic mix. In the Pacific States live about 40 per cent of the nation's Chinese, Japanese and Mexicans, and approximately 12 per cent of the Indians. The largest Oriental community in the United States is the Chinatown of San Francisco, a teeming ghetto where the suicide rate is considerably greater than the already high San Francisco city-wide rate. Los Angeles is often called the second-largest Mexican city; its Mexican-American community is larger than that of any Mexican metropolis except Mexico City. All over California the Mexican-Americans are in sociological limbo, neither accepted nor rejected. They themselves appear to prefer separate folkways to integration, and their leaders have not been so militant as those of the Negroes. The prominent Mexican-American community leader or civic figure is the exception.

The mass migration of Mexicans to the state came long after their own government had been pushed out of California. The migration swelled during the 1910-1917 Mexican Revolution and

reached a peak in the 1920s, when the contrast between American prosperity and Mexican famine was at its greatest. Immigration was encouraged by California farmers, for the Mexican is an uncomplaining worker and even the lowest U.S. wages seem large to him in contrast to those of his homeland. Mexican farm laborers in the West have been of two types: the legally imported worker, called the bracero; and the illegal entrant, known as the wetback (an expression that derived from a favored method of unlawful entry: swimming or wading clandestinely across the Rio Grande). Employment of wetbacks on California farms reached a peak in 1954; in that year more than a million wetbacks were apprehended in the United States and returned to Mexico. At one time federal immigration authorities used chartered planes to fly wetbacks to the Mexican city of Guadalajara, 1,000 miles below the U.S. border. Enterprising U.S. aircraft operators were often near at hand to sell the deported Mexicans return-flight tickets to the United States. The crackdown on illegal Mexican labor in the mid-1950s reduced the numbers of wetbacks; in the ensuing decade the bracero, protected under a treaty between the United States and Mexico, was the main migrant-labor source on California farms. Although the bracero program ended in 1964, several

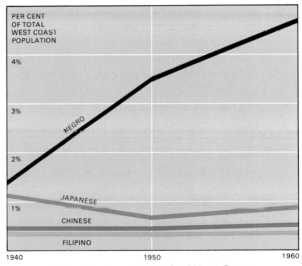

Minority groups on the West Coast

Minority groups comprise a significant percentage of the West Coast's population. The heavy lines above show the percentages made up by four such groups in recent censuses. Chinese and Filipinos increased at about the same rate as the total population and their lines are nearly level. Negroes increased greatly, while Japanese decreased, largely because of World War II relocation. A fifth group, people of Mexican or Spanish descent, is not shown; mostly restricted to California, it comprises some 11 per cent of the state's population.

thousand Mexican laborers are periodically admitted to perform seasonal labor on farms in the Imperial and San Joaquin Valleys.

The heart of American Mexico is in eastside Los Angeles communities like Belvedere, Boyle Heights and City Terrace. These are the homes of Mexican-American factory workers whose families are in the difficult transition from the agricultural society of Mexico to the industrialized one of the United States; here the man is away at the factory, instead of at home on the farm, and it is the woman who must control the home in his absence. The older members of these families are still close to the fields, and in times of unemployment will revert to their native occupation, following the California harvests.

One of the brighter facets in the California racial picture has been the achievement of Japanese-Americans in recapturing a place in society since their internment during World War II. In a panicky overreaction to Pearl Harbor more than 75,000 American citizens of Japanese descent and another 35,000 Japanese aliens were uprooted from their West Coast homes and imprisoned in "relocation centers" on the West Coast and elsewhere.

Many of the Japanese were forced to sell their property hastily at great loss; others were unable to sell at all. Some Japanese-Americans were permitted to work outside the centers. Others served with distinction in the United States armed forces. The federal government eventually reimbursed the Japanese for their losses at an average rate of about 30 cents on the dollar. But the inland relocation centers did not begin to close down until October of 1945, and it was not until then that those Japanese who had remained in the camps were able to begin straggling back to the West Coast to start over. Many of them went elsewhere; only an estimated 65,000 came back. Their old communities overrun, they resettled in the cities of Southern California. Before the war some 85 per cent of the Japanese had been farmers; with the loss of their lands most of them gave up that way of life and today only about 10 per cent are engaged in agriculture. Others are scattered throughout the business and professional worlds of the area. With infinite patience and forbearance they have managed to grow more prosperous than before.

The Indian, by contrast, has been able to achieve little. Decimated and segregated by the pioneers, the Indians moved on into an almost equally deadly phase; they were forgotten and ignored by Westerners. Indolent and defeated, they subsisted on reservation lands or departed for low-scale industrial jobs in the cities, where today they are integrated into the poorer communities in the three states. Pockets of Indian prosperity do exist. Only about 100 members of the Agua Caliente tribe remain, but their 28,000-acre reservation lies in and around the Palm Springs resort area. Some Agua Caliente land has been sold or leased for the white man's resorts; the tribal land today has an estimated value of $50 million.

The Indians of the Colorado River reservation, which lies partly in Southern California and partly across the river in Arizona, are also well off. With miles of their newly irrigated lands along the California bank being leased for farming, they are moving from mud huts into new houses. They plan their future tribal development in a headquarters building that has wall-to-wall carpeting, wired-in music and a handsome fountain. In Oregon the Indians of the Klamath Falls area have received more than $70 million for the sale of their timber-rich reservation lands.

The most serious modern conflict with the Indians in the Pacific States has been over tribal fishing in Northwest rivers, a right guaranteed by federal treaties. The Indians contend that the treaty protects their traditional fishing rights; sportsmen and state conservation authorities argue that the modern, efficient nets that the Indians now stretch across the rivers will deplete the salmon schools.

Offbeat religious sectarianism, which has tended to center in Southern California, is no longer a part of the Western style; it has declined steadily since World War II as new migrants have evinced less and less interest in exotic worship. In the past, hundreds of diverse stairways to heaven were offered in the Los Angeles cultist market. The best-remembered evangelist is Aimee Semple McPherson, who moved up from tent revivals to her own 5,400-seat Angelus Temple in Los Angeles, performing ecclesiastical legerdemain with great flair. So beloved was this evangelist by her followers that she even managed to survive the gossip that surrounded a 36-day disappearance in 1926 that she subsequently described as a kidnapping but which appeared instead to have been an adulterous holiday. In that period her Angelus Temple probably had 35,000 members. She died in 1944 after taking an overdose of sleeping pills. Today the Temple counts a membership of about 20,000.

While not so large as it once was, the audience for evangelism has not entirely disappeared elsewhere in California. Faith healers still attract thousands, and evangelical advertising rises to ludicrous levels of sensationalism. Revivals feature women preachers on white horses or in gold cages descending from high ceilings. Even conventional denominations resort to unusual salesmanship. Free buses roam across California cities to bring worshipers to churches. In San Francisco an Episcopal bishop retained as public relations counsel a man whose other major clients had included Bay Area race tracks. In San Diego a Baptist minister conducted services in the surf, with baptisms recorded on film from a hovering helicopter.

Neither evangelism nor organized religion has prospered in the Northwest. No social stigma attaches to the nonchurchgoer. But the influence of the church in the Northwest is still evident—for example, in state liquor laws. Bottle sale of liquor is state-controlled. Stores in Oregon are open only about eight hours on weekdays and are closed on Sundays. In Washington no liquor is sold either by the bottle or by the drink from midnight Saturday until 6 a.m. Monday, and no woman may sit at a public bar. Although attacked by the Washington convention and tourist industry, this strict regulation has prevailed against all opposition.

The high incidence of divorce on the West Coast is perhaps not unrelated to the tenuousness of the church tie. But like the high suicide rate it has some out-of-state genesis. California, in particular, inherits from other regions more than a normal share of couples who have decided to make one last fresh start in the West. But a bad marriage is seldom saved by a change of scene, and so the final break occurs in the West, away from prying eyes. The divorced often salve their loneliness with one another, as at Mission Beach, in San Diego, where two women recently took an apartment together after they had been divorced from the same man. A Pasadena hairdresser relates that he overheard one of his clients tell another: "We got to talking, and found out my father used to be married to his mother."

The same casualness that marks social relationships among the milling hordes in California cities extends to sexual matters. All of the enabling factors are there to expedite easy sexual relations: plenty of cars, a year-round benign climate, miles of beaches and, above all, affluence. The motel is everywhere. For many months not long ago, the house publication of a California-based motel chain listed the standings of its motels by percentage of room occupancy. Many motels consistently reported occupancies greater than 100 per cent—an indication that rooms were being rented more than once a night. After a San Diego newspaper began reporting the standings, they were no longer made public.

The California libido was once associated with

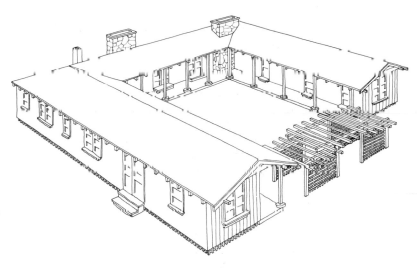

The California redwood bungalow, with its strong emphasis on simplicity, convenience and integration with the outdoors, was first developed by two brothers, the architects Charles and Henry Greene. Searching for a design suitable to the local climate and terrain, they built the house shown above in Pasadena in 1903. Based on the Spanish adobe style, the house was composed of a string of rooms around three sides of a patio. Many builders soon produced variations but often cheapened the Greene brothers' clean design. By 1915 the original style had lost favor, but not before it had influenced much of California—and American—architecture.

the Hollywood influence, but that issue is now subject to argument; foreign films, not Hollywood's, have recently been pushing back the traditional limits of propriety. The reputed bacchanalia of the Hollywood of the past seems tame today. The town has grown a little seedy, and its image is becoming that of a place to work. Revelry now seems lustier if it is reported from the Riviera, Madrid, or Puerto Vallarta in Mexico.

But California has found replacements for the Hollywood lust symbol. California newsstands stock a flood of salacious magazines published within the state. The focus of the San Francisco newspapers has grown blatantly libidinous. In 1966 in Sausalito, across the bay from San Francisco, a woman named Marcia Owen ran a respectable fourth in a field of six in one of her periodic races for a city-council seat; as usual, the San Francisco dailies made much of the fact that she had been better known under the name of Sally Stanford as the last of San Francisco's fabled madams. But most of all, the banner of sex has been unfurled by California youth, the generation born to the great wave of World War II immigrants. These young people, having grown up amid the permissiveness of the free-searching Western society, represent the furthest American swing from the Puritan ethic. Their symbol is the surfer, the tanned youth whose life is as unfettered as the board he skillfully guides over the waves of the Pacific. He is the most spectacular representative of the new generation; 300,000 to 500,000 California youths regard themselves as surfers. But the genuine, competitive surfers of California, who fly to Hawaii and Australia for international meets, have sought to free themselves from any delinquent image, disassociating themselves from the not uncommon youth who carries a sawed-off surfboard protruding from the trunk of his car but never goes near the water. It is this poseur who contributes to the spiraling California rate of juvenile delinquency and who helps to provide the rumor and the fact of teen-age sex orgies, drug addiction, crime and suicide.

California youths are at the forefront of the national teen-age emancipation because of their generally high income, their numerous automobiles, and their widespread rebellion against home and family ties. In 1964, when the Free Speech movement erupted on the University of California campus at Berkeley, the word "Berkeley" became a synonym for student revolt. Whatever else may be said about them, the youth of California have been among the leaders in their generation in voiding the dire prediction that, having been born and reared in the television age, they would become a generation of spectators, not participants.

It should not surprise California parents that their offspring are probing new frontiers of hedonism. The Western style is so leisure-oriented that the pursuit of pleasure has become a regional trait. The Western manual of conventional leisure is *Sunset*, a monthly magazine with handsome ranch-style offices in Menlo Park, south of San Francisco. *Sunset* is a symbol for many Westerners, a bible of how-to-live-Western. Its subject matter is restricted to food, travel, and house-and-garden topics. To attract advertisers primarily interested in reaching the Western market, its circulation is confined almost entirely to the West; only one in 20 copies goes east of the Rocky Mountains. But it is suggestive of the heralded spread of the Western style that a *Sunset* book entitled *Landscaping for Western Living* was revised with changes on only 10 pages, with the result that the same book had a lively sale in the East under the title *Landscaping for Modern Living*.

Disneyland is the most ballyhooed fun shrine in the West, but its importance as a playland pales in comparison to the natural settings of water and mountains that are the heartland of Western leisure. At last report there were more than 340,000 pleasure motorboats registered in California, as well as uncounted sailboats and small outboards; there are even more pleasure boats in the Northwest. Marinas cannot accommodate the number of boats being launched in Southern California—not even with giant Marina del Rey, near Los Angeles, which has 6,000 boat slips. Snow skiers are even more numerous than boatmen. In the deer season California hunters trek to southern Utah by the tens of thousands. More fishing licenses are bought in California than in any other state, although most fishermen regard the trout and salmon fishing of the Northwest as infinitely superior to that of California. At Crowley Lake on the barren east Sierra slope, opening day of the trout season brings out as many as 12,000 California fishermen; their boats almost block sight of the water. To a Southern California sportsman accustomed to such crowding, trout fishing in the rivers of the Northwest or sailing among the spacious channels of the San Juan Islands in Puget Sound can be the ultimate diversions.

The leisure search has caused overcrowding in the parks, both state and national. No more extreme example exists than Yosemite, where on summer weekends the valley floor is jammed with as many as 30,000 visitors. Rationing of visits to the more popular parks has been proposed. There have been serious proposals to stagger weekends to minimize the crowding on freeways, beaches and mountains. Another solution is a massive private development of new summer and winter resorts such as the Mineral King venture of Walt Disney in the Sierra Nevada, which is designed to accommodate an eventual total of 2.5 million visitors each year.

It is clearly impossible to keep the Westerner at home for any extended period. He has an almost total disregard for distance. Several thousand Southern Californians live in the San Diego area but commute daily by car to jobs in Los Angeles, a round trip of more than 200 miles. Others commute by air; one aerospace firm for a time offered a free air shuttle between the cities as an enticement to employment. A slightly more complex commuting task was undertaken by a painting contractor who kept daily office hours in San Diego, Los Angeles and San Francisco, traveling almost 1,000 miles a day. Many Californians are almost as much at home in one city as another, and are on first-name terms with bankers and headwaiters over a 500-mile range. Such a businessman from San Diego bought his wife a suit for Christmas in San Francisco; with it, knowing that nothing he had ever bought her had fit quite properly, he enclosed a round-trip plane ticket to San Francisco.

Despite a 40° February chill, Oregonians gather on Agate Beach, named for the semiprecious stones sometimes found in the sand. Some enthusiasts, for whom a winter's ride or picnic is too tame, have made swimming and surfing year-round activities.

People avid for the active life

The people of the Pacific States pursue every activity with a startling vitality. Given a choice of weekend sports, many a West Coaster simply avoids the decision: he skis on Saturday and surfs on Sunday, driving hundreds of miles in the process. Not everyone is this avid—many West Coast residents have never skied or surfed —but the same kind of zeal can be felt at a PTA meeting or a society ball, by a trout stream or at a crowded campsite. This fervor may be a legacy from early settlers. Like pioneers everywhere, they had to struggle merely to stay alive, but the beauty of the land must have lent them an extra measure of inspiration, as it does their descendants today. Even their homes, the best of which seek to harmonize man's work with nature's, reflect the magnetism which draws West Coasters toward the outdoors.

Sails taut, tall sloops and yawls maneuver at the start of the
1,430-mile race from San Diego to Acapulco, Mexico. More than
500,000 private craft cruise the region's lakes and coastal waters;
one of every four families in Washington owns a boat.

Crowded with anglers, the Klamath River in Northern California yields salmon and trout for all. With ocean, streams and lakes within easy reach, fishing is one of the most popular forms of recreation; there are 1.7 million licensed fishermen in California alone.

In vigorous pursuit of outdoor pleasures

Virtually every person in the Pacific States seems bent on perfecting some sporting skill. This is not surprising; the opportunities for outdoor activity are great. West Coast people need not wait for the seasons to change, because somewhere in their vast territory it is always winter, somewhere summer. There is skiing in Washington in July, swimming in California in December. If the breeze is too light for sailing, the day is probably perfect for riding. With such opportunity for sports, it is no wonder that the region contributed more than one third of the American entries in the 1964 Olympic Games.

Members of the Palm Springs Desert Riders, one of hundreds of riding clubs on the West Coast, jog their horses through the foothills of the San Jacinto Mountains. The club members usually breakfast in the open before returning home.

The energetic, affluent young— a West Coast specialty

The young people of the Pacific States, a group larger than the entire populations of all but seven states, share one characteristic—a boundless, almost frightening energy. The climate and geography that make the West Coast so inviting to all who live there, and the mobility that is so much a part of West Coast life, are even more accessible to the young. Lacking the family responsibilities of their parents, and aided by an affluence uncommon among members of their generation, they travel, play, work, buy and devote themselves to the idealistic causes of youth with a startling vigor.

A favorite meeting place, the bridge over the skating rink at Lloyd Center, a 50-acre shopping complex in Portland, Oregon, is crowded with teenagers. Aware of this lucrative market, many shops lure the young with displays of the latest clothing fads.

Showing off tans, muscles and glistening machines, shirtless cyclists meet on a Santa Monica beach. One fifth of the country's motorcycles are registered in California; riding them has become, like surfing, a cult among the youth of the West Coast.

Light and uncluttered, the Sausalito, California, house of Professor Caroline Shrodes seems to float among the tops of trees whose roots are anchored far below in the steep hillside, provoking the feeling that life indoors is a perpetual camping trip.

A handsome fusion of architecture and landscape

Early in the 20th Century a few California architects perceived that the Coast was evolving a new way of life—relaxed, casual and with a great emphasis on the outdoors—and began to create an architecture to harmonize with this new living pattern. Early pioneers such as Charles and Henry Greene used local wood and stone to integrate their houses with the rocks and trees surrounding them. Later, other architects attempted to blend indoors and out with walls of glass and indirect lighting. They also integrated patios and gardens with living areas, a device that has become popular across the country in recent decades. Choosing such apparently hostile sites as steep hillsides, West Coast designers have created functional, multilevel homes frequently supported by stilts and graced by cantilevered terraces that add to the sense of openness. Most recently, architects—ever more conscious of the need to preserve the natural beauties surrounding their buildings—have placed their communities in spacious tracts, leaving untouched large areas of field and forest.

To the sound of Pacific waves crashing on the rocky Northern
California coast, a visitor reads in the living room of a condominium
apartment in a handsome modern development called Sea Ranch.
Laid out by the landscape architect Lawrence Halprin, Sea Ranch is
in the best tradition of West Coast architecture—functional,
comfortable, and at home in the land it stands on.

Looking as though it were a natural part of the shoreline, this Sea
Ranch structure is radical even by West Coast standards. Its 10
apartments, which include the one shown above, all have a view of
the sea, and skylights dispel any hint of gloom even on dark days.
According to the architect's plans, two thirds of the 5,200-acre tract
on which Sea Ranch is being built will remain wild and undeveloped.

97

The West Coast's social whirl

If West Coasters generally are enamored of sports and the outdoor life, they nonetheless organize and enjoy glittering cotillions and balls. The relaxed citizens of Washington and Oregon have evolved a relatively informal social style, but their neighbors to the south, especially in the cities of San Francisco and Los Angeles, throw themselves into a whirl of social events with greater frequency. Los Angeles' big affairs have much of the aura of excitement of Hollywood extravaganzas; San Francisco, considerably more staid and traditional, stages parties of impressive and dignified elegance.

Despite their reputation for casual living, the people of Los Angeles are well able to put on sumptuous parties such as the $150-a-plate charity ball held in 1966 in the Century Plaza Hotel's immense ballroom. Called the Century Ball, it brought together 800 Los Angeles social leaders and members of the film colony.

In an atmosphere befitting a coronation, debutantes are presented at the annual cotillion in San Francisco's Sheraton-Palace Hotel. Since its inception in 1932, the white-tie ball has been San Francisco's biggest social event. To qualify for her debut, the girl, or at least one parent, must be a native Californian.

5

An Innovative Economy

Westerners like to say that their region is one that men have built by using their wits alone. This is a romantic simplification, for the West's economic growth has been aided by rich natural resources, the vagaries of history and the bounty of the federal budget. But there is truth in the simplification, for Western ingenuity has coaxed the most from each source.

Agriculture has been more sophisticated than it has been elsewhere. Industry has overcome the obstacles of remoteness. Financiers have proved adept at innovation. From the mammoth Boeing aerospace empire in Seattle through the plywood plants of Oregon to the corporate citadel of Montgomery Street in San Francisco and the diversified industrial complex of Southern California, there is strong economic muscle. In 1965 twenty of the nation's 200 largest industrial corporations were located in the Pacific Coast states, as were 10 of the 42 commercial banks in the country with assets of one billion dollars or more. Industrial wages in the region are substantially higher than the national average.

Assembling astronauts' quarters, North American Aviation technicians in Downey, California, prepare part of an Apollo spacecraft for a voyage to the moon. Aerospace, employing more than half a million persons, is the West Coast's largest industry.

The level of prosperity is startling even in America.

California, in particular, seems to establish new records of economic achievement each year. "New Yorkers," *The New York Times* reported in 1965, "must suffer still another indignity at the hands of Californians, who outnumber New Yorkers, own more cars, buy more life insurance and shamelessly loll in more swimming pools. Now the proud residents of the Golden State can boast that it has firmly established its lead over New York as the nation's top exporter of manufactured goods." In the same year the total personal income of Californians passed that of New Yorkers to become the highest in the nation. From 1955 through 1965 employment in manufacturing industries in California rose by more than 25 per cent, compared to the national rise of 6.5 per cent. Los Angeles County, with 2.1 million people at work in 1964, led all 3,043 U.S. counties in the number of persons employed. What economists might call the state income—the dollar value of the goods and services produced by Californians in a given year—is exceeded, in the world at large, only by the national incomes of the United States, the Soviet Union, West Germany, the United Kingdom and France. California has more people who own shares in companies listed on the New York Stock Exchange than any other state. Californians are dominant in agriculture and aerospace, wine making and film production. Their opulence can be substantiated by less-heralded facts; partly because of their high divorce rate, they are the nation's biggest spenders for legal fees.

For the first half century after the discovery of gold in 1848, the economy of the West Coast was almost colonial. Mining and agriculture were the dominant industries. Only the emerging railroad dynasties gave portents of what was to be the pyrotechnic pattern of Western growth. In the minds of many of its settlers, California seemed able to provide little but gold. Recalling in 1865 that the forty-niners had adopted a practice of shipping their laundry to China to be washed and returned months later, a speaker before the Mechanics' Institute in San Francisco noted in addition that "onions and potatoes came from the Sandwich Islands . . . our eggs and butter [were] brought from Boston, our lumber from Australia, and our bricks from New York." Much of the food for early miners came by ship from the Willamette Valley in Oregon. Prices were exorbitant and profits great. At the mine camps a pound of produce sold for more than the price of an acre of land. A young physician from the East Coast named J. D. B. Stillman wrote home from the mine country in the spring of 1850: "Eggs and milk are to be had—the former at six dollars a dozen and the latter at one dollar a quart; we use them only for patients. Butter is down to one dollar a pound."

Agriculture was slow to develop in California, and from the start it was more of a large-scale industry there than elsewhere, for the difficulties of production in an arid climate, and of shipment over long distances, were too burdensome for small farmers. Owners of large farms, however, were able to surmount such problems, and the wheat grown during the hot, rainless summers was so dry and hard that it easily withstood the long voyage to the East around Cape Horn. The rich potential of Western crops soon began to be apparent. In 1863 the historian John S. Hittell reported in amazement that he had seen a 10-pound carrot, a 26-pound turnip, a 53-pound cabbage, a 118-pound beet and a 260-pound squash in California. He did not say whether such overgrown freaks of the state's sunshine were edible, but there were other products that were eminently salable; by 1870 California vineyards were producing close to three million gallons of wine each year.

Industry in California first evolved from the demands of miners for machinery and equipment.

Until the Gold Rush, mining had not been a major factor in the American economy; there was little machinery available for extracting and refining the gold and there were interminable delays in bringing what there was of it to the coast. Entrepreneurs were quick to respond to the need; the manufacture of mining machinery rapidly became a California industry. From iron foundries and machine shops around San Francisco came equipment to meet the special requirements of Sierra Nevada mining. By 1870 San Francisco had even begun to export mine machinery. Sawmills produced lumber for the mines and for houses and wagons. Tanneries converted cowhides into harnesses, saddles and boots.

Isolated and prosperous, Californians early developed a rare degree of economic self-reliance. To expand, the young Coast industries needed investment capital, and they usually found it readily available close to home. But the dollars that built California were not so much those obtained from mining profits as those derived from the development of farmland, cattle ranches and, above all, railroads. Westerners have always seemed to be in a hurry. Even while rival stage lines were slashing hours from their schedules and steamship lines were running up huge profits in passengers and freight,

Exotic harvest of the Pacific States

California, Washington and Oregon grow virtually the entire U.S. crop of the six foods shown below. Artichokes, olives and dates come almost exclusively from California; Monterey County alone produces some two thirds of the nation's artichokes. All three states grow apricots and account for 97 per cent of the total U.S. production. Garlic and nectarines are grown in Oregon and Washington, but California has the largest crop.

a clamor went up for a transcontinental railroad. In the brief but dashing era of the Pony Express in 1860 and 1861, it was possible to send mail from the West Coast to Missouri for forwarding elsewhere by rail in the record-breaking time of 10 days. But the need for a transcontinental railroad grew more pressing. For most of their transport to and from the East, Californians were dependent on the Pacific Mail Steamship Company and its rail line across the Isthmus of Panama; a typical Pacific Mail trip consumed 33 days. Finally in 1862 the exigencies of the Civil War helped sway the United States Congress and President Abraham Lincoln to authorize the granting of land subsidies and loans for construction of the first railroad lines to span the continent.

The knowledge that a railroad could cross the forbidding Sierra Nevada was the outcome of years of surveying by a young engineer, Theodore D. Judah, who is one of the most overlooked heroes in Western history. It was he who persuaded the quartet of Sacramento merchants who came to be known as the Big Four—Charles Crocker, Mark Hopkins, Collis P. Huntington and Leland Stanford—to pledge initial funds for the Central Pacific, which was to be built eastward from Sacramento. In addition, Judah was instrumental in persuading Congress to pass the subsidy-and-loan bill that made the railroad possible. But a rift developed between the Big Four and Judah. As chief engineer of the Central Pacific, he refused to certify to federal authorities that track had been laid between Sacramento and the Sierra Nevada, a prerequisite for the payment of the first federal moneys. The line was in fact 20 miles short of the Sierra, and the Big Four thereupon arranged for the California state geologist to make the certification. Judah was outraged. En route to the East Coast in 1863, apparently in search of capital to buy out the Californians, he contracted yellow fever in Panama and died in New York, unrewarded and unrenowned, long before the railroad was completed. But the Big Four profited beyond their dreams. They and their associates invested only $159,000 in the Central Pacific, and yet the railroad reached a capitalization of $139 million under their management. The federal government gave the Big Four more than 11.5 million acres of land subsidies in California alone, and loaned them more than $27 million. Their profits solely from construction of the railroad—they hit upon the happy device of setting up their own construction company and awarding liberal contracts to it to carry out the actual building of the road—amounted to more than $200 million.

CHARLES CROCKER

MARK HOPKINS

COLLIS P. HUNTINGTON

LELAND STANFORD

The "Big Four" railroad magnates

The men who controlled the Central Pacific were all small-town merchants before they decided to speculate in railroad construction. Largely backed by government loans and subsidies, they amassed fortunes—estimated at $19 million for Hopkins and $40 million for Crocker.

Close to 15,000 Chinese were imported for the tedious and dangerous work of blasting a way for the roadbed over and through the Sierra Nevada and beyond to meet the westbound track being laid by the rival Union Pacific. On May 10, 1869, the tracks of the two lines were officially joined at Promontory, Utah. The isolation of the West was ended; more irrevocably than even the discovery of gold had done, the railroad brought the Pacific Coast into the United States. Soon a familiar phrase of early settlers—"back in the States"—would pass from the language of the West Coast.

With its subsidiary, the Southern Pacific Railroad, the Central Pacific became the dominant economic force on the West Coast for the next half century. It managed to exclude rival railroads from Los Angeles until the Atchison, Topeka and Santa Fe reached there in 1887. No other line ran trains east from San Francisco until 1910 or north from there until 1931. North of the Columbia River the reigning railroad baron was James J. Hill, whose Great Northern line reached Seattle from St. Paul, Minnesota, in 1893. He and Henry Villard of the Northern Pacific, which had linked Portland to the Midwest in 1883, played the role of benevolent princes, constructing churches and introducing nursery stock, blooded cattle and seeds, as well as establishing banks and building sawmills. The Southern Pacific erected vacation resorts around Monterey on the California coast and launched *Sunset* magazine in 1898 as a publicity organ to promote the sale of railroad lands and stimulate passenger and freight traffic. The railroad fortune of Leland Stanford built Stanford University and railroad money founded company towns like Tacoma. The Southern Pacific assumed control of utility firms and, frequently, of the state legislature. In 1873 the author Charles Nordhoff made clear the immensity of the sudden wealth and power of the railroad owners when he warned visitors to the West: "The railroad will seem to you the great fact. Man seems but an accessory; he appears to exist only that the road may be worked."

Although they abused their power the railroads moved the West rapidly toward a balanced economy. They brought lumber tycoons to the West to buy railroad-owned forests. They opened Eastern markets for Western sheep, cattle and wheat from the seemingly endless fields of the Great Central Valley and of eastern Washington—which had become, with steam-operated combines, the scenes of the most mechanized agriculture in America. Over the new rails, Northwest apples and berries and Southern California citrus fruits found their way

east. Yet the same railroads that boomed Western agriculture brought ruin to some fledgling Western manufacturers who could not compete with the flood of Eastern goods shipped westward with new ease and speed—some 20 miles an hour, on the average—over the rail lines.

In the 1890s the entire region continued to grow. The Southern California economy brightened as oil strikes were made in that area. Lumber production in Oregon and Washington increased tenfold between 1880 and 1905, partly because of mechanization. The salmon industry became a staple of the Northwest economy. Seattle, port of embarkation for the Klondike gold rush of 1897 and for the Alaska rushes of 1899 and 1902, began to compete with Portland for economic dominance over the Northwest hinterlands.

In its first half century as part of the United States, the West Coast had achieved astonishing economic momentum—a momentum that accelerated with the start of the 20th Century. San Francisco rebuilt itself boldly after the earthquake and fire of 1906. Agriculture became the backbone of California wealth. Gold and silver were already giving way in 1900 to industrial mining; petroleum, iron ore, sand and gravel, salines and cement minerals were being extracted in place of the precious metals. Unimagined at the time, the Hollywood film industry was destined to leave an indelible mark on California and the world. Growing hand in hand, transport and tourism were finding on the West Coast a trove of unsuspected treasure. The West Coast financial community was still a stripling in the eyes of Wall Street, but from it an unsuspected giant, Amadeo P. Giannini, was about to emerge.

At the turn of the century Giannini was a successful young produce dealer in San Francisco. In 1904, at 34, he opened a one-room bank to serve the Italian colony of that city's North Beach section. As a newcomer to banking he saw no reason why a bank should not act as a money store for people of moderate means; the concept was bizarre in that era, and Giannini grew notorious for his naïveté in granting small personal bank loans to seemingly unpromising applicants. His experience in produce had given him a basic understanding of the peculiar potential of branch banking in California. In branch banking each branch is able to call on the resources of all the other branches in the system. California agriculture was already both specialized and diversified. A Kern County farmer might grow only potatoes, while a farmer in nearby Fresno County grew only grapes. One grape crop

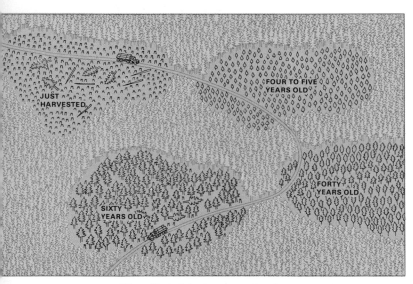

Many of today's lumbermen are tree farmers, growing crops of trees that will later be harvested. One of their techniques is "patch cutting," which is used in the Northwest's stands of Douglas fir. A small area of forest is cut over which will reseed itself from the surrounding trees. The young trees thrive in the sunlight of the open "patch." When partially grown, the trees are thinned so that those which remain will grow more vigorously. This and other methods will enable farsighted lumbermen to grow more timber than they cut annually.

DAVID W. GRIFFITH

MACK SENNETT

CARL LAEMMLE

JESSE L. LASKY AND ADOLPH ZUKOR

Moguls of the early movies

Hollywood became the center of the American film industry largely because a number of early moviemakers moved west and happened to settle on the then-sleepy Los Angeles suburb. Among these pioneers was David Wark Griffith, a highly original director who first made extensive use of such now-basic cinematic tricks as long shots, close-ups and fade-outs. Feeling constrained by the 12-to-24-minute limit usually put on films by the era's major producers, Griffith joined an independent company and made his 144-minute *The Birth of a Nation* (1915), which has become perhaps the most celebrated movie of all time. In these same early years another director, Mack Sennett, the great genius of comedy, was making films with his Keystone Cops and discovering such famous stars as Charlie Chaplin and Gloria Swanson. Meanwhile some of the early producers were founding companies—and making fortunes. Carl Laemmle, who started as a nickelodeon operator, spent many years fighting film monopolies in the courts and thus helped to establish much of the law that today protects the motion-picture business. Another former nickelodeon operator, Adolph Zukor, organized a company that turned a number of classic tales, like *Tess of the D'Urbervilles*, into movies. In 1916 he joined with Jesse L. Lasky to form the company that eventually became Paramount Pictures.

failure could bankrupt Fresno farmers and endanger the assets of a local bank. But if the bank were a member of a branch system, overall solvency could be insured by a good potato crop that season in Kern. In 1910 Giannini's little Bank of Italy began to expand, opening a branch in San Jose. In 1913 he startled Californians by invading Los Angeles, which was still regarded with condescension by the financial community of San Francisco. Giannini's timing was superb. Water had just come to Los Angeles from the Owens Valley. A period of labor strife had just ended. The new Los Angeles harbor was beginning to handle almost as much cargo as San Francisco's. Three enterprising young men —Samuel Goldwyn, Jesse L. Lasky and Cecil B. DeMille—were planning the production of a film called *The Squaw Man*. Giannini moved in on Los Angeles near the start of a period of great economic growth.

His subsequent rise all over California was phenomenal. In one year, 1927, his bank—which after an intricate series of mergers eventually became known as the Bank of America—expanded from 98 to 289 branches. Before his death in 1949, Giannini had withstood Eastern corporate raiders and had seen his one-room bank grow into the largest nongovernmental banking institution in the world.

By 1966 the Bank of America had more than 900 branches in California, more than seven million deposit accounts and total resources in excess of $16 billion. Its loans sustained half of the California agricultural industry.

Other corporate giants were launched at the turn of the century. The Pacific Gas and Electric Company was founded in 1905. Today PG&E has 80,000 miles of power lines serving 4.3 million customers in central and northern California. A corporate neighbor in the San Francisco financial district is Standard Oil of California, the leading Pacific Coast petroleum company. It built its first refinery on San Francisco Bay in 1902, serving it by pipeline from Bakersfield, in the Great Central Valley.

California oil wells were already producing four million barrels a year by 1900, and in 1920 new oil fields were tapped in Southern California, near Long Beach. California was the country's leading petroleum-producing state from 1900 to 1936, and the second-ranking state until 1958. (Now California ranks third, behind Texas and Louisiana.) In Los Angeles oil wells pump night and day beside the fairways of the stylish Los Angeles Country Club on Wilshire Boulevard and in the shadow of Century City, a new high-rise community adjacent to Beverly Hills. Oil production in this century has greatly

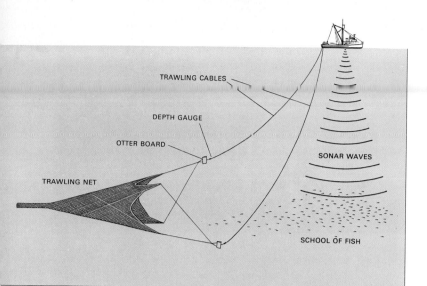

To aid commercial fishermen, a system that gives them "eyes" to see into the depths has been developed on the West Coast. Instead of dragging their nets blindly through the water, fishermen with sonar can now find schools of fish at intermediate depths, from 300 to 600 feet down, and lower their nets unerringly, guided by a depth gauge on the net that relays its measurements through special trawling cables. The net, too, is newly designed and has hydrofoils, called otter boards, to keep its mouth open. One type of fish discovered in quantity at these depths is hake, which may become popular in the United States now that huge amounts are available.

contributed to California's economic growth and has not been unrelated to the prompt and overwhelming acceptance by Californians of the automobile. But the state's reserves have been slowly depleted over the years, and fuel is being imported into California today. Natural-gas lines cross the Southwest desert from Texas and New Mexico to serve West Coast cities. California utility systems are now using large amounts of the gas as fuel for their steam-generating plants, and are presently developing nuclear-power sources.

In the Northwest, with less strain from population expansion, the depletion of natural resources has been less abrupt, except for the cutting of virgin forests. In this, 1900 was a fateful year. That was when a German immigrant named Frederick Weyerhaeuser, who lived in St. Paul, Minnesota, next door to James J. Hill, the railroad man, founded what is today the largest corporate forest empire in the Northwest. Hill was anxious to sell forestlands granted him by the federal government as a subsidy for building the Great Northern railroad; Weyerhaeuser and a band of associates bought 900,000 acres from Hill and opened offices in Tacoma under the Weyerhaeuser name.

Lumbering dominates the economy of Oregon, which has more than one fifth of the nation's entire supply of sawtimber. Washington ranks directly behind, second among states, with one sixth of the supply. Almost half of the land area of Washington is in commercial forestland; in Oregon the proportion is only slightly less. Within Oregon alone are enough trees to rebuild every house in the 50 states. Not so diversified as Washington, Oregon sees its economy thrive or decline with national building trends.

Large corporations like Weyerhaeuser, Georgia-Pacific of Portland and Crown Zellerbach of San Francisco have been absorbing the small lumbermen and mill operators of the Northwest; huge capital reserves are required for reforestation, and reforestation is a necessity if a company wishes to stay in business more than a few years. Alarmed by the rapid disappearance of Northwest timber, the Weyerhaeuser firm established the nation's first tree farm in 1941 near Aberdeen, Washington; it became the model for more than 28,000 other such operations across the nation. Tree farms and pest and fire controls enable Oregon to grow an increasing number of trees each year. The state produces close to 70 per cent of the nation's plywood; in Washington emphasis has been on the pulp-and-paper section of the industry. Despite increasing mechanization, one third of the Washington manufacturing payroll goes to workers in the lumber industry, as does more than half of Oregon's. But as new techniques are introduced, fewer employees work in the forests and more are in semiautomated factories. The industry weathered a recession after World War II and has since moved forward again with sophisticated techniques like those for converting waste—sawdust, bark and chips—into composition board, paper, wax, pressed logs and alcohol. So profitable have these products become that major companies now buy waste material from smaller operators for conversion.

As Weyerhaeuser and his associates had bought timber-rich railroad lands in the Northwest in 1900, California syndicates acquired huge tracts in that state. Very little California land found its way into the hands of homesteaders. By 1880 the railroads had been granted more than 11 million acres of federal land in California, much of it rich farm, timber or oil land. The railroads sold vast amounts of it to the highest bidders. Southern Pacific sold with the rest; so extensive were its holdings, however, that as late as 1919 it remained the largest landowner in the state. In addition, more than eight million acres of federal land in California were deeded to the state. Some 6.7 million acres of this land were intended for schools and other public buildings; the state instead sold most of it off at a pittance. The remainder—much of it classified as useless "swampland" by government surveyors bribed by speculators—found its way into the hands of large landowners like Henry Miller, a former butcher whose Miller & Lux combine acquired an empire within the state that was as large in area as Belgium.

Such large landholdings did not become farms but agricultural assembly lines. In 1871 the political economist Henry George wrote that "California is not a country of farms but a country of plantations and estates. Agriculture is speculation. . . . There is no state in the Union in which settlers in good faith have been so persecuted, so robbed, as in California. Men have grown rich, and men still make a regular business of blackmailing settlers upon public land, of appropriating their homes, and this by power of the law and in the name of justice." The estates were farmed by pools of cheap labor, typically Chinese or Mexican. The cleavage between corporate landholders and the farm workers widened and resulted in labor strife that continues to this day. Rural slums grew up and squatters rioted when landowners attempted to evict them.

Despite such conflict California has developed the most productive agriculture in the world, and one of the most diversified. The state grows more than 200 agricultural products, from artichokes to zucchini. This diversity is possible because of the variety of soils and climates in California, and because of the extensive use of irrigation. There are about eight million acres of irrigated farmland; even pastures have been irrigated. The state is a vast controlled hothouse. Most farms specialize in one or two crops as a result of tedious experimentation to determine the best use of the local soil, climate and water supply. Winter apples are produced at Watsonville, on Monterey Bay, for instance, and summer apples are harvested north of San Francisco around Sebastopol. Salinas claims the title of lettuce capital of the world, and Castroville, near Monterey, bills itself as the international artichoke capital. Dates come from the Coachella Valley. Orchids are raised in commercial quantities at Ojai, near Santa Barbara, and poinsettias at Encinitas, near San Diego. Specialization extends even within single crops: one variety of fig is raised for drying and another is grown for canning.

Also because of the different climates and soils, California farmers have successfully grown plant species brought to the state by immigrants from all over the world: avocados and tomatoes from Mexico; flax from India; dates from Algeria, Egypt

Ladders for fish to climb dams

Leaping from pool to pool, salmon work their way up a fish ladder toward spawning beds in the upper reaches of a fresh-water stream. Fish ladders were devised to enable salmon—and other fish that live in the sea but spawn in rivers—to surmount man-made dams. Without such devices the fish would exhaust themselves trying to swim up the dams' steep spillways, and die without spawning, thus jeopardizing the West Coast salmon industry. All ladders consist of a series of pools separated by low barriers called weirs which the fish can easily negotiate. In the center of each weir on many ladders is a raised section which creates a backwater where the fish can rest. Near the bottom of each weir are one or two openings through which the fish can swim if they do not jump. These ladders are effective only on low dams. For higher dams, special elevators or trucking systems carry the fish past the obstacles.

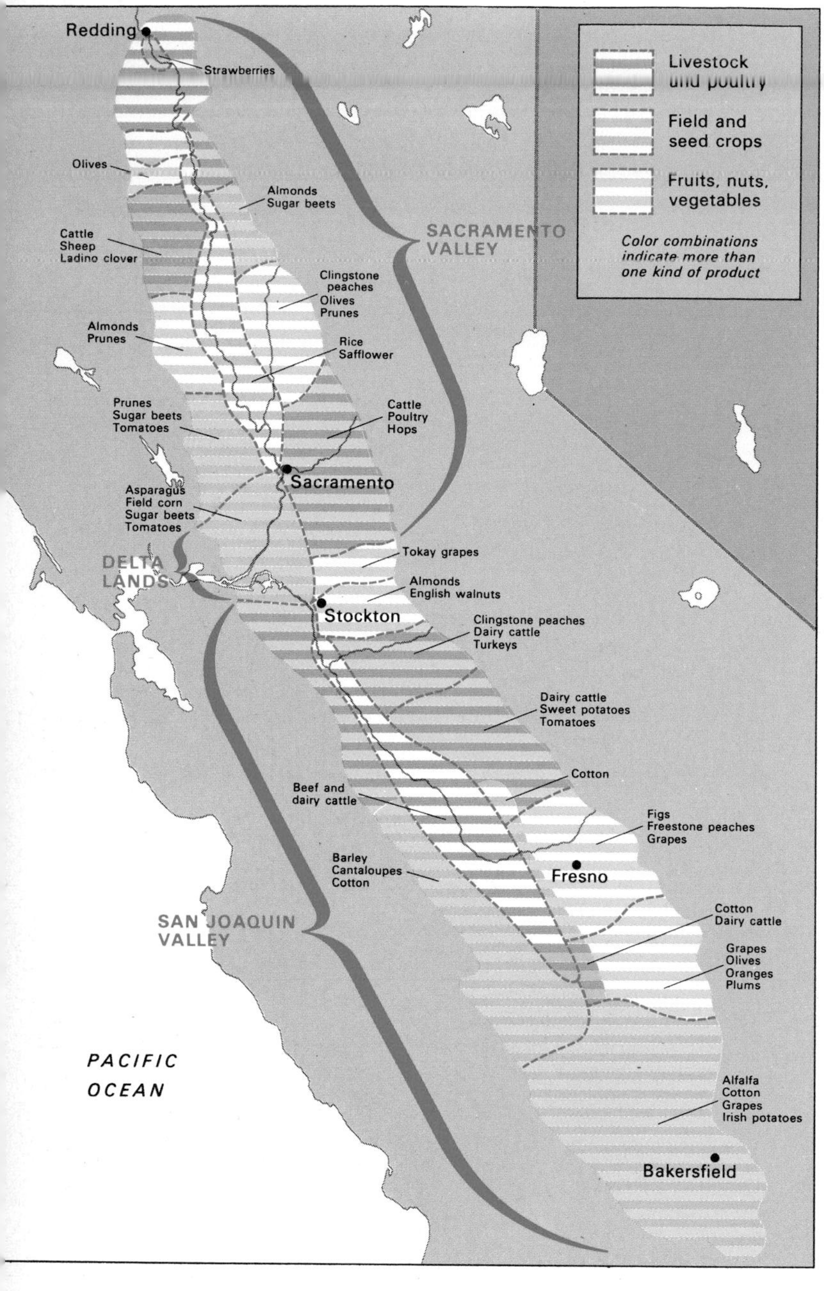
Redding
Strawberries
Livestock and poultry
Field and seed crops
Fruits, nuts, vegetables
Color combinations indicate more than one kind of product
Olives
Almonds
Sugar beets
SACRAMENTO VALLEY
Cattle
Sheep
Ladino clover
Clingstone peaches
Olives
Prunes
Almonds
Prunes
Rice
Safflower
Prunes
Sugar beets
Tomatoes
Cattle
Poultry
Hops
Sacramento
Asparagus
Field corn
Sugar beets
Tomatoes
Tokay grapes
DELTA LANDS
Almonds
English walnuts
Stockton
Clingstone peaches
Dairy cattle
Turkeys
Dairy cattle
Sweet potatoes
Tomatoes
Cotton
Beef and dairy cattle
Figs
Freestone peaches
Grapes
Barley
Cantaloupes
Cotton
Fresno
SAN JOAQUIN VALLEY
Cotton
Dairy cattle
Grapes
Olives
Oranges
Plums
PACIFIC OCEAN
Alfalfa
Cotton
Grapes
Irish potatoes
Bakersfield

Farming the Great Central Valley

California's farmlands of the Great Central Valley comprise one of the most remarkable agricultural areas in the nation. This immensely fertile region produces a great variety of fruits and vegetables and much of the nation's barley and cotton. The valley is also a major producer of beef and dairy cattle. Areas specializing in the three major types of agriculture are shown above; where the three overlap, only the two most important are shown. Labels on the map indicate areas where extraordinary amounts of a crop are grown or where a specialty crop, like safflower, dominates. The distribution of the various kinds of agriculture depends largely on the availability of irrigation water and on the soil. Thus the valley's dry borders are fine for cattle, while the soil in the delta of the San Joaquin and Sacramento Rivers is excellent for tomatoes and asparagus.

and Persia; walnuts from Chile; grapes and prunes from France; milo from Japan; rice from China; alfalfa from Chile. Much of the research that led to the successful production of such transplants was done by agronomists at the University of California campus at Davis, near Sacramento. The California wine industry, which produces 80 per cent of the wine consumed in the United States, works closely with the Davis Department of Viticulture and Enology, whose faculty of 14 is larger even than that of the University of Bordeaux Enological Station in France.

The California citrus industry, which ranks second to Florida's in the production of oranges, was saved from virtual obliteration in the 1940s by the University of California's Citrus Experiment Station at Riverside. The state's orange trees had been dying by the thousands; after two years of investigation plant pathologists at the Riverside campus traced the cause to a virus known as tristeza. The threat to the industry was eliminated by grafting rootstock from the Troyer citrange, a variety capable of tolerating tristeza, to the disease-prone varieties. Today, about five million California orange trees are the descendants of two Troyer citranges still growing in the nursery on the University's Riverside campus.

Many mechanical devices used on the farms of California are the invention of University of California researchers. There are pneumatic tree-shakers to harvest nuts, and rubber hands that reach out to "feel" heads of lettuce and activate a cutting blade if the lettuce is ripe. Tomatoes are grown in winter under cone-shaped "hot caps" that shield them from cold and give the fields the look of little cities of miniature tepees.

Although emphasis upon mechanization has tended to boost California agricultural productivity, the industry is not without critical problems. Labor is in irregular supply, and growers are largely dependent upon migratory workers. Efforts to unionize agricultural workers began to achieve some success in 1966 after years of bitter strife, but it is likely that there will be a continuing period of labor unrest and discord. Even more critical in the long view is the conversion of farmland to nonagricultural uses, currently at the rate of about 140,000 acres each year in California. About 15 million acres in the state are being farmed or are potential farmland, but much of the land adjoins expanding urban areas, and growers predict that one third of it will be taken out of agricultural use by the year 2000. In 1966 eight major American food processors, including several with extensive acreage in

California, were experimenting with pilot farms and processing plants in Mexico, where labor is cheaper and more abundantly available, and where farmland is relatively as underdeveloped as was the Great Central Valley in 1900.

Much of the farmland conversion in the Pacific Coast states is caused by the need to make room for the sprawling new aerospace industry and the communities that it spawns. The growth of aerospace has been an economic boon to the region; in the years before World War II the West Coast had lagged behind the rest of the country in large-scale manufacturing. The great Northwest shipyards of World War I had been shut down completely by 1925. The lumber industry sagged between the two World Wars, and labor trouble plagued the Coast. San Francisco employers smashed the maritime unions of San Francisco in the early 1920s. But under the radical leadership of Harry Bridges the International Longshoremen's Association surged back in 1934, staging a coastwide maritime strike that year and precipitating a general strike in San Francisco. Booms in oil and real estate came and went in Southern California, but the movie industry began to add substantial strength to the economy of that area as Hollywood entered a golden era. Box-office revenue from motion pictures reached a peak of $1.5 billion in the mid-1940s, when almost 400 movies a year were being made in Hollywood. But it was not until the World War II years that industrial growth—largely of aircraft plants and shipyards—attained explosive proportions on the West Coast.

Aircraft plants were no novelty to the Coast. Glenn L. Martin had begun manufacturing planes in Los Angeles in 1912. Lockheed Aircraft started production in Santa Barbara in 1916, and that same year William E. Boeing began building planes in Seattle. By 1937 California led the states in the production of aircraft; by 1940 almost half of the airframe, engine and propeller workers in the nation were employed in the metropolitan areas of Los Angeles, San Diego and Seattle. Shipyard employment rose in all the major coastal cities during World War II. The West offered room, raw materials, climate and electric power. With a loan from the federal government, Henry J. Kaiser built the first West Coast plant capable of carrying through the entire steel-manufacturing process. Aluminum and magnesium industries sprang to life in Washington.

After the war, unemployment rose sharply, as expected. But the trend was soon reversed. Because of the influx of migrants, record levels in residential construction were established in California. Retail

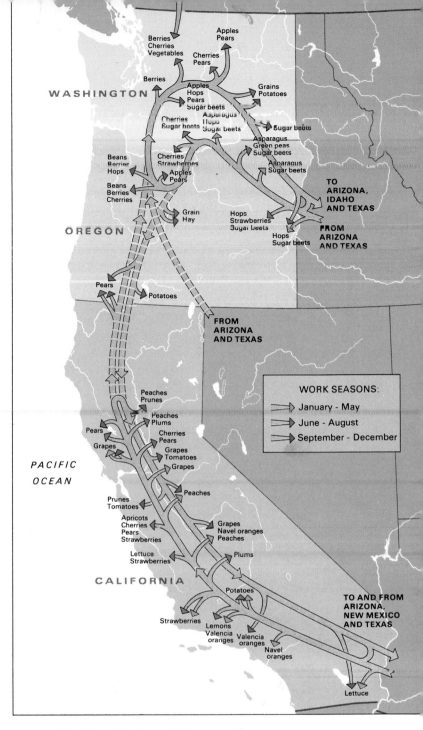

The flow of migrant labor

Streams of migrant laborers flow up and down the states of the West Coast each year, cultivating and harvesting the region's varied crops. Many come from the Southwest; some are of Mexican origin. The major routes followed by these laborers, and the seasons in which they work, are shown on the map above. Large numbers of migratory workers are needed because many of the area's crops must be cultivated and harvested by hand, because the crops mature at different times, and because many of the fields and orchards are enormous. Migratory labor is useful to West Coast farmers; the system, however, has grave defects. The laborers' living conditions vary from fair to intolerable—studies made in the 1960s show that 80 per cent of the housing provided for them is inadequate. The same studies report that the average family income is only $1,432 a year.

and service trades prospered. Branch plants were built by Eastern industries. By 1956 aircraft employment in Washington was greater than that in the lumber industry. Although by 1963 California contained a little less than 10 per cent of the country's people, 20 per cent of the workers in defense and related industries were Californians. In 1965 eighteen of the top 100 American defense contractors were in California, including Lockheed Aircraft, the nation's leading defense contractor. During the mid-1960s, when almost 40 per cent of all federal research-and-development funds were going to California-based firms, lawmakers from other regions protested against the West Coast's pre-eminence. Government spokesmen asserted that the sole reason for the apparent disproportion was that research-and-development facilities and a high proportion of research people working in matters important to the Defense Department were centered on the West Coast.

The defense dollar remains an important bulwark of the West Coast economy. The nation's economists continually prod the cities of the Coast to seek diversification and lessen the tendency toward boom-and-bust that has grown to haunt many industries in the region that are dependent upon defense contracts. Yet the economic maturity of the Pacific Coast states is less often disputed nowadays. Business surges have been fueled by the soaring population. The speed and relative ease of postwar economic conversions, and the subsequent breakneck industrial growth, have surprised many of these same economists.

Economic growth in nondefense areas continued on the West Coast in the 1960s. Between 1960 and 1965 the Pacific Gas and Electric Company increased its assets by more than $100 million each year. In 1965 Los Angeles reached a long-sought milestone when it supplanted San Francisco as the Western financial center. In the three critical measurements of growth—total loans, deposits and savings—Los Angeles banks exceeded those of San Francisco. Western steel output from Kaiser and from the Bethlehem plant near Oakland grew larger, despite increasing competition from Japanese imports. In Washington, Boeing took a position of world dominance in the manufacture of commercial jet airliners. Tourism became a billion-dollar-a-year business in Southern California alone, with California hotels and motels second only to those of New York in their annual gross income. With one million persons a year unable to find room on its crowded beaches and parks, California in 1966 estimated that it would spend $500 million within

20 years for recreational expansion. Other funds for major public works—the estimated two billion dollars to be expended through the 1960s and 1970s for the California Water Project, and the $10 billion to be spent in those years for more California freeways—were sure to be an economic prop.

There have always been large amounts of aid made available to the West from federal sources in such forms as railroad land grants, subsidies, research funds and money for the construction of dams. But federal spending in the region has undergone a transition from the era when the West was regarded as a colony rich in mineral wealth. Federal money today is spent on the Coast not only because of its natural resources but because of its wealth of human resources—brains and skills.

In turn, because the money is being spent there, additional numbers of qualified people tend to move to the Coast. Industry has often been established in the West because management or potential employees choose to live there. Many space-age industries are relatively foot-loose, freed by the nature of their product from any necessity to locate near rivers or railroads, population centers, or coal and iron deposits. The environment in its entirety, intellectual as well as physical, has been a basic factor in West Coast economic growth. "It's quite fair to say that California will continue to be an attractive place for technologically oriented business and industry," David Packard, board chairman of Hewlett-Packard, a manufacturer of electronic measuring instruments, observed in 1964. "This is true because of the state's strong universities and because there's a [national] shortage of technological people who can [therefore] command a fair choice of where they work—and who like the California climate." The attraction of West Coast living has had a profound effect in promoting the region's industrial development in recent years.

So has the relative lateness of the industrial history of the West. The American economist Thorstein Veblen observed in 1915 that 19th Century Germany had gained an advantage over Great Britain by its late start in industrialization. Germany was able to apply new technological innovations and profit by the experience of older industrial economies. In the same way the tardiness of industrialization in the Pacific States has ruled out, for the time being, the inertia of tradition. Instead, there is an affinity for new methods, new products and new marketing techniques. The freshness of Western products has led to ready sales in other regions. So long as the West remains energetically different, its economic future would seem assured.

Spreading over a reshaped hillside, houses in a development called
Laurel Hills go up near Hollywood. In the mid-1960s, attacking their
landscape on a mammoth scale, California builders constructed
an average of 236,000 housing units each year.

Industries marked by ingenuity

From home construction to lumbering, West Coast industries are distinguished by ingenious solutions to special problems. Modern loggers have developed mechanized monsters to conquer the giant trees of their areas, enabling Washington, Oregon and California to remain the top lumber-producing states in the country. Faced with rising costs and shipping bills, West Coast farmers remain competitive by utilizing new machines; California's mechanized farms annually produce three billion dollars' worth of agricultural products, the nation's largest crop. Much of it remains at home to feed the state's burgeoning population. An average of 1,500 people move to California each day—and the state's construction industry rises massively to that challenge by erecting more housing units annually than are built in any other state.

Launching an experimental V-shaped balloon, loggers prepare to airlift logs near Reedsport, Oregon. When towed through the air the balloon achieves aerodynamic lift similar to that of an airplane's wing, enabling it to carry as much as 10,000 pounds of timber at one time—more than three times the weight a round balloon would be able to lift. Besides saving road-building costs in remote lumbering areas, moving logs by balloon prevents damage to young trees and leaves the ground undisturbed for future forest growth.

Mechanization in the woods to keep an industry modern

The forests of the West Coast contain perhaps the most magnificent stand of timber in the world, and from them loggers annually harvest some 3.8 billion cubic feet of timber—almost one third of the nation's supply. The loggers' willingness to try innovations aids them to attain that output, and also helps them to turn out a variety of products. More than half of the harvested timber is made into lumber used in housing and in other construction projects. About 25 per cent becomes wood pulp, from which paper, cardboard and composition board are produced. Some 10 per cent is made into plywood.

Moving toward a mouthful, a loader prepares to pick up a stack of logs at a plywood plant in southwestern Washington. This loader is able to raise some 35 tons, and the largest models can lift 65 tons. They replace machines that handle only one log at a time.

Depositing a log on its conveyer belt, an automatic chipper works on the Clatsop Tree Farm near Seaside, Oregon. The chipper moves the log up the belt, strips it of bark and branches, then cuts it into small pieces from which wood pulp will be made.

A strong and growing industry from an ancient art

Among the nation's fastest-growing nondefense industries in recent years has been plywood manufacturing, which is largely a West Coast industry. The first American plywood plant was built in Oregon in 1905. Today, of the 360 plants in the country, 182 are on the Coast. These plants yearly turn out some 12 billion square feet of plywood—roughly 85 per cent of the national output—for use mainly in home construction (the average new house uses more than 3,800 square feet). Although a relatively new invention, plywood traces its origins to the ancient Egyptian art of veneering. A veneer is a layer of a valuable wood glued to a cheaper wood to improve the appearance of the finished product. Plywood—as shown by these pictures taken at International Paper's plant in Chelatchie Prairie, Washington—consists of several layers of wood glued together to achieve strength. This is done by running the grain of each layer at right angles to the next.

Coming from the drier, sheets of wood move to a sorting turntable developed at International Paper in 1964. The better sections will become the face sheets of the plywood panel, while those with large knotholes or other imperfections will be used for core sheets.

A ribbon of wood is skinned off a solid piece called a "block" during a process known as "peeling the log," one of the first steps in making plywood. A block 30 inches in diameter unwinds into a sheet as thin as one tenth of an inch and up to 800 feet long. The sheet is then cut into short lengths and sent to a drying machine.

"Laying up" wood sections, workmen make sandwiches of exterior, or face, sheets and interior, or core, sheets. The glistening sheet atop the pile has just gone through a glue spreader to the left of the men. The sandwiches next go to a hydraulic press (right background), which will squeeze them to form the finished plywood panels.

Myriad machines
to increase farm productivity

Agriculture is big business on the West Coast, and especially so in California, which produces more than 200 crops and since 1943 has ranked as the nation's top farming state. While mechanization is widespread in U.S. agriculture, it is particularly prevalent in California, where the shortage of labor has brought about the development of huge factorylike farms, replete with bizarre machines.

Demonstrating new citrus-fruit pickers, three men ride scissor-extender booms in Oxnard, California. Suction tubes used with such apparatus enable three men to pick 900 boxes of fruit a day—about seven times what three hand workers can pick.

A factory in the field, a lettuce packer on the Bud Antle ranch in Salinas, California, helps 26 farm hands to do the work of 45. As the workers move across the field, the packer seals the lettuce heads in plastic film and deposits them, boxed, for pickup.

Driving a two-row picker in the San Joaquin Valley, a farm hand harvests California's biggest single crop, cotton, which brings in almost 10 per cent of the state's agricultural income. Such a picker, complete with power steering, can outperform 80 hand pickers.

Apples in field bins travel by conveyer to be washed in a modern packing plant in Wenatchee, Washington. The state supplies 25 per cent of the nation's apples, and sells many of them to neighboring California, which buys some half billion a year.

Fresh from the vine, grapes are dumped into a hopper in Napa, California. The grapes are moved by a conveyer to a machine that removes the stems, then to a crusher. After fermentation, the juice is aged for several years in redwood casks before bottling.

Ancient crops changed by modern methods

Even such ancient crops as wine grapes and apples are being affected by the West Coast's emphasis on mechanization and research. In Washington apple orchards, picking and sorting are still done by hand. But in many areas in the state, machines take over after the harvest, carting, washing, polishing and storing the fruit before it reaches market. To take advantage of market trends, growers are constantly developing new varieties that ripen at different times of year, store better or taste sweeter.

Similarly, research in California universities has supplied that state's vintners with better yeasts for fermentation as well as superior varieties of grapes and increased knowledge of the best soil in which to grow them. Already producing 85 per cent of the nation's wines, California vintners have begun using mass-production methods to increase their output.

A technician records temperatures and other information necessary to control the aging of champagne in the modern Paul Masson winery in Saratoga, California. While most wines in other parts of the country come from native vines, California's are produced from vines originally imported from Europe. They have done so well in their new home that when a blight almost wiped out European vineyards in the early 1870s, California roots were used to develop the blight-resistant strain that now produces most of Europe's wines.

BRUT CELLARS
00,000 BOTTLES
AGING

Tooting earnestly, the ladies of a "kitchen band" support the
financial "plan" of Dr. Francis E. Townsend during a Los Angeles
rally in 1938. Townsend was one of many West Coasters to propose
radical (and often loony) schemes to relieve the Great Depression.

6

Politics
in Disarray

During a roll-call vote at the California Democratic Council convention in 1964, a delegate from a mountain county rose and spoke in a shrill, nasal twang. "In the great tradition of our great state of California," he announced, "and in the great tradition of our great Democratic governor, our delegation is divided!" He sat down amid laughter and applause. With one stroke of whimsy he had touched the core of California politics: Californians rejoice in their political disarray.

Political divisiveness is a trait common to the entire Coast. In their probing for the ideal society the people of the Pacific States have experimented and cast aside, gone to ludicrous extremes, achieved noble reform and managed to remain a perpetual conundrum in American politics. They show scant inclination to follow rigid political folkways; the only predictability is the overriding flexibility of the electorate. Oregon has been called the "political experiment station of the nation." Washingtonians voted for Republican candidates for President in 1956 and 1960, and in the same years elected a Democratic governor; in 1964 they voted for a Democratic President and a Republican governor. Western voters behave in ways that appear haphazard and irresponsible to outsiders. They do not conform to traditional political laws. They cross party lines with regularity; they will not be machine-organized or bloc-delivered. They are prone to experiment with extreme swings to left or right, and to unite only against some familiar danger or behind some bland, moderate candidate.

Neither Right-Wing nor Left-Wing extremism has made any profound or lasting imprint in the region. Moderates have held sway, and the few extremists who have risen to state office have been tempered by their contact with responsibility. "California is not lunatic or bizarre," wrote the political novelist Eugene Burdick. "It is just slightly skewed, asymmetrical, off-center in almost every way." The skewing is seen in an emotional commitment to individualism. Despite his widespread dependence on the federal dollar, the Westerner is more distrustful of federal intervention than is the Easterner. "The Westerner has come [West] because he is an individual," says Richard Nixon, the California-born former Vice President. "He thinks he can get along all right by himself, with less central government than the voters of some other regions are accustomed to."

The prospect that continuing population growth in this unconventional West will give California more political power than any other state is alarming to many observers in more politically mature states. They note that California has given no evidence that its people take their growing influence soberly. The image of California politics is often one of extremism, of film-stars-turned-politicians, or of madcap antics at Presidential conventions—like those of the 1964 Republican delegates pledged to Barry Goldwater who took their seats in the Cow Palace outside San Francisco clad in imitation life jackets. While any danger of drowning is remote, it is true that California politicians of both parties are quick to set sail without a compass.

The individualistic style is by no means new to the Western political scene. In the 1880s the British historian and diplomat Lord Bryce visited California and wrote that its people were impatient with "the slow approach of the millennium." Neither there nor in Oregon and Washington did either the Republican or Democratic Party manage to establish dominance in the early years of statehood, although Washington soon earned a reputation as a socially progressive state. Oregon also developed continuity in handling its social and economic affairs. Democrats gained control for short periods, but Oregon was to remain a predominantly Republican state until midway in the 20th Century, voting for both Republican governors and Republican Presidents. The Populist reform movement came to the state in the mid-1890s, ignited by the farmers' discontent with the power of the railroads and industrial interests, and by drunkenness and debauchery in Salem, the state capital. Led by William S. U'Ren, a religious mystic and onetime Prohibitionist, Oregon Populists channeled enthusiasm for reform into the establishment of machinery

to enable the voters to legislate directly; in 1902 Oregon voters approved the initiative and referendum petition system by a margin of 11 to 1. Under what came to be known as "the Oregon system" 107 measures were taken directly to the people in six subsequent elections; Oregonians voted to limit the working day for women to 10 hours, to prohibit free passes on railroads, to control freight rates and establish taxes on utility companies, and to set up an industrial-accident commission. Oregon's citizens were the marvel of the nation for their devotion to the study of politics. "Every . . . community is being trained to a knowledge of politics," wrote the political scientist Frederic C. Howe in 1911 in describing Oregon as "the most complete democracy in the world." In that same year Woodrow Wilson, then Governor of New Jersey, referred to the laws of Oregon as seeming "to point the direction which we must also take." Washington was quick to follow Oregon's lead, its voters presently accepting the direct primary and initiative and referendum. They also adopted workmen's compensation and woman suffrage.

The spirit of reform had also been rising in California. There the Southern Pacific Railroad, in an effort to support high passenger and freight rates, had built an immense political machine that controlled governors, senators, congressmen and even judges. Such special-interest political rule was then common all over America, but reform attempts came quickly in the West, where oppression did not seem to be a tolerable state of affairs. The first significant attempt at reform in California was launched by the Workingmen's Party, which was founded in 1877 in San Francisco by Denis Kearney, an Irish immigrant and former seaman. His reform program was tainted with violence and racism. He pressed for "a little judicious hanging" for Nob Hill millionaires and launched the slogan, "The Chinese Must Go!" Although the state enacted a "gag law" to suppress Kearney, his new party elected some candidates to the legislature and forced adoption of a new state constitution that established a railroad commission; within six years, however, the party had disappeared.

Other reform movements in California in the 1890s proceeded from the opposite end of the economic spectrum. Two of San Francisco's reform mayors, Adolph Sutro and James D. Phelan, were millionaires. So was Dr. John R. Haynes of Los Angeles, a doctor who founded the Direct Legislation League in 1895 to challenge the Southern Pacific machine. But it was from the melodrama unfolding in a San Francisco courtroom that a lawyer

A great California political figure, Hiram Warren Johnson twice was elected governor of the state and five times U.S. senator. Born in Sacramento in 1866, he was nominally a Republican, but he broke with the G.O.P. to become Theodore Roosevelt's running mate on the Bull Moose ticket, and he actively supported President Franklin D. Roosevelt during Roosevelt's first term.

named Hiram Johnson emerged to become the historic hand of reform. Graft had grown so open in San Francisco that "Boss" Abraham Ruef was able to get a violinist named Eugene Schmitz into office as a puppet mayor in 1901. When Ruef and Schmitz were brought to trial on indictments of graft in 1907, the chief prosecutor, Francis J. Heney, was shot and nearly killed in the courtroom by a former convict. The prosecution was taken over by Johnson. Although Schmitz's indictment was dismissed on a technicality, Ruef was to spend nearly five years in San Quentin. Hiram Johnson had made his mark. A group of civic reformers had founded the Lincoln-Roosevelt League in 1907 with the aim of capturing the state government; in 1910 they backed Johnson for governor. Promising virtually nothing but to "kick the Southern Pacific Railroad out of the Republican Party and out of the state government," Johnson won.

His victory set the course of California politics to the present day. Guiding with a firm hand, Johnson introduced an arsenal of legislative and constitutional devices designed to inhibit political machines, prevent effective party organization and minimize patronage. Most of them have prevailed, and are basically responsible for the debilitating excesses of nonpartisanship and the comically lengthy array of proposed legislation often confronting California voters. Because of the Johnson measures, every California election shows symptoms of a free-for-all, and California parties appear to be in constant chaos. But the result has also been to foster moderation in government while at the same time providing usually harmless forums for screwballs and extremists. The Johnson package included the initiative, referendum and recall, as well as the direct primary that replaced the machine controlled political convention. Johnson's administration also established the cross-filing system that allowed candidates to run in both the Democratic and the Republican primaries and thus sometimes to assure themselves of victory by winning both nominations—an institution that was not abolished until 1959. The election of judges was made nonpartisan, and patronage was virtually wiped out when state and local offices were placed under civil service.

The Johnson legislation went far beyond political reform. An avalanche of progressive laws came out of the 1911 legislature as it set out to implement the platform of the Lincoln-Roosevelt League that had launched the reform movement. The railroad commission was strengthened so that it could control rates and its authority was extended over all public utilities; this effectively diminished the power of the railroads. The workday for women was restricted to eight hours, and child labor was prohibited; free textbooks were authorized for the public schools. Funds were voted for flood control and reclamation, and a Water and Power Conservation Act was passed to halt the destruction of natural resources. Legislators established employers' liability and old-age pensions and gave local communities control of the sale of alcoholic beverages.

Almost immediately California found itself in the vanguard of the states pressing for liberal social and political legislation. Former President Theodore Roosevelt referred to the work of the 1911 lawmakers as "the most comprehensive program of constructive legislation ever passed at a single session of an American legislature." What the lawmakers could not manage, the voters approved through constitutional amendments. Twenty-three amendments were passed in 1911, including one granting the suffrage to women. In 1913 the next legislature continued the progressive surge, establishing commissions concerned with industrial accidents and laborers' welfare, and with conservation, housing and immigration. No other major state had moved so boldly in political and economic reform.

Part of the effect of Hiram Johnson's rousing leadership was the firm entrenchment of the Republican

An early West Coast union agitator, James B. McNamara *(far left)*, awaits trial for the 1910 dynamiting of the Los Angeles *Times* building in which 21 employees died. McNamara was defended by the fiery lawyer Clarence Darrow *(sitting beside him)*. The case developed into a bitter battle between labor and capital—until McNamara unexpectedly confessed, thus dealing a crippling blow to organized labor and making Los Angeles especially hostile to unionism for many years.

Party. Until 1898 most California governors had been Democrats. Thereafter, except in the Depression-year election of 1938, no Democrat gained the governorship for 60 years. Republicans virtually dominated California delegations in Congress, as well as the state legislature, for half a century. Yet party politics seemed secondary to Johnson. The party umbrella came to provide only leaky refuge for candidates, and party labels were minimized in the more practical interest of straddling party lines and seeking wider voter support. Visiting California in 1911, Woodrow Wilson remarked: "I can't, for the life of me, in this place be certain that I can tell a Democrat from a Republican."

With Democrats flocking to his support, Hiram Johnson became the first master of the strangely neutered political system he had helped to devise. He learned to capitalize on the voters' belligerent independence. Californians developed a suspicion of political parties and a reliance upon individuals. Johnson led the California reform movement until 1917, when he resigned as governor to serve as a United States senator; he was returned to that office with huge majorities—95 per cent of the total California vote in 1934—until his death in 1945. But it had been the Johnson era in Sacramento that had attracted national attention and had set the high-water mark in California political achievement.

By the early 1920s, however, progressivism was finished in California. Between the two World Wars the progressive mood gave way to one of fundamentalism. Prohibition became a major issue up and down the West Coast, and prejudice against racial, religious and political minorities grew. The devices of reform became the weapons of discrimination as extremist factions used direct legislation to enact laws aimed at the minorities. A Kansas publisher described California and Washington in the mid-1920s as two of the most reactionary states in the nation. The Ku Klux Klan thrived in Oregon. The rapid swing and sway of West Coast politics was again in evidence, abetted by trends in migration. New York and Massachusetts had long provided more Californians than any other states; now people from Illinois, Missouri, Texas and Oklahoma became the leading migrants to California. A Bible Belt of fundamentalism grew up in Southern California. Northwest progressivism was diluted by the immigration of rural Southerners to logging communities. The presence of such voters enabled the forces of Prohibition to carry all three states. In 1922 Oregon voters passed a compulsory public-school attendance law sponsored by Freemasons and aimed at destroying parochial schools; before it could take effect, however, it was declared unconstitutional by the United States Supreme Court. Evangelical religious sects came to be associated with extremist political measures, especially in Southern California. But this wave did not last long; the political appeal of Prohibition and prejudice began to decline in the late 1920s.

The Democratic victories of 1932 were echoed in the West, most notably in the Presidential election: the West voted as conclusively for Franklin D. Roosevelt as it had for Republican Presidential candidates in the 1920s. But all three West Coast states moved sharply to the right in their choice of state officials in the mid-1930s. In Washington, politics reached a low ebb in 1932, when the Democratic landslide swept numerous incompetent candidates into power. One of the new legislators had been elected while serving a jail sentence for the rape of a 12-year-old girl. Victor Aloysius Meyers, who had been leader of a Seattle night-club dance band, became the lieutenant governor. In an earlier campaign for the city mayoralty, Douglass Welch, a reporter for *The Seattle Times*, had prevailed upon Meyers to enter the race to parody the ineptitude of the available candidates. Although Meyers failed to win that election, he went back into politics without the support of the *Times* and presided over the

Washington senate for five terms as lieutenant governor; later he was elected secretary of state. The saga of Meyers remains a favorite of Washingtonians, who take pride in their fresh and breezy politics. In 1936 Mayor John Dore of Seattle gave free beer to sailors when a Navy fleet sailed into port. Dore referred to Dave Beck, the Teamsters' Union boss who later served a prison term, as "our public citizen Number One." Such antics evoke a fondly remembered allegation of Rudyard Kipling, who visited Tacoma as a young newspaperman and wrote, "They are all mad here, all mad."

Beneath the madness, however, the state preserved its progressive tradition. Washington voters have supported Republicans as well as Democrats, but more often have sought out Republicans from the liberal wing of the party. They have firmly supported education and welfare programs and have been sympathetic to labor unions. During the Depression of the 1930s an amalgamation of Left-Wingers and jobless citizens, known as the Unemployed Citizens' League of Seattle, almost won control of the Democratic Party.

The Depression years in California were politically uproarious. Class conflict flared as labor strife increased and the poverty of migrant farm workers deepened. The pendulum swung entirely away from the euphoria of progressivism. During those years, the historian Earl Pomeroy has written, "the old idea that the West led the nation in opportunity and in democracy seemed out of date. . . . The great opportunities, and then the great problems and their solutions, all seemed to be in the East. On the eve of their greatest growth, Westerners worried about the future of their economy and wondered whether it might in fact be hard to find uses for the water and power the New Deal had given them." The depressed mood of California was not unlike that which had prevailed in 1877, when Kearney and his Workingmen's Party had suddenly blazed forth to exploit unrest. This time the insurgent was the Socialist writer Upton Sinclair, who moved into the Democratic Party and won its nomination for governor in 1934 with a crusade of "production for use." He called his movement EPIC, for "End Poverty in California." Widespread farm strikes in 1933 and 1934 and the San Francisco general strike of 1934, followed by vicious repressions on the part of landowners and employers, played into Sinclair's hands. Bitter partisanship wrenched the state, with the aged, the poor and the Left-Wingers siding with Sinclair. Despite smear charges that he was "an anarchist, a free-lover, an agent of Moscow, a Communist, an anti-Christ," he almost won election.

Sinclair's EPIC was not the only panacea offered to Depression-weary Californians. Another was Technocracy, a movement that called for the country to be run by engineers and technicians. Its meetings swept the state, but its proposals made no dent in government. Technocracy was followed by the Utopian Society, which at its peak claimed half a million members, most of them in Southern California. Its gospel was that private ownership and the profit system should be supplanted by a controlled society in which the national product would be supplied through the performance of only three hours of work each day by all those between 25 and 45 years of age. It too went quickly out of vogue. Soon came Dr. Francis E. Townsend, a retired physician from Long Beach, who prescribed another cure for the Depression: simply give $200 each month to every person more than 60 years old. The absurdity of the Townsend Plan doomed it, but in 1938 and again in 1939 almost one third of the California electorate voted to adopt a proposal known as Thirty Dollars Every Thursday, or Ham and Eggs—a plan that would have awarded a weekly pension of $30 to all unemployed persons over 50. Support of the plan had helped win election in 1938 for Culbert Olson, the first Democrat to be elected governor of California

Sitting in his cell in the 1930s, labor organizer Thomas J. Mooney works on an appeal of his sentence for the bombing of a World War I Preparedness Day parade in San Francisco which killed 10. Although much of the trial testimony was later proved false, Mooney's reputation as a labor agitator during a period of severe labor strife helped keep him in prison from 1917 until his pardon in 1939. As an unjustly jailed man, he became a martyr for the labor cause, and said himself that he did the movement as much good in jail as out.

since 1898. When the issue came up again in 1939, however, Olson turned against Ham and Eggs. Its defeat at the polls marked the end of California's most perilous political decade.

Olson, however, had been discredited by his vacillation. He was succeeded by Earl Warren, a moderate Republican who for his time seemed a counterpart of Hiram Johnson. Warren raised the state budget, paid off the state debt, expanded the educational and highway systems, and successfully carried out a program of prison reform. Old-age pensions and unemployment insurance were adopted by the state and a fair-employment practices commission was set up. Warren was elected governor for an unprecedented three terms and was appointed Chief Justice of the United States in 1953, being succeeded by his lieutenant governor, Goodwin J. Knight. But with Warren gone, the California Republican Party became divided and impotent. In 1958, when Edmund G. "Pat" Brown won the governorship in a Democratic landslide, the Republicans who had controlled the state almost continuously since the turn of the century found their long dominance broken.

World War II had changed the Pacific States more than any event in history. As newcomers moved chiefly to the cities, the rural vote became less significant. Voter registration in California had become predominantly Democratic in 1934; by 1950 all three coastal states had Democratic majorities. Since World War II the electorate has seemed more a part of the national mainstream. Throughout much of the Depression the California state government had been so out of sympathy with the New Deal that it had declined some available funds. With postwar recognition of the vital role of military and aerospace funds in Western growth, rapport between California and the federal government improved. Nonetheless, there have been federal-state clashes. The problem of water— too much or too little—has been the most stubborn and recurrent political issue, one in which federal intervention has been frequent and inevitable.

In California, as in some other states, a major federal-state issue has involved offshore oil deposits. In 1945 the federal government claimed that it held title to all underwater oil deposits within the three-mile offshore line traditionally regarded as the territorial limits of the nation. The California constitution, approved by act of Congress, had defined the state's western boundary as three miles out in the Pacific; nevertheless the United States Supreme Court in 1947 ruled that the federal government held "paramount rights" in the offshore waters. With millions of dollars at stake in California alone, the Republican controlled 83rd Congress in 1953 carried out a G.O.P. campaign promise to restore the rights to the states. Litigation began again in 1963. California claimed that it held rights not only to submerged lands three miles off its coast but even to a point three miles beyond its offshore islands—a claim that, if upheld, would have extended the state's boundaries and oil rights some 50 miles offshore. Not until 1965 was the issue resolved, when the United States Supreme Court declared that California was entitled only to lands within the three-mile coastal limit and to three-mile belts extending around each of the offshore islands. The rest of the submerged lands between the islands and the coast, the Court ruled, belonged to the federal government.

The people of the West Coast were long more concerned with resident foreign nationals than with national foreign policy; but the role of the West in World War II, especially in the Pacific, did much to eliminate provincialism. Yet the West Coast has been slow to contribute an appropriate share of national political leadership. In the Senate the most prominent men from the Coast have been the Californians Hiram Johnson and William Knowland and the crusty Oregonian Wayne Morse, a classic embodiment of Western unconcern for party organization (long a Republican, Morse became an independent in 1952 and in 1954 shifted his allegiance to the Democratic Party). Richard Nixon came out of California to the Congress and then to the Vice-Presidency, and Earl Warren went from the California governorship to the United States Supreme Court. Yet California, as Nixon declared in 1962, "has hardly scratched the surface of its potential influence and impact on the nation." The Pacific States, still relatively young, have been until recently too obsessed with local affairs, too remote from the national capital, and above all, too divided and unpredictable to achieve real political leadership.

Yet the politics of California have become a center of national curiosity and concern. Many observers believe that California is slowly growing more like the rest of the nation in its political metabolism. The abolition of cross-filing in 1959 stimulated partisan party activity. But California possesses still another political oddity—the volunteer party organization, an institution that usurps some of the roles fulfilled by the parties in other states. Law forbids the official party structure to endorse any candidate prior to the primary election, and so unofficial groups have sprung up, like the Republican Assembly and the Democratic Council. Their members are fiercely loyal to their chosen candidates, whom they endorse before the primaries, and may raise and spend campaign money and form slates of delegates to political conventions; politicians must vie for the support of these organizations. Eventually some rebels secede and form rival groups. In the mid-'60s the volunteer organizations of both parties were almost torn apart by the activities of extremist minorities. The trend toward fragmentation in these groups would tend to undermine both the Democratic and Republican Party structures except that the California electoral machinery is rigged against third parties, and warring intraparty factions make some pretense of togetherness at election time.

The rootlessness of West Coast society explains much of the far-Left and far-Right extremism so often heard expressed in California. "Shorn of tradition and the moderating influence it exercises," said a 1966 report issued by the liberal Republican Ripon Society of Southern California, "the new Californian casts about for an alternative. Some find this alternative in the uncompromising principles of extremism. To a member of the John Birch Society or to his Leftist counterpart, there are no questions, only answers; no problems, only solutions." The Birchers are best known for their activities in California, but they have not been absent from the scene in the Northwest. The Birchite attacks on so-called "big government" emanating from the area are interpreted by some as an ironic echo of the old Populist "anti" sentiment. Political extremism in California revolves around questions like the menace of Communism and the welfare state. When a newcomer senses the lack of community in California, he may turn his attention from local affairs to national issues; such externally oriented interest has been exploited more successfully by the far Left and far Right than by the moderates, who are more likely to be coming to grips with common regional problems like smog, water shortages, taxation, conservation, education, minorities and transportation.

There is seldom much to divert the newcomer toward an interest in local politics. Urban politics in California are notably uncorrupt and often pallid. Machines are almost nonexistent because the precincts are full of mobile strangers who do not remain on the scene long enough to become organized into voting blocs. Municipal and state jobs are bestowed by civil service, not by political bosses.

The shame of local politics is more the apathy of newcomers than the corruption of the entrenched. This apathy makes it difficult to deal with the increasing problems caused by rapid growth.

As local bodies have proliferated and their responsibilities have overlapped, the need for regional cooperation has grown greater. In Los Angeles County, with its 76 separate but inseparable cities and towns, there is some interest in the Southern California Association of Governments, an organization of city governments dedicated to exploring the possibilities of regional integration; it has a counterpart in the San Francisco area in the Association of Bay Area Governments. But the two groups have had minimal success in arousing interest in their activities and in achieving cooperative action in their respective areas. Their organizational task is even more formidable than that of a United Nations; not only do the cities fear the loss of their sovereignty under regional government, but officeholders anticipate (and naturally resist) the extinction of their jobs.

All over California, voter apathy is assaulted by the neck-snapping techniques of paid professional campaign organizers, who have developed yet another California industry: manipulating the public interest for a fee. California is vulnerable to their services because the size of the state makes personal-appearance campaigning a formidable problem in logistics, because party loyalties are tenuous and party power is diffuse, and because the state has a tradition of forcing the electorate to settle many issues—both trivial and important—by placing them on the ballot through the process of the initiative and referendum.

Among the California companies specializing in political management are Spencer-Roberts, Baus and Ross, and Whitaker & Baxter. This last group claimed 70 successes against only five defeats between 1933 and 1955. Retained by the railroads to defeat a "full-crew" provision of the state constitution in 1948, Whitaker & Baxter distributed 10 million pamphlets and leaflets, mailed 4.5 million postcards and sent 50,000 letters to influential individuals. In addition it bought 70,000 inches of advertising in 700 newspapers, 3,000 radio spot announcements and twelve 15-minute network radio programs. Whitaker & Baxter also purchased space on 1,000 billboards, distributed more than 18,000 smaller posters, and arranged for the showing of slides and trailers in 160 theaters. The full-crew provision was repealed by an overwhelming majority.

Such firms will guarantee to clients that they will place a measure on the ballot by securing the signatures of the required number of voters: 8 per cent of the votes cast in the preceding gubernatorial election. The basic fee to the client is 40 to 60 cents per name. At such prices special interests can coolly calculate the cost of new laws; in the 1960s one campaign firm's charges for placing proposals on the ballot and then shepherding them through to passage ranged from an estimated minimum of $25,000 to more than two million dollars. Such a firm bills a candidate about $40,000 for a campaign for the state assembly and up to $1.5 million to manage a campaign for a state-wide office. Operating techniques are pseudoscientific. In 1966 one firm drew up its charges to a candidate on a formula of "reach"; the firm "reached" an estimated 92 per cent of the electorate through newspapers and broadcasting media in Los Angeles, San Francisco, Sacramento and San Diego. The rest of the electorate was reached through small-town media or by direct mail.

The dangers of professional campaign management are legion, and more ominous in their potential than any other California political aberration. Possessed of a keen understanding of the way to win elections, the professional campaign managers inevitably set out to change the public image of a candidate and gradually assume responsibility for his position on vital issues. In 1965 an advertisement appeared in a Los Angeles newspaper that began: "You can be elected state senator. Leading public relations firm with top-flight experience in state-wide campaigns wants state senator candidate." The public relations man who placed the advertisement, Hal Evry, claims that he guided 35 of 39 candidates to election over a period of 10 years by keeping them out of the public limelight and centering campaigns around catchy slogans. "If a candidate is articulate and wants to talk," Evry says, "maybe it's all right. But often it doesn't pay. He makes a speech and then exposes himself to foolish questions from some nut who makes him look bad."

With such political counsel readily available on the California market, it is understandable that party leaders have grown apprehensive. The Ripon Society has observed in a report that the professional campaign managers are "approaching the point where they will be able to 'sell' a prospect a 'campaign package' for Congress or the assembly or whatever, [and where] they will be dictating candidate selection with the Party only able to protest weakly and attempt to pick up the pieces afterward." Yet the system thrives because California political candidates cannot rely on a party machine

for campaigning, or even on any dependable backlog of straight-ticket voting; understandably, they tend to bypass the official party structures and seek personal merchandising as peddled by professional firms. The system is not unique to California, but nowhere else is it so advanced.

One other factor which plays into the hands of such professionals is the sectionalism of California. A candidate for state-wide office from the north of California may expect trouble in the south unless he is presented dramatically to the electorate throughout the state; a candidate from the south experiences similar difficulties in the north. Sectionalism is so fierce that there have been serious and recurrent attempts to split California into two states. In 1965 twenty-five Northern California state senators supported legislation that would have divided the state at the Tehachapi. The growing size of Southern California's population has heightened the schism. In 1960 voters of the south swung passage of the $1.75 billion bond issue that launched the diversion of Northern California water to the south; the vote in the north was heavily against the proposal. Conservative strength is centered in the south, particularly in Orange and San Diego Counties; in the Republican Presidential primary of 1964 Northern California supported Governor Nelson Rockefeller of New York, but Southern California tipped the scales for Senator Barry Goldwater of Arizona. To many Northern Californians a kind of political death knell was sounded by the reapportionment of the California state senate in 1965 on the "one man, one vote" formula ordered by the U.S. Supreme Court. Thirteen of the 40 senate seats that had belonged to the sparsely settled counties of Northern California were transferred to Los Angeles County, and a 14th seat was assigned to Los Angeles and Orange Counties jointly, establishing a massive concentration of legislative power in Southern California.

Yet in California, despite all the sectionalist feuds and other uproars, the bulk of the citizens are oblivious, unmoved by issues that may seem cataclysmic to the political scientist. The California voter prizes stability and is offended by roughhousing. One rule of California politics, the journalist Gladwin Hill has written, is that the "nice guy" always wins; he is the one who manages to seize the defensive, making his opponent seem contentious and crotchety. The winner is the man who "can come out first for home, mother and highway safety, and deflect all criticism into attacks on such verities." In their admiration for such candidates, California voters have generally stood united.

Discussing their own futures, Negroes, Mexican-Americans and Indians serve on the Yakima Valley Council for Community Action in Yakima, Washington. Many West Coast cities are racially diverse; some have similar programs for improving community relations.

The mobile melting pot

The states of the West Coast have attracted all sorts and conditions of men: young and old, rich and poor, and people with a variety of racial and ethnic backgrounds. The young have been lured by the many thriving industries, the elderly by the genial climate and by communities planned expressly for retired people. Many Negroes and many immigrants from foreign lands have also sought new lives in the West. California has more Orientals than any other state. Washington ranks third in number of Japanese. San Francisco has a large Italian-American community. Some of these migrants have battled their way to success. But too many, Negroes and Mexican-Americans particularly, have been shunted into ghettos where their frustration at being barred from the region's affluent ways has erupted in violence.

Tom and Susan Croson settled in Newport Hills in 1962. An insurance underwriter, Croson moved to the Seattle area from Idaho in 1954 to seek better business opportunities.

Fred and Sally Crawford, who have four children, moved from nearby West Seattle in 1961. Crawford, assistant manager of the Port of Seattle, liked the good schools.

Don and Eunice Wheeler moved to Newport Hills from Tacoma in July 1965 so Wheeler could be nearer his job as project engineer with the Lundberg Construction Company.

A retired Air Force captain, William Preston, his wife, Patricia, and three children came from Virginia in the fall of 1965, when he accepted a job as an engineer with Boeing.

For David Engstrom and his family Newport Hills is the fifth home in 10 years. Engstrom, a geologist for Standard Oil of California, was transferred to the area in 1965.

Stephen and Bettye Ragar moved to Newport Hills in 1962 because of a love for Northwestern summers. Now an engineer with Boeing, Ragar had been in Texas with the Air Force.

A community of people from somewhere else

The movement of people to the West Coast in the last two decades has been perhaps the largest migration in the history of the world. In one recent five-year period one fifth of all the persons who moved from one state to another were bound for Washington, Oregon or California. Once on the Coast many of these migrants continue to move about, seldom settling in one spot for long. While the Coast does have its old settled communities, more and more it is a land of new and nearly identical suburban developments, with nearly identical schools and supermarkets, and with populations in constant flux. Since these communities are so alike, the new Westerners find it easy to uproot themselves frequently and move from one to another.

Fond of the Northwest after a trip to Seattle, Leonard Culjat, a retired Navy man, and Margaret, his wife, moved from Maryland in 1963. Culjat is an employee of Boeing.

Deacon Anderson and his wife, Mary, moved from San Francisco in 1965 so Anderson could take a job as managing news director for the King Broadcasting Company.

Kenneth and Mildred Niebauer and their children moved to the area from Pittsburgh in 1956 and settled on the block in 1962. Niebauer is a supervisor of engineers at Boeing.

Clifton and Mabel Brandt left Minnesota for Newport Hills in 1965 simply because they liked the area. Mrs. Brandt works for Over Lake Realty, of which Brandt is co-owner.

James Posz, a Boeing engineer, was transferred to the area from Kansas in 1965. He, his wife, Elizabeth, and their children like the camping facilities of the Northwest.

Oklahoman Noah Johnston has lived in the Northwest since 1943. He and his wife, Patsy, and their children moved to the block in 1963. Johnston works for a construction firm.

California-born Harold Welch is a Corporate Management Facilities Assistant for Boeing. He and his wife, Gloria, and their children moved to Newport Hills in 1962.

Newport Hills, a middle-class suburb of Seattle, is, like many others on the West Coast, a community of transients. Its 800 houses, many occupied by newcomers to the Coast, change hands often as newer arrivals replace families who may have lived there only a few months. The majority of newcomers have been lured by jobs at nearby offices and industries. There are fringe benefits, too: the climate is pleasant, recreational facilities are plentiful and schools are good. One block of S.E. 54th Street (above) provides a cross section of the community. Of the 13 families on the block in mid-1966 the one with the longest tenure had arrived in the spring of 1961; eight had come from outside the Pacific States. Five of the men worked for Boeing, largest employer in the vicinity. Among them the residents had 32 children, 29 of whom had changed homes at least once during their young lives.

131

Tending their gladioli, Mr. and Mrs. Henry Ernst putter in the garden in front of their house in Altadena, California. Originally from Switzerland, the Ernsts have lived in California for 20 years. Both are active in a senior citizens' center and both attend classes.

Peering across Lake Washington, Horace B. Coburn enjoys the view from the apartment he and Mrs. Coburn have taken in Seattle's Park Shore, a 15-story building for people 62 and over. High-rise apartment houses for older people are a West Coast innovation.

A happy place for "senior citizens"

For more than 80 years the Pacific States have had a special magnetism for the people who once were called "the elderly," or simply "old folks." During the last decades of the 19th Century California was looked upon as a vast sanatorium whose mild climate made life easier for the aged. But today the over-65 population does not act its age. Rest homes and rocking chairs are out of style, and retired people do everything from playing golf to taking graduate courses in political science. And the region has led in the evolution of a whole new life-pattern for the retired—large self-contained communities specially designed for older people which, in addition to conveniently laid-out housing units, provide facilities for a wide variety of sports and activities.

The practice green at Laguna Hills Leisure World, south of Los Angeles, is crowded with golfers waiting to tee off. One of the largest communities for older people, Leisure World also has two swimming pools, hobby rooms—and plans for 18,000 apartments.

A supplier of Mexican foods, Alejandro Banuelos *(above),* who came to California from Mexico in 1920, inspects one of his assembly lines. He and his wife bought a *tortilla* factory in 1949 for $450; it now grosses close to two million dollars a year.

A civil engineer, Professor Tung Yen Lin of the University of California at Berkeley stands before a viaduct in Oakland that he designed. Before coming to the U.S. in 1946, Lin helped design railroads and bridges in China, where he was born in 1911.

A distinguished horticulturist, Jan de Graaff owns and runs the Oregon Bulb Farms in Gresham, Oregon, a suburb of Portland. De Graaff, member of a Dutch family that has specialized in flower growing since 1790, came to Oregon to live in 1932.

An aerospace instrument maker, Russian-born Boris Korry arrived in the U.S. in 1923 and managed to get an education while doing a variety of odd jobs. He founded his firm, which makes electrical and electronic components for aircraft and missiles, in 1956.

Successful immigrants to a region of varied opportunity

The West Coast has been enticing immigrants from many lands since the middle of the 19th Century. Mexicans from the south, Orientals from across the Pacific, and men of European and African origin have flocked to the region. In 1860, just 10 years after statehood, eight out of 10 persons in California had been born outside the state, and half of those came from foreign countries. Thousands were Chinese who came in search of gold. The Japanese, who today outnumber the Chinese, arrived after 1890, many to work on the region's immense truck farms. Land-starved men from southern and eastern Europe came seeking soil to till. Today Scandinavians are still settling in the Northwest. Over the years the reception given these groups has not always been friendly, and animosities still persist, but a number of immigrants have achieved success—in pursuits as varied as their lands of origin.

A prominent vintner, Louis M. Martini owns some of California's finest vineyards. He came to the United States at the age of 13 in 1900 from his native Italy and worked in the San Francisco fishing industry before returning briefly to Italy to learn wine making.

Children of a Mexican-American family play outside their deteriorating house in Pico Rivera. Mexican-Americans, living mostly in the southwestern U.S. have been generally overlooked by federal antipoverty programs. A few of the 600,000 who live in Los Angeles County succeed in getting satisfactory jobs, but the plight of the group as a whole is as bad as that of the Negroes.

Answering a call, Los Angeles police break up a fight in Watts. True or not, claims of police brutality, such as sparked the 1965 riot, are merely a symptom of Watts's problems. The neat one- and two-story houses fronting on wide, sunny streets belie the fact that unemployment in Watts averages nearly 40 per cent and that the incomes of two out of five families are in the poverty range.

A disillusioned search for a better life

Into the southern districts of Los Angeles pours a steady stream of Negroes, mostly from the U.S. South, seeking work and a decent place to live. With the same hopes, Mexican-Americans continue to crowd into the city's eastern sections. The severe unemployment and poor education plaguing the people of these areas attest to the failure of their quest. It was the tragic disparity between the Negroes' hopes and the reality they found that helped fuel the 1965 riot in the Negro ghetto of Watts, an outbreak that awoke Angelenos to problems many had not known existed. Since then plans have been proposed which, hopefully, will break down the isolation of these groups from the white community.

The Watts Towers, a mammoth sculpture completed in 1954 by a Watts tilesetter, serves as the meeting place for a children's painting class, part of a program instituted since the riot. Long scorned by local residents and visited only by curious whites, the towers have recently become a symbol of strength to Watts Negroes, and a drive is underway to make them the focal point of a 15-acre cultural center, the first such effort of any consequence the district has known.

7

The Intellectual Climate

Late in 1964 the University of California at Berkeley was the scene of a student rebellion of major proportions. In protest against a university ruling that students could not use campus facilities for political and social-protest activities, undergraduates called a strike that halted classes. Some 800 students and their sympathizers were forcibly removed from the administration building during an all-night sit-in and were jailed. The governor of the state sent highway patrolmen to restore order. In the difficult months that followed there were somber warnings that the university was irreparably divided. Yet in May 1966 a study of graduate schooling by the highly regarded American Council on Education described the Berkeley campus as "the best-balanced distinguished university" in the country. Such a rating was all the more remarkable because the university was then still two years shy of celebrating its first centennial, a bit too young by traditional academic standards to have achieved greatness. The paradoxes of California again had emerged to puzzle the nation.

At the Berkeley campus of the University of California, a revolving stage swings a physics demonstration into view as the professor lectures via closed circuit TV. The stage allows one demonstration to be conducted while others are set up backstage.

But for more than a decade the academic world had been aware that some kind of intellectual renaissance was underway on the West Coast. In the 1950s a westward migration of scholars and scientists from the most renowned campuses of the Midwest and East had signaled the beginning of an unprecedented period of academic pirating. Between 1957 and 1961 fifteen professors were lured from Ivy League faculties to Stanford University alone; many more were attracted to the diverse campuses of the far-flung University of California. The professorial stars of older campuses, especially the physical scientists, moved to California at such a rate that academic boastfulness took the form of number games, as when the University of California noted that it could count 12 Nobel laureates among its faculty in 1966, more than at any other university in the nation; on its San Diego campus in the same year one in 10 professors was a member of the prestigious National Academy of Sciences. The California Institute of Technology could claim that it had the highest percentage of members of any American college in the same National Academy of Sciences. The brilliance of such faculties was paralleled by that of the staffs of numerous nonacademic organizations formed for research—"brain factories" and "think tanks" such as The RAND Corporation

One of the West's pioneering educators, Asa Shinn Mercer was the first and for a time the only teacher at the University of the Territory of Washington, which became the University of Washington. Born in Illinois in 1839, Mercer emigrated to the Territory in 1861, after being graduated from Franklin College in Ohio. In Seattle he got a job helping construct the university's first building, but while it was being completed he was asked to instruct the first 31 students. The next year, 1862, he became the struggling institution's acting president. One of his duties was to travel to logging camps to recruit students. In time more students came, but Mercer by then had left the area; he eventually became a rancher in Wyoming, where he died in 1917.

of Santa Monica and its offshoot, System Development Corporation, and others in the Santa Barbara, San Diego and Stanford areas.

Bright young Western scholars began to shrug off bids—once highly prized—to join the faculties of Eastern universities; the West was producing its own share of academicians, and providing the funds and facilities needed to hold them in the West. Suddenly the West seemed to provide an exciting environment for the scientist. "If you are to make a good life in this part of the West," said Dr. Frederic de Hoffmann, an executive with a division of General Dynamics in San Diego, "you realize it will be by having intellectually bright enterprises that will constantly stay up with the future. Everywhere I go in the West, this sort of world is much more in evidence than it is in the East." By 1966 the leadership of California in space research and in other federal research-and-development work was unchallenged. The state was reaching the goal set in 1948 by Robert Millikan, a founder of the California Institute of Technology, on his 80th birthday: ". . . if Southern California is to continue to meet the challenge of its environment . . . its supreme need . . . is for the development here of men of resourcefulness, of scientific and engineering background and understanding—able, creative, highly endowed,

highly trained men in science and its application."

Both the work of educational pioneers like Millikan and the affable climate had helped this startling scientific swing toward California, but so had a long tradition of generous public support of higher education. State aid for public institutions of higher learning has soared past $580 million. In the mid-1960s the state ranked second only to sparsely settled Alaska in per capita state- and local-government expenditure for higher education.

The quest for knowledge is stressed all along the West Coast. One thing that binds together the people of California and those of the Northwest is their almost mystical faith in education. Oregon and Washington are close behind California in many key educational measurements, and ahead in others: their classrooms are less crowded than those of California and they have fewer youths who fail to pass the mental tests of the military draft; their per capita expenditures for education are closely aligned with California's. They are as interested as Californians in higher education. After Charles Odegaard came from the University of Michigan in 1958 to assume the presidency of the University of Washington, that stately campus emerged from an era of provincial regression. Largest in the Northwest, the university attracts superior faculty members from other regions much as do the campuses of California. "They want laboratories and libraries along with Mount Rainier, though," Odegaard has warned the taxpayers of his state. "You've got to keep moving to hold them. The climate goes for you, but it's nowhere near enough." Oregon's Reed College, a small independent school in Portland, has been ranked with the California Institute of Technology and Pomona College, near Los Angeles, as among the 19 most selective institutions in America; the Reed student body has been rated one of the six most academically capable in the nation.

Both in the Northwest and in California such educational attainment arouses fierce and widespread pride. An important element of Western life has been a compulsion to excel, and knowledge is regarded as the key. The new Westerner is oriented to education and the campus. He grasps the ideal of lifelong learning—and he enrolls in adult-education courses at an unparalleled rate. His status symbol may often be some kind of intellectual activity, or the support of one. When in the early 1960s the future of Robert M. Hutchins' idealistic Santa Barbara retreat, the Center for the Study of Democratic Institutions, was jeopardized through the depletion of its Ford Foundation grant, scores of wealthy Southern Californians underwrote its continuing operation with large pledges. By no means were all of these patrons themselves college graduates; a number were businessmen who lacked degrees.

There are those who do not regard all these apparent manifestations of interest in educational and intellectual matters as evidence that any broad intellectual community yet exists in the West. The region remains a target for the same kind of criticism that the East received in years past from the older scholarly centers of Europe—that of immature scholarship. While the schools and colleges of the West became the region's "most efficient agencies of social mobility, its most powerful engines of assimilation," the historian Earl Pomeroy has written, the region has been "more successful in legislating a high average of educational attainment as measured by years in the classroom than in raising the intellectual level of society outside the more formal channels."

The California renaissance of the 1950s and 1960s was predominantly in the sciences; in the humanities, predictably, there remained deficiencies. The vast federal funds that helped to elevate the sciences were not available to the humanities. Still, certain regional specialties have developed: strong departments of Asian studies exist, for example, at the University of Washington and at the Berkeley campus of the University of California. Despite such achievements there is nagging evidence that intellectualism is regarded by many in the prosperous West as a commodity to be purchased rather than as an ideal to be attained. "If certain kinds of intellectuals are uneasy here," the critic Clifton Fadiman wrote in a biting appraisal of Los Angeles, "that may be a sign that the future does not need them. If challenged to do so, we will import them by the bale, reward them, bid them a friendly, casual farewell as soon as it becomes evident that their attachments are to things dead or dying." Scientific research has often been encouraged in the West solely because it brought dollars. Faculties of great universities have been expected to serve the community in practical capacities that are not directly related to the ivory tower. Perhaps it is because the West is still not long past the frontier that knowledge is sometimes regarded as merely utilitarian.

The origins of public educational systems along the West Coast were brisk and forthright, foreshadowing their rapid rise. With the characteristic bravado of the Gold Rush, delegates to the first California Constitutional Convention at Monterey

The little school that grew

The University of California, so varied it has been dubbed a "multiversity," was chartered by the state legislature in 1868. The first classes were held in temporary quarters in the fall of 1869. Four years later the entire school —40 students and 10 teachers—moved to the fledgling institution's first campus at Berkeley. Today there are nine campuses and innumerable research centers, more than 10,500 full-time and part-time teachers and a student body of nearly 80,000. The inverted family tree below illustrates the growth of the university in terms of its major components: the general campuses (those that offer both graduate and undergraduate programs) and the most important research centers. The dates indicate when each facility was established in its present form or annexed by the university.

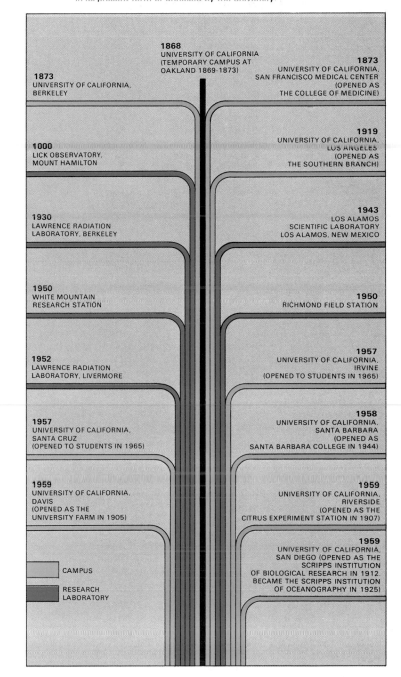

1868
UNIVERSITY OF CALIFORNIA
(TEMPORARY CAMPUS AT
OAKLAND 1869-1873)

1873
UNIVERSITY OF CALIFORNIA,
BERKELEY

1873
UNIVERSITY OF CALIFORNIA,
SAN FRANCISCO MEDICAL CENTER
(OPENED AS
THE COLLEGE OF MEDICINE)

1000
LICK OBSERVATORY,
MOUNT HAMILTON

1919
UNIVERSITY OF CALIFORNIA,
LOS ANGELES
(OPENED AS
THE SOUTHERN BRANCH)

1930
LAWRENCE RADIATION
LABORATORY, BERKELEY

1943
LOS ALAMOS
SCIENTIFIC LABORATORY
LOS ALAMOS, NEW MEXICO

1950
WHITE MOUNTAIN
RESEARCH STATION

1950
RICHMOND FIELD STATION

1952
LAWRENCE RADIATION
LABORATORY, LIVERMORE

1957
UNIVERSITY OF CALIFORNIA,
IRVINE
(OPENED TO STUDENTS IN 1965)

1957
UNIVERSITY OF CALIFORNIA,
SANTA CRUZ
(OPENED TO STUDENTS IN 1965)

1958
UNIVERSITY OF CALIFORNIA,
SANTA BARBARA
(OPENED AS
SANTA BARBARA COLLEGE IN 1944)

1959
UNIVERSITY OF CALIFORNIA,
DAVIS
(OPENED AS THE
UNIVERSITY FARM IN 1905)

1959
UNIVERSITY OF CALIFORNIA,
RIVERSIDE
(OPENED AS THE
CITRUS EXPERIMENT STATION IN 1907)

1959
UNIVERSITY OF CALIFORNIA,
SAN DIEGO (OPENED AS THE
SCRIPPS INSTITUTION
OF BIOLOGICAL RESEARCH IN 1912.
BECAME THE SCRIPPS INSTITUTION
OF OCEANOGRAPHY IN 1925)

CAMPUS

RESEARCH
LABORATORY

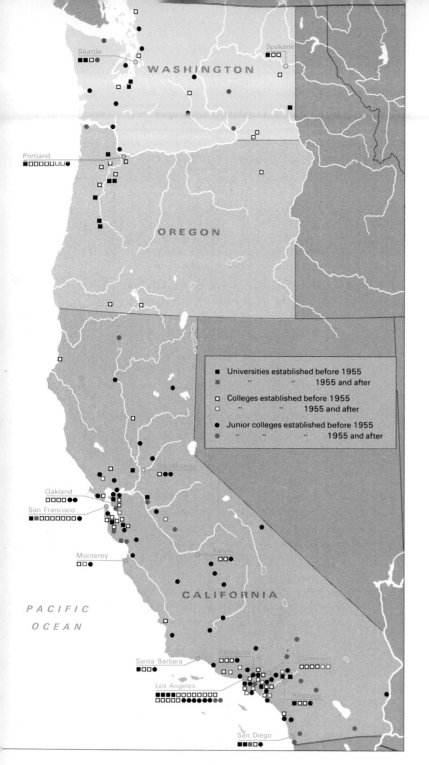

Recent growth of the colleges

The rapid spread of West Coast universities and colleges is shown on the map above. The three states possess 223 accredited two- and four-year institutions of higher education. Of these, 16.6 per cent were founded in 1955 and after, with the greatest increase among junior colleges. The institutions vary from specialized schools like the California Podiatry College to sophisticated universities that offer courses in many fields. They range in size from Deep Springs College with 21 students to the Berkeley campus of the University of California with more than 26,000. On the map, cities with three or more institutions are named. The highest concentration of colleges and universities is in the Los Angeles area.

in 1849 discussed establishing a university. "If we have the means here we can procure the necessary talent," one delegate said. "We can bring the president of the Oxford University here by offering a sufficient salary." Such funds, however, materialized slowly. In 1862 the U.S. Congress passed the first Morrill Act, by which public lands were donated to the states so that proceeds of their sale could be used as a perpetual fund to help sustain so-called land-grant colleges and universities. These institutions were to teach not only the traditional humanities and sciences but also agriculture and mechanic arts and military tactics. The pattern of higher education in the Pacific States was in part shaped by this act and others like it; no strong private institutions had come into existence before the introduction of this governmental aid, and state-supported institutions have ever since been dominant. Only a small minority of college students in the Pacific States attend private institutions. The dominance of public campuses has contributed to the Westerner's expectation that his universities will be functional; it has also brought about the creation of a comprehensive higher-education system that allows qualified students to work at the loftiest levels of study at public expense.

Despite the enthusiasm and the brave talk of the early Californians, it was the frontier territory of Washington that achieved the distinction of launching the first public institution of higher learning on the West Coast. Washington was a raw, sparsely settled land, a most unlikely place for a university. But the territorial legislature petitioned the federal government in 1854 for land to be used in the support of a university. The grant came quickly, and after a period of haggling among several towns, Seattle was chosen as the site of the University of Washington. The first classes were held late in 1861. There were 31 students and a faculty consisting solely of a young college graduate named Asa Mercer. Oregon, which was slower to exploit its land-grant opportunities, opened its state university at Eugene in 1876; by then more than a score of modest private institutions—the majority of them church-supported, like Willamette College of Salem—had opened their doors.

The forerunner of the University of California was an academy opened in an Oakland dance hall in 1853 by a Congregationalist clergyman from Yale, Henry Durant. Debt haunted his project, and he sometimes lost patience. One of his outbursts might well have been recalled by his successors in times of turmoil with taxpayers. "Individuality is carried to an extreme in California," he said. "Our fast living may almost all of it be referred to intense selfishness. Indeed, sentimentality and idealism seem lost from the mass of the people. They are sensualists and materialists, or nearer that than anything else—the very condition on account of which the Spirit of God forsook the antediluvian world."

In 1868 Durant's College of California was designated as a state land-grant institution and became the University of California; in 1873 classes began on the present campus at Berkeley. The legislative act and ensuing constitutional provisions that established the university gave sweeping powers to a Board of Regents that sets policy for the entire institution. Of the board's 24 members, 16 are appointed by the governor of the state for 16-year terms. As supervisors of a vast domain—the university now includes multiple campuses and research stations scattered over the thousand-mile length of California, scientific establishments as distant as Los Alamos, New Mexico, and research vessels cruising the oceans of the world—the regents achieve a prestigious rank that has been called the closest thing to knighthood in California. The constitutional insulation from political caprice that has been granted the regents through their long terms of office has been of immeasurable help to the university, for from the start the institution showed headstrong tendencies. In 1870 it took the radical step of admitting women. In 1874, after a fiery controversy over whether the university should lay primary stress on "agriculture and mechanic arts," President Daniel Coit Gilman, backed by the regents, succeeded in establishing the principle that it should instead offer a comprehensive and liberal program of education. In leading the fight for diversification Gilman showed perspicacity with the cry, "Science is the mother of California."

The university nevertheless grew slowly. So did the separate and independent University of Southern California, which was established by the Methodist Episcopal Church at Los Angeles in 1880. Another private institution soon moved to the forefront. In 1887 Leland Stanford, one of the Big Four railroad builders and by then a United States senator, stood by as the cornerstone was laid for the first building of Stanford University, which at the time was the most richly endowed educational institution in the world. Stanford and his wife initially conveyed properties appraised at six million dollars, invested another $1.25 million in buildings and promised additional funds in the form of bequests. Overriding skepticism that the new institution could draw an adequate student body or a competent faculty, Stanford University moved swiftly under its forceful first president, the ichthyologist David Starr Jordan. The importance of scientific research was stressed; the example helped to prod the University of California, located across San Francisco Bay, toward achieving its later scientific distinction.

From the time of the completion of the first transcontinental railroad in 1869 until near the turn of the century, it was traditional among more aristocratic Westerners to send their sons to Eastern colleges, but the rapid development of Western campuses in the early 1900s began to stem some of the eastward flow. Two presidents dominated the University of California in the first half of the new century. One was Benjamin Ide Wheeler, a vigorous autocrat who between 1899 and 1919 was the architect of rapidly emerging academic prestige. He improved and expanded the faculty and oversaw the growth that foreshadowed the future "multiversity." In his tenure the University Farm School was established at Davis, the Citrus Experiment Station at Riverside and the Scripps Institution for Biological Research at La Jolla; today all have been expanded into full general university campuses. By 1923 the University of California—with 14,061 students at various locations—was the largest in the world.

Robert Gordon Sproul headed the university from 1930 to 1958. He was a master of persuasion; at his urging the state legislature boosted university salaries to equal the highest in the nation. During Sproul's administration Professor Ernest O. Lawrence brought the first of many Nobel Prizes to Berkeley for his invention of the cyclotron. Berkeley's achievements in advanced scientific research were acknowledged in 1943 when the campus was selected to operate the Los Alamos Scientific Laboratory in New Mexico.

The scientific tradition in California owes much to an eccentric millionaire, James Lick, who in 1874 donated $700,000 to build an astronomical observatory for the university. The site on Mount Hamilton, south of San Jose, was chosen partly because Lick owned a flour mill nearby. The 36-inch refracting telescope at the Lick Observatory is, after the 40-inch Yerkes instrument in Wisconsin, the most powerful of its type in existence. Scientists longed for something like it in the less fog-bound skies of Southern California. In 1917 the astronomer George Ellery Hale, with the help of funds supplied by wealthy friends in Pasadena, completed an observatory with a 100-inch reflecting telescope on Mount Wilson, north of Los Angeles. For three decades this was the world's largest telescope. With the aid of Robert A. Millikan and others, Hale also interested Southern California philanthropists in underwriting the costs of a scientific institute at Pasadena; by 1920 Hale and Millikan were well along in the task of transforming a small campus known as the Throop College of Technology into what was to become one of the world's leading centers of scientific education, the California Institute of Technology. But the growth of Los Angeles began to thwart astronomers on Mount Wilson; as the basin below became a saucer of light that interfered with viewing conditions, Hale looked elsewhere; in 1928 the Rockefeller Foundation granted six million dollars for a still more powerful observatory—with a 200-inch reflecting telescope—that went into service on Palomar Mountain in San Diego County in 1948 after years of meticulous preparation.

California also was quick to develop at lower education levels. In 1863 the kindergarten system appeared in San Francisco, just 26 years after its introduction in Europe. The junior-college system was born in California in 1907 when high schools were authorized to offer postgraduate work; 10 years later the two-year junior college was integrated into the state school system. Support has always been strong for public schools on the West Coast. In the 1912-1913 academic year only 12 American cities paid elementary teachers annual salaries of more than $1,000; seven of the cities were in California, and one each in Oregon and Washington.

The severest test of public-school support came with the unparalleled population growth after World War II. For many years California was building new schools at a rate of one each day. Yet communities sprang up so rapidly that new schools were filled to capacity on opening day and plans immediately had to be launched to build more. Among the areas showing the greatest strain was San Diego, which throughout the 1950s carried out one of the largest school construction programs, on a per capita basis, the nation had ever seen. Nevertheless, with new housing going up even faster than schools, classes sometimes had to be held in three-bedroom houses intended for sale as tract homes. Enrollment in the San Diego school district doubled between 1950 and 1960, and new schools proliferated at such a rate that not even the members of the board of education could stay abreast of the growth. In the fall of 1965 a member of the San Diego board proposed naming a school for the distinguished Negro scientist George Washington Carver; an aide checked the records and announced that San Diego already had a school named for Carver.

To staff these expanding systems, West Coast school administrators send out teams of teacher-recruiters each winter, concentrating on the Midwest in times of snow and sleet; when the new teachers arrive the following summer, civic gatherings and other activities are frequently arranged to welcome them to their new home communities. About 50 per cent of California teachers come from outside the state. Teacher shortages will probably continue to exist; California educators have estimated that throughout the late 1960s they will have to make up an annual deficit of about 7,000 teachers by importation.

Rapid growth has necessitated experimentation. In Oregon, where Portland schools have long commanded nationwide respect, a Ford Foundation grant in 1961 made possible a sweeping modernization of school techniques under the name of the Oregon Program. The program's aim was to improve the classroom environment by utilizing new methods, and to lighten the teacher's load by passing on some of the work to nonprofessional employees. Experiments have encompassed team teaching, flexible scheduling, self-instruction and advanced audio-visual aids. In California in 1966 first-graders of the Brentwood School at Palo Alto became the first public-school pupils in the nation to receive instruction by computers on a regular basis. The computer curriculum was developed by the nearby Stanford University Institute for Mathematical Studies. Pupils are assigned by their teachers to consoles that include a typewriter, television screen, another movielike screen and a headset, from which the child receives spoken commands, suggestions and encouragement.

The top echelon of the public-school system is the junior college or community college, equivalent to the first two years of regular college. Only the extensive development of this system in the West has made it possible for four-year colleges and universities to cope with the multiplying number of college applicants. By 1966 there were 78 of these two-year colleges in California, and so many more were planned that it was estimated that up to 75 per cent of the number of high-school students intending to further their education in public institutions would eventually be accommodated by junior colleges.

Although the two-year college was introduced

in California in 1907, its role was not clearly delineated until the mid-1950s when educators and lawmakers began a series of studies that culminated in 1960 in the California Master Plan for Higher Education, many of whose features are being adapted by other states. The plan staved off the incipient chaos implicit in the combination of competitive educational institutions and spiraling student enrollments by clearly marking out the roles of the three public higher-education systems: the University of California, the four-year state colleges that are independent of the university, and the junior colleges. Under the Master Plan the numerous campuses of the University of California began to accept only the top one eighth of high-school graduates, and retained supervision over all doctoral degrees; the four-year state colleges—18 of them in 1966, with an administration responsible to state authorities—began to draw students from the top one third of high-school graduates. The junior colleges took the rest; although many graduates of the junior colleges are able to transfer easily to four-year campuses after their two years in order to qualify for a bachelor's degree, many do not, and training in technical skills is therefore a major aspect of the junior-college curriculum. Sensing the increasing concentration on graduate studies at the University of California campuses—especially at Berkeley—some of the state's educators began to predict that the time would come when no first- or second-year students would be accepted by the university. If that occurs, the academic responsibilities of the state and junior colleges will become even heavier.

Like the two-year public colleges, university extension services have been developed to unusual complexity in California. The universities of the Pacific States engage in wide-spectrum activities involving large numbers of people of diverse age levels and from varied segments of society. Most prominent among the extension services is that of the University of California, which in 1966 had almost 220,000 enrollments in more than 7,000 courses, given in about 250 locations. With a $15 million budget for such activities, California is the recognized leader in university extension work. The typical student is a college-educated adult who is not necessarily studying for academic credit but who is paying substantial fees for advanced learning; 55 per cent of the extension enrollments are in graduate professional courses, and the knowledge sought is often so newly established that textbooks are not yet available. In such areas University of California Extension is attuned to the technological emphasis of California. Industry leans heavily on Extension to continue the education of its professional people, and spends nearly two million dollars annually to support Extension programs in engineering and physical science. "California is now the leading center of technological population," says Dr. Simon Ramo, who heads The Bunker-Ramo Corporation of Canoga Park, one of California's many research-and-development groups. "But California can maintain its position and meet its responsibilities only by sponsoring University Extension programs on a level with regular daytime college work. U.C. Extension is completely indispensable to California."

Extension courses are not all science-oriented. Almost the entire roster of city officials in the town of Buena Park once enrolled in an Extension course on city management. One of every two California physicians and lawyers was enrolled at one time or another in 1965 for Extension studies of the newest developments in their professions. Labor studies are included, and at least one firm—Lockheed Aircraft—reimburses its employees for three fourths of their University Extension tuition fees, including those paid for courses in labor-union leadership. Correspondence students of more than 50 nations are enrolled in University of California Extension courses. The overall income from fees makes it possible for the California Extension system to operate with a smaller state subsidy than that of most similar state university programs. In 1966 the state contributed only 7 per cent of the total California Extension budget.

In Los Angeles several years ago 14 men—each a Doctor of Philosophy—went to University Extension officials requesting a night course in the theory of games. Extension officials consulted The RAND Corporation at Santa Monica and chose a RAND physicist to teach the course. In such ways there is correlation between continuing adult education and the "brain factories" of California.

Protected by uniformed guards, RAND's thinkers work in a long, low building only a few blocks from some of the finest beaches in Southern California. Their employer is a nonprofit research corporation designed to advance "scientific, educational and charitable purposes" in behalf of the public welfare and security of the United States. RAND's name is taken from the words "research and development"; an old company story is that the name means "research and *no* development." RAND was formed shortly after World War II at a time when Air Force generals were becoming disturbed because scientists who had helped win the war were going back to their campus laboratories. The idea of gathering scientists for studies vital to national security in a university-like setting rather than in an industrial environment was then unprecedented. Today the RAND staff totals almost 1,200, and there are other centers similar to it.

The Russians, it is said, once described RAND as "an American academy of death and destruction," but the description seems ludicrous when one enters the building; men looking like professors —and many have been—sit in modest offices thinking, reading, sometimes talking or writing, more often silent. Their research is involved with matters of national security—air defense, nuclear weapons, metallurgy, communications and space—and yet their work veers naturally into economic and political affairs, both of this nation and of others.

The vigorous existence of institutions like RAND in the purportedly unintellectual West points up a continuing anomaly. Like any new land, the West Coast is many things. While thousands of people seek to advance their understanding through extension studies, and scholars probe the outermost limits of knowledge at centers like RAND, political fights in local schools are set off by radical Right-Wingers who rage at the threat of smutty library books, Communist sympathizers or one worlders. There still exists in the Pacific Coast states an inclination to conformity—to accept society as it is rather than to try to change it. Some charge that campuses studded with Nobel Prize winners are emphasizing research to the detriment of teaching, in the interests of enhancing institutional prestige and gaining more taxpayer support. Others insist that in a zeal for new techniques, the Western educator pays too little heed to tradition and may lack an understanding of the historic debt that the West owes to the Eastern parts of the country. Many believe that West Coast university students graduate with less feeling of dedication than Eastern students—with less of a sense of being an elite trained to run the country. Some people hold that the West Coast is not yet in the national mainstream, not yet imbued with a sense of destiny; they believe that the West's intellectual renaissance has its roots in materialism and spiritual shallowness. They recall that both the Ford Foundation and Mortimer Adler's Institute for Philosophical Research moved their headquarters to California and then retreated eastward, while Adler warned against the pitfalls of the "mellifluous climate" and of the emphasis on quantity above quality.

But Western educators are pioneering in the crucial area of maintaining academic standards in the face of a massive onslaught of students. It is a crisis which California, through no choice of its own, has had to face earlier than the rest of the nation. The educational techniques that Westerners are devising to cope with this flood of students have become influential in the overall U.S. educational establishment. No eyebrows were raised in 1965 when the dean of academic planning for the University of California declared: "What I want is a society that is all university. . . . The whole *state* is the university!" The mood for that dream had been set a century before, when those who drafted the first California constitution took the position that public education is an indispensable inheritance, a bulwark of American culture. In this environment, whether because of mass-produced knowledge or esoteric research or both, trends continue to emerge which are reflected in the nation as a whole.

There are some moments when the dream grows bright—though they often occur under characteristically West Coast circumstances. One such event came in 1965 on the infant campus of the University of California at San Diego, when the historian John Galbraith was installed as chancellor. It was the first formal academic procession to be staged on the campus. No auditorium or stadium had yet been built; the setting was a campus cliff beside the Pacific. It was a balmy day in November, and folding chairs had been set out in the open air. The grove of academe was a forest of dusty eucalyptus trees. A Marine Corps band played Elgar's "Pomp and Circumstance" as the gowned scholars marched toward a makeshift podium and students hung over the balconies of surrounding buildings to watch. Amid it all came the steady drone of cars and diesel trucks from the nearby Pacific Coast Highway. But witty and scholarly addresses were heard, and applause drowned out the sounds of traffic. A mood of aspiration permeated the affair; even in the benediction, sensing an opportunity to underline a current campus budget plea, a local bishop invoked the help of God toward speedy development of the campus library. Then faculty members and community leaders sat down for lunch in a new, high-ceilinged dining hall, whose design had been enhanced through a bequest from a generous friend of the university. On the wall, bearing witness to the continuing support of higher education in California both from public funds and from private benefactors, was a plaque that stated wryly: THIS ROOF WAS RAISED TWELVE FEET BY AN ANONYMOUS DONOR.

Pupils at Los Angeles' Eastman Avenue elementary school race between movable temporary classroom units which enlarge the original school *(background)*. A fifth of the city's classrooms are portable, providing space while permanent structures are built.

A bold demand for knowledge

A bracing climate of intellectual endeavor pervades the three West Coast states. In education both quantity and quality are sought increasingly. Between 1954 and 1965 in the three states, college enrollment ballooned by 700,000 students—and the colleges have recruited some of the nation's greatest scholars to teach them. All three states are building new public schools or enlarging old ones at a furious pace, both to house increasing numbers of pupils and to provide them with finer facilities. But the pursuit of knowledge goes beyond the normal academic channels. The West Coast has attracted many independent research organizations, such as The RAND Corporation, where scholars and scientists explore rarefied realms of pure theory or search for answers to the pressing problems of our time.

147

Idea "factories" that help solve 20th Century problems

Examining an aerial photograph, electronics experts at The RAND Corporation discuss problems of reconnaissance in Vietnam. Although many of RAND's projects are theoretical, some, like this one, are intended to supply ideas for action on current dilemmas.

A remarkable group of research organizations has recently grown up in California. These are the so-called idea factories, or "think tanks." No smokestacks grace their buildings, no railroad sidings mar their lawns, for the only products of these companies are ideas. Oldest is The RAND Corporation in Santa Monica. Conceived by the Air Force in 1948 to plan long-range strategy, the organization employs experts in many fields to ponder, among other things, the economics, sociology, psychology and politics of war. Since RAND's success, other think tanks have been established, like the Center for the Study of Democratic Institutions in Santa Barbara. The Center's basic purpose is not to recommend any specific course of action. Instead its members seek new insights on such subjects as education, democracy and the American character.

In the RAND "war game room," two teams of researchers act out military strategy. Separated by a partition that hides their moves from each other, the teams deploy troops, arms and supplies on a world map, while a referee decides whether each move is possible.

At the daily discussion period, members of the Center for the Study of Democratic Institutions listen to the Dean of the UCLA Graduate School of Business Administration, Dr. Neil H. Jacoby *(far left)*, outline problems facing the University of California. Following the one-hour talk, the Center's members discussed the university's problems for another hour. The Center hopes that by confronting experts and issues in this manner new ideas will emerge that will strengthen cultural and intellectual forces everywhere.

Firms in search of knowledge through experimentation

Like the think tanks, the research-and-development firms on these pages seek answers to many sorts of problems. But while think tanks usually search for general solutions, R & D firms (as they are called) spend much of their time hunting cures for specific maladies. To help in the search, whether the problem involves life sciences, nuclear physics or industry, R & D firms employ both theorists to conceive new ideas and scientists and engineers to test them by experimentation. Although other areas of the U.S. have R & D firms, no state can boast as many scientists doing this work as California. So many have migrated there in recent years that other parts of the nation have complained of a "brain drain."

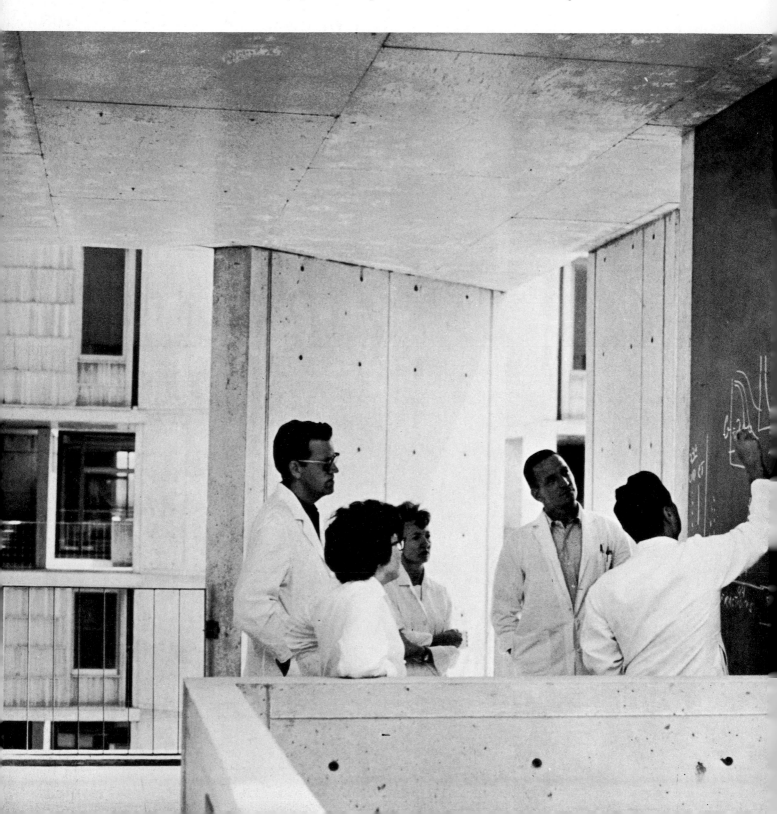

Pig-tailed monkeys romping in a special
enclosure at the Oregon Regional Primate
Research Center in Beaverton, Oregon, are
observed by Dr. George Kittinger, a
biochemist who studies monkeys to find new
preventives and cures for human disease.

Looking for structural changes in radioactive
materials, technicians work in the radio
metallurgic laboratory of Battelle-Northwest
in Richland, Washington, a research firm
that studies a wide variety of scientific
problems for both government and industry.

Associates of Dr. Jonas Salk, developer of the
first polio vaccine, discuss multiple sclerosis
at the Salk Institute for Biological Studies
in San Diego. The Institute was founded in
1960 to give leading biologists equipment
and opportunity to pursue their own research.

A planned integration of a city with a university

A new concept of coordinating education and city planning is being made a reality at the 88,000-acre Irvine development near Los Angeles. There the University of California in 1964 began building a new campus, while developers were busy laying out industrial parks, residential areas and recreational facilities. The project is being built according to a master plan conceived by William Pereira, a prominent Los Angeles architect. Approximately 10,000 acres surrounding the campus will become a university-focused community of some 150,000 residents, thus integrating the centers of intellectual activity with the life of the people as a whole.

Students at the University of California at Irvine stroll past two strikingly modern buildings—classrooms and offices—designed by William Pereira for the Social Sciences and Humanities section. The campus opened in 1965 with just a few of its buildings completed and only 1,500 students on the undergraduate and graduate levels, but enrollment is expected to hit 27,500 by 1990.

The site of the University of California at Irvine and other areas in the extensive Irvine development project are shown below. The current uses of completed buildings and areas are shown in roman type; future developments are shown in italics. The whole project is to be completed in carefully planned stages; completion dates of one set of university buildings are given in parentheses.

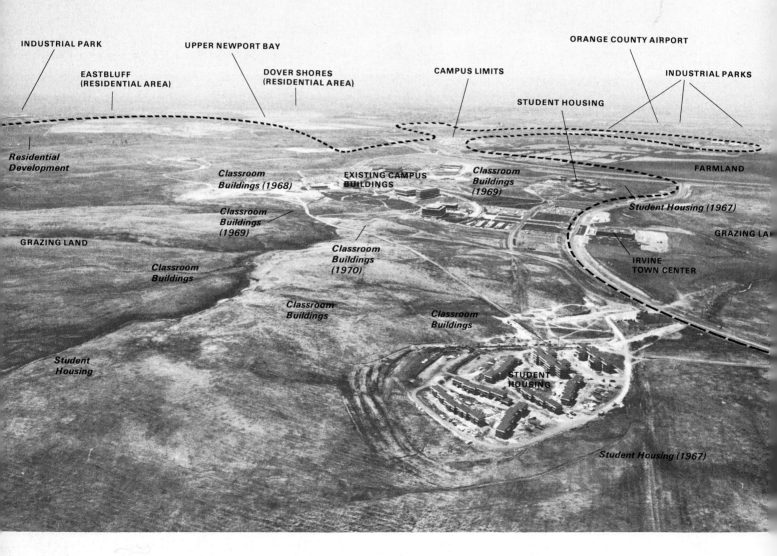

8

The Putty Culture

More than 150 years ago President John Adams said, "I must study politics and war, that my sons may have liberty to study mathematics and philosophy [as well as] commerce and agriculture in order to give their children a right to study painting, poetry, music, architecture, statuary, tapestry and porcelain." Much as he foresaw, such cultural opportunities are now widely available to Americans. The trend throughout the country is to provide abundant facilities to shelter the creative and performing arts, and to encourage those who seek to participate in them.

Now doubts arise. Is quality being submerged in quantity? Does this surge of mass participation doom the arts to mediocrity? Or does it strengthen the base of support and widen the audience for the creative professional? The Pacific States, with their high levels of affluence and education, their driving aspirations and their new, egalitarian society, have become a proving ground for such questions.

"After New York," goes a saying attributed to the humorist Bugs Baer, "everything is Bridgeport."

First-nighters line the balconies and mingle in the foyer of the San Diego Civic Theatre's Grand Salon. This fine modern theater, which houses San Diego's symphony and opera company, was built through the farsighted efforts of civic leaders.

Clearly that would be an overstatement in contemporary America. But the West has always been on the cultural defensive. No notion has echoed more persistently through West Coast society than that a new and vital culture would someday emerge on the Pacific Coast. Much professionalism today exists in the West, and some creativity; more significantly, there is widespread public involvement with the arts. In music and in painting, Los Angeles is the do-it-yourself capital of the world; it teems with community orchestras, chamber-music societies and weekend artists. Amateur theatrical groups are everywhere. High-school band directors recruit trumpeters as fervently as coaches seek out quarterbacks. One writers' conference is succeeded by another; part-time poets lurk beneath every palm. Businessmen form Dixieland groups and make recordings. New grand-opera companies in San Diego and Los Angeles supplement the performances of the venerable San Francisco Opera Company.

In a cacophony of festivals, chamber-music concerts are given in a Napa Valley vineyard, jazz performers gather in Monterey, and new symphonies are performed at the University of Washington. La Cienega Boulevard in Los Angeles is an art market surpassed in the United States only by the strings of galleries on upper Madison Avenue in New York;

155

Mark Tobey, one of America's most important painters, has long considered Seattle his home. Born in 1890 in Wisconsin, Tobey did portraits and fashion illustration before settling on the Coast, where he began to paint highly individual abstractions. Many of his works, such as the one shown behind Tobey above, are in a style Tobey calls "white writing," which is indebted to Oriental calligraphy. Untroubled by those who do not understand his work, he has said, "I can't understand doctors or lawyers, why the hell should anyone understand me?"

the Puget Sound area boasts more than 25 art galleries and museums. In Portland four old firehouses are now used as community centers for contemporary dance and music, and the audiences have grown so large that in 1966 the public-recreation director of the city requested that still another firehouse be converted to cultural use.

Governmental interest in the arts has not lagged in the region. In 1963, following the lead of New York State, the California legislature set up the California Arts Commission to establish "the paramount position of this state in the nation and in the world as a cultural center." The commission surveyed the cultural resources and activities of California and proclaimed in 1965, in the words of its chairman, Dr. Abbott Kaplan, that the "upsurge of interest in the arts is apparent throughout the country; but nowhere . . . more so than in California." It found symphony orchestras from California cities touring the agricultural towns of the Imperial Valley, classical Spanish ballet being taught in the city of Chula Vista, near the Mexican border, and repertory companies active everywhere. In San Francisco a wine warehouse and a wax factory, as well as stables, churches, garages, movie houses and dance studios, had been converted into theaters.

In Southern California evidence of interest in the arts is even more abundant. There local government and private interests have combined to support a variety of cultural projects. More than $12 million was collected from private sources to help build the Los Angeles County Art Museum, which opened in 1965; the county budgets $1.5 million annually to operate it. In its first year the museum attracted more than twice as many people as did the Louvre in Paris. The Los Angeles Music Center, whose first building was opened in 1964, received private contributions totaling more than $11 million. The county spends close to half a million dollars a year to support it and various other musical projects.

The tax-supported state universities are also active in cultural matters. The arts program of the University of California seems under virtual siege, with more than 300,000 people a year coming to the university campus at Los Angeles to attend lectures, dance recitals, concerts, plays and films. The UCLA Theater Group has become the leading resident theater of Southern California.

The widespread interest in the arts on the West Coast is relatively new; prior to World War II there was a mood of indifference and sometimes of hostility toward musicians, artists, writers and actors —particularly in California. While the attitude has changed, and the region as a whole seems engaged on a culture-appreciation binge, facilities for appreciating the work of creative and performing artists are not everywhere available. The novelist Martin Dibner, who led the California Arts Commission survey, found many areas of the state in which there still were "informed, interested, culturally alive people who have never seen a live concert or a professional theatrical company or an art show." Nor has the changed attitude toward the arts and artists brought about universal excellence. The same legislature that set up the California Arts Commission went on to name as poet laureate of the state an assemblyman who responded with a scrap of doggerel not atypical of his work:

> *The lark, the nightingale, the thrush,*
> *Have nurtured poets with lyric mush,*
> *But sweetest of all woodland notes,*
> *Are in the words, "He's got the votes."*

So thrive the people's arts in California, with lapses between the good and the worthless. Tolerant and eager to know, the vast numbers of new Californians are a shapeless mass, yeasty and in ferment. In the eyes of the designer Charles Eames, they have made of Los Angeles an "esthetic nightmare"—not because the people of that city are "a less sensitive group than any other," but because of the absence of social and physical restraints. "This would happen in the hands of any group freed from the restraints of tradition and with no new restraints to take their place," Eames told a California audience in 1963. "This is happening in varying, but increasing, degrees all over the world. The problem, of which Los Angeles is such a dramatic example, will soon be a universal one."

The missing restraints are diverse in type. In architecture, for example, the mild climate and the easy availability of building materials of most kinds, coupled with the heterogeneous nature of the populace and the highly varied California terrain, have brought into existence a motley collection of styles. Some handsome work, however, has been done. The contemporary California ranch house of redwood and glass is a descendant of the California bungalow, perhaps the Pacific States' most important architectural contribution. The landscape architecture of Thomas Church has also been excellent and influential, and the well-designed housing tracts of Joseph Eichler have been widely praised.

But the pleasing combination of such houses on handsomely laid-out sites is not universally accepted. Lacking local traditions or intertwined civic responsibilities, each person is free to burden the community with his own esthetic mistakes as long as his house is sanitary and earthquake-resistant. Eames has attempted to explain the cultural nihilism of California by drawing an analogy with the work of a sculptor. Hard granite, Eames points out, resists the sculptor's chisels. With granite, he says, it is "very difficult to do something bad"; but in plasteline, a spineless material, "one can do any imaginable variety of bad without half trying. The material puts up no resistance and whatever discipline there is, the artist himself must be strong enough to provide." The analogy extends into all the arts in the region. The California culture is a putty culture, not yet hardened into shape.

Caustic criticisms have been directed against this yeasty culture over the years. Nathanael West pulverized the old romantic Los Angeles legend three decades ago in *The Day of the Locust*. F. Scott Fitzgerald and Budd Schulberg both stripped bare the Hollywood ethic. Evelyn Waugh found morbid comedy in the Los Angeles of *The Loved One*. The California landscape architect Garrett Eckbo laments, "We are producing with staggering velocity and astonishing self-assurance, the most mechanical, regimented, sterile, uncultured, inhuman urban environment in the history of the world...."

Yet in this unrestrained society many capable artists appear to thrive. The painter Ed Ruscha

The striking towers of Watts

Among the most intriguing structures in a city filled with the unusual are the Watts Towers in Los Angeles. Built singlehandedly by an immigrant tilesetter named Simon Rodia, they consist of three lacy spires, the tallest 99.3 feet high, four smaller towers, fountains and arches. Made of reinforced concrete, they are encrusted with mosaics of materials Rodia gleaned from the city dump and from beaches: glass, bits of tiles, seashells.

Rodia, born in Italy in 1879, came to the U.S. as a boy and, after serving in the army in World War I, began his masterpiece. Climbing aloft without scaffolding, he worked on his towers with simple hand tools, revising and elaborating as his ideas changed. In 1954, after 33 years of work, Rodia deeded the property to a neighbor and disappeared. The towers were threatened with destruction as unsafe, but artists, critics and museum curators came to their defense, calling them a "unique work of folk art." Rodia, found living in Northern California, was reluctant to talk of his work, saying, "If your mother dies and you have loved her very much, maybe you don't speak of her." He died in 1965.

Resting from his prodigious labors, Simon Rodia stands within the mammoth sculpture he put together in the back yard of his home in the now largely Negro district of Los Angeles called Watts. On March 7, 1963, the towers were declared a historic monument.

157

Helen Hunt Jackson, born in 1830 in Amherst, Massachusetts, published her first poetry in 1865 but became famous with her extremely popular novel *Ramona* (1884), which reflects her outrage at the many injustices done the California Indians by the federal government. She died in 1885.

Some noted West Coast writers

From the earliest days of West Coast settlement, the region has produced a succession of novelists, short-story writers, poets and historians. Although they have never formed a West Coast "school," many have been highly individualistic and vigorous writers and have gained worldwide recognition. Some, like Edwin Markham, who wrote the famous poem "The Man with the Hoe," were born on the West Coast; others, like the novelist and reformer Upton Sinclair *(The Jungle)*, who was born in Baltimore, lived in the West for many years. A few of the better-known writers who were born in, or have become associated with, the region are shown on these pages.

The adventurer Jack London was born in San Francisco in 1876. Some of his tales were based on his own escapades along the San Francisco area waterfront. He was most famous for his stories and novels of rugged frontier life, also written, to some extent, out of his own experience.

One of the most famous West Coast writers was Bret Harte. He wrote some of his best mining-camp stories, including "Tennessee's Partner" and "The Outcasts of Poker Flat," for the *Overland Monthly,* which he edited. Harte was born in Albany, New York, in 1836; he died in 1902.

insists that "the greatest thing about Southern California is that the pressure is just nonexistent." The San Francisco Ballet, founded in 1933, is the nation's oldest classical ballet; from California have come the dancers Isadora Duncan, Martha Graham, Ruth St. Denis, Ted Shawn, and Maria and Marjorie Tallchief. More professional writers live in California than in any other state but New York. "When writers begin to feel secure in their trade they migrate to California," the literary critic Joseph Henry Jackson once wrote. The state has been no less attractive to musical artists, having numbered among its residents the violinist Jascha Heifetz and the cellist Gregor Piatigorsky, the soprano Lotte Lehmann, and the composers Arnold Schoenberg and Igor Stravinsky. The San Francisco Symphony, whose international reputation declined after the departure of its renowned conductor Pierre Monteux in 1952, is being revitalized under the direction of Josef Krips, and the Los Angeles Philharmonic is achieving increasing recognition under the brilliant young conductor Zubin Mehta. For some the indulgent freedom of the region is a catalyst, and for others a target. Although the ebullient amateurs sometimes seem to hold the cultural reins, there appears to be no irreconcilable conflict between the pursuit of artistic

excellence for its own sake and the mass stampede to take advantage of cultural opportunities. As J. George Harrar wrote in a Rockefeller Foundation report on the arts in 1965, "We live at a time when among the new attitudes developing in our society, there is one demanding not only excellence in the arts, but the availability of those arts to new audiences, in new places."

The West Coast always has abounded in such new audiences and new places. Its few cultural traditions long were centered in San Francisco, which had precocious beginnings in journalism, literature, music and the theater. As Walt Whitman wrote, early San Francisco society was "fresh come, to a new world indeed, yet long prepared." Miska Hauser, a violinist from Bohemia who toured the Gold Rush towns in the mid-century, received $3,000 to $4,000 a concert—although, he wrote in his travel journal, "somehow the people seem to prefer my variations on 'The Bird in the Tree' to a Beethoven sonata." The theater of Gold Rush days grew quickly from minstrel and vaudeville shows to a more solid repertoire as the lure of easy money drew to California such classical actors as John Wilkes Booth and his brother Edwin Booth, and such stage personalities of the day as Lola Montez and Mathilda Heron.

A journalist and popular historian, Stewart H. Holbrook was born in Vermont in 1893 but lived from the 1920s until his death in 1964 in the Northwest, on which he based much of his work, like *The Columbia*, a study of the river.

Pulitzer and Nobel Prize winner, John Steinbeck was born in Salinas, California, and has based many of his novels and short stories on the working people of his home state, such as Oklahoma migrants in *The Grapes of Wrath*.

Novelist, short-story writer and playwright, William Saroyan was born in Fresno, California, in 1908. A buoyant nonconformist, he refused to accept the Pulitzer Prize awarded his ebullient play, *The Time of Your Life*.

Soon the theater circuit included Oregon City, Portland and Seattle.

The most renowned of early regional traditions, however, was in journalism. The first newspaper on the Pacific Coast was a Democratic Party organ published in Oregon City. In the 1850s, before the Gold Rush abated, more newspapers were being published in San Francisco than in London; besides those in English, there were two daily newspapers in French and others in German, Italian, Swedish, Spanish and Chinese. The drama of the new California had magnetic appeal to journalists and soon to writers of more literary talents. Like the miners, early California writers were from elsewhere—the lusty storyteller Bret Harte, born in Albany, New York; the novelist Mark Twain, born in Florida, Missouri; the poet Joaquin Miller, from Liberty, Indiana; and the caustic columnist and short-story writer Ambrose Bierce, from Meigs County, Ohio. In the 1860s and 1870s they found rich material in California.

San Francisco, with money, publishers, libraries and an eager reading public, became the literary capital of the vast Western frontier as its writers mined the lore of the new society. *Golden Era*, a weekly founded in 1852, became the first medium for Harte and others in the early literary galaxy.

The *Overland Monthly*, launched in 1868 with Harte as editor, contained the purest jewels of early Californiana. Fiercely Western in content and picturesque in style, it brought new vigor to American writing and worldwide fame to Harte. In their realism, stories like Harte's "The Luck of Roaring Camp" foreshadowed the California tradition of forthrightness; in the West no period since then has seen so significant a body of regional writing.

Two writers of the same generation as Harte voiced an emerging social consciousness. Helen Hunt Jackson, an antagonist of United States Indian policy, swept the nation with *Ramona*, a romanticized account of an Indian girl. The political economist Henry George cried out against land monopolies and the greed of landowners.

The next generation of writers included a trio of novelists who carried on this spirit of social protest. Jack London, a storyteller of the first rank, was also a Marxian socialist and revolutionist; Frank Norris, charging that "we have done nothing to get at the truth about the West," portrayed California conflicts of class and culture in *McTeague* and *The Octopus;* Upton Sinclair lashed out in a string of powerful but rather graceless novels against a variety of what he considered America's ills. A tenuous lineage may be drawn from these writers to the later social protest expressed in the books of John Steinbeck. The writing of the naturalist John Muir set the tone near the turn of the century for the wave of conservation and park legislation.

A concern for architectural esthetics emerged in San Francisco in the 1870s and 1880s and opulent public buildings were created; the city's attractive bay-window, gingerbread style appeared. San Francisco's concern has sometimes approached narcissism, but it has always been infinitely more tolerable than indifference. It is traditional to compare the San Francisco that flourished before the earthquake and fire of 1906 with Athens and Florence in their days of greatness; there was a self-awareness and a receptivity toward the arts.

The bizarre cultural growth pattern of Southern California—"tradition" would be too stable a word —began with the arrival of artists, writers and novelists imported by the railroads to serve as troubadours of the area. One of the first of them was Charles Nordhoff, who came from the staff of the New York *Evening Post* to work for the Southern Pacific; his articles, published first in *Harper's Weekly* and later in book form in 1873, won Southern California much attention. Another enthusiastic writer was Charles Fletcher Lummis, who walked across the continent in 1885 as a prelude to editing

The Land of Sunshine, which was first subsidized by the Los Angeles Chamber of Commerce and was for years the principal cultural voice of Southern California. Such subsidization of writers and periodicals did much to build the make-believe image of the area that stubbornly persists; the image was later reinforced by the ballyhoo of Hollywood. But the region has never much resembled that which has been written about it. Much early writing was obsessed with the scenic and picturesque; in that tradition the hordes of insignificant Southern California poets remain among the most saccharine offenders. California has, however, produced one poet of note: Robinson Jeffers, whose verse vigorously evokes the Big Sur country.

Drawn by movie money, many able writers came to California after Hollywood converted to sound in the late 1920s. Oddly, their coming signaled a decline of true creativity in Hollywood. The film industry had originally been lured to Los Angeles by clear skies and photogenic scenery. For a time movies mirrored some unmistakably California traits: a lack of inhibition, a sense of space, the euphoria of a new-found land. "We can see, looking back," says the director and producer John Houseman, "that it was a rather curious image—the code of the West plus the electric refrigerator, the middle-class sentimentalities of the *Saturday Evening Post* enacted in the cool magnificence of tiled bathrooms, the smooth power of multicylindered Cadillacs combined with the elemental violence of Mafia morality. It is true that none of these elements [was] specifically or exclusively Californian—but California did supply the solvent, the atmosphere of unbounded self-confidence in which this strange uninhibited synthesis was made possible."

In the 1930s, despite the influx of distinguished literary figures like William Faulkner and Robert Sherwood as screenwriters, Hollywood began to veer away from this spontaneity. Producers shied away from original work and began to lean more heavily on successful novels, dramas and musicals. The old self-confidence faded. When the full force of competition from television struck in the 1950s, Hollywood had grown so devitalized that it offered minimal resistance to the new medium. There was no longer a Hollywood tradition to defend. Many of the greatest talents drifted away. Houseman himself became the director of the experimental Theater Group at the University of California at Los Angeles. But hundreds of others, notably film writers, stayed on, caught up in the pervasive narcotic of the film and television industry.

In the 1940s the two contemporary novelists most associated with California, John Steinbeck and William Saroyan, left the state. Most of the younger writers had been in California for so short a time that they had little success in making the regional culture meaningful in their work; more often they turned inward in isolation and disaffection. Among their ranks were the members of the Beat school of Jack Kerouac, which flared and faded in San Francisco in the 1950s. In postwar San Francisco there was nevertheless for a time some of the creative excitement of past decades. Much of the revival, particularly in poetry, was in the hands of Quakers and other conscientious objectors who had been held in a camp at Waldport, Oregon, during World War II. Like the military, they had visited San Francisco on leave and settled there after the war.

Nor was this rebirth solely literary. Under the guidance of Douglas MacAgy a group of Abstract Expressionist painters began to work with the support of the California School of Fine Arts and the San Francisco Museum. At Mills College, in Oakland, the composer Darius Milhaud taught GI-Bill students—among them Dave Brubeck and Paul Desmond, who soon led jazz in new directions strongly influenced by the training in classical music that Milhaud had given them.

Experimental theater came to life in San Francisco, with one group, the Interplayers, moving *in toto* from the Waldport camp. In 1952 the Actor's Workshop, under the directors Herbert Blau and Jules Irving, had its beginnings in Ebenezer Church, a little frame building in a Negro neighborhood; 13 years later Blau and Irving and members of their troupe moved across the country to the multimillion-dollar Vivian Beaumont Theater at Lincoln Center in New York. They had made of the Actor's Workshop a successful company whose repertoire ranged from Aristophanes to Bertolt Brecht. With a paid staff and company and the help of volunteers, the Blau-Irving company was for years the only West Coast theater of its kind to survive on a professional level. Yet the writer Mark Harris, a San Francisco resident, charged: "Nothing in San Francisco resembles a theater of community. Most people watch television. Society goes to the opera. Suburbanites go to the suburbs." Still, the San Francisco culture, in the opinion of that city's poet-artist Kenneth Rexroth, remained "incomparably richer and of higher quality *proportionately* than New York's."

The departure of the Actor's Workshop for New York became a *cause célèbre* because for many decades California theater had been mainly restricted to the offerings of Broadway touring companies and to bland performances by little-theater groups, with their prevalence of incompetence. The Northwest had attempted to deal with the lack of good theater some years before. Seattle, which often found itself ignored by Broadway touring companies, developed its own theater even before San Francisco. In 1940, under the direction of Glenn Hughes, the University of Washington School of Drama built the nation's first theater-in-the-round, the Penthouse Theater. The community enthusiastically supports the Penthouse and two other university theaters, the Playhouse, which employs a thrust stage, and the Showboat, which uses the traditional proscenium; each of the three theaters presents between four and eight productions a year.

In Seattle in 1950 Gene Keene, a university drama graduate, founded the Cirque Playhouse, which offers a yearlong series of plays with local performers. Finally, with the stimulus of the Seattle World's Fair of 1962, the Seattle Repertory Theatre was launched. Its home is the 800-seat Seattle Center Playhouse, which was built for the fair. The Center Playhouse's impressive offerings of both classic and contemporary theater, first under the direction of Stuart Vaughan and later under that of Allen Fletcher, have met with resounding success and established the theater as a leader in regional repertory. Portland is somewhat less active than Seattle; its single substantial theater is the Portland Civic Theatre, formed in 1926. A similar civic company is the charming Old Globe Theatre of San Diego, which operates throughout the year in a replica of the Globe theater of Elizabethan London, where Shakespeare's plays were first performed.

Other areas of the West Coast have more recently become active in theatrical programs. With the help of a $300,000 Rockefeller Foundation grant, the Stanford Repertory Theater was launched in 1965 in conjunction with a new graduate school of theater at the university. The Repertory Theater is a professional company placing emphasis on contemporary drama. There are admirable summer Shakespeare festivals at Ashland, Oregon, and at the Old Globe in San Diego.

Less ambitious theatrical undertakings are so numerous as to defy cataloguing. Los Angeles newspapers list an average of 50 offerings in Los Angeles County each week, and in San Francisco there are sometimes even more. Many of these productions are underwritten by private contributions and membership dues. Not unexpectedly, their directors complain that they must emphasize light theatrical fare in order to attract audiences. But their

The poet of the Big Sur

Enclosed in his study, Robinson Jeffers seems almost a part of the rough gray granite from which he built his home, Tor House, near California's Big Sur country. Much of Jeffers' rugged verse reflects his love of nature, its cruelty as well as its peaceful beauty. Born in Pittsburgh in 1887, Jeffers moved to California in 1914. He died there in 1962. In "Tor House," reprinted below, he mused on the future of his beloved home.

Tor House

If you should look for this place after a handful of
    lifetimes,
Perhaps of my planted forest a few
May stand yet, dark-leaved Australians or the coast
    cypress, haggard
With storm-drift; but fire and the axe are devils.
Look for foundations of sea-worn granite, my fingers
    had the art
To make stone love stone, you will find some remnant.
But if you should look in your idleness after ten
    thousand years:
It is the granite knoll on the granite
And lava tongue in the midst of the bay, by the mouth
    of the Carmel
River-valley, these four will remain
In the change of names. You will know it by the wild
    sea-fragrance of wind
Though the ocean may have climbed or retired a little;
You will know it by the valley inland that our sun
    and our moon were born from
Before the poles changed; and Orion in December
Evenings was strung in the throat of the valley like
    a lamp-lighted bridge.
Come in the morning you will see white gulls
Weaving a dance over blue water, the wane of the moon
Their dance-companion, a ghost walking
By daylight, but wider and whiter than any bird
    in the world.
My ghost you needn't look for; it is probably
Here, but a dark one, deep in the granite, not
    dancing on wind
With the mad wings and the day moon.

number testifies to the laudable effort on the West Coast to give its people greater access to the performing arts. The author Nard Jones of Seattle says: "We have a tremendous will to grow intellectually, to create while we compete, and to become superior to 'tribes' elsewhere in the nation."

In California that mood has developed sophomoric and irrelevant overtones in a provincial debate over whether Los Angeles is assuming cultural pre-eminence over San Francisco. The traditional self-assurance of the San Franciscan seemed nettled in the mid-1960s by the completion of the Music Center Pavilion and the County Art Museum in the southern city, by the loss to New York of the core of the Actor's Workshop and finally by a convincing defeat at the polls in San Francisco of a proposed $29 million cultural center. Passage of that measure, San Francisco Mayor John F. Shelley had said, would make Los Angeles "think it's again a little Mexican village." The failure of the measure caused the San Francisco *News Call Bulletin* to run a series headlined "L.A.'s Culture Conquest." "San Francisco," added Dean Wallace, art and music editor of the *San Francisco Chronicle*, "is rapidly becoming known from coast to coast as the place where everyone talks about culture and nobody does anything about it." Such observations seemed excessive. But it was true that while impressive private collections were growing in Southern California, as was the number of museums and art centers, there were few collections of modern painting of national importance in San Francisco.

In painting itself, the entire region was making notable strides. In the Northwest Mark Tobey and Morris Graves, both under strong Oriental influences, established international reputations in the 1940s and 1950s, as did Guy Anderson and Ken Callahan, who are still painting vigorously. Younger men like Paul Horiuchi, Richard Gilkey and William Cumming are today developing individualistic styles. San Francisco painters like Richard Diebenkorn, Elmer Bischoff and the late David Park seemed to be establishing a school of figurative painting. In Southern California, where the late Rico Lebrun, strongly influenced by Goya and Picasso, enjoyed a lonely eminence after his arrival in 1938, a strong new style began to emerge. More recently a still newer style, which might be called far-out surrealism, has appeared. Seen in such works as the brutal tableaux of sculptor Edward Kienholz, it conveys a sense of immediacy, of American art at its frontier.

The art world of Southern California is currently in ferment. That world is being bolstered by the addition of artists and art historians to the faculties of universities and by large gallery programs in which the public so openly demonstrates its involvement in art affairs that the creative fervor is nourished and sustained. "Visiting the galleries along La Cienega," wrote the New York art critic Barbara Rose, "one begins to picture Europe as the Renaissance, New York as the avant garde and L.A. as the 'orgiastic future' that year by year becomes more actual and immediate, replete with an art already actual and immediate."

The measure of Western maturity is being found in the support and creation of art without regard to fashions made in the East. The people of the region thrive on change, and change, the designer Henry Dreyfus wrote, is an ideal climate for design; it may prove so for other arts as well. The immense popularization of the arts in the Pacific States cannot be dismissed as insignificant; it brings a large segment of society into closer touch with much that is good. It helps to create a tolerant attitude that readily accepts the experimental or avant-garde.

On his last visit to California the late British novelist T. H. White wrote: "I don't mind if the beauty is a bit cockeyed sometimes, like the Grauman Theatre or even the wildest excesses of de Mille. The point is that the money *is* being spent on culture of some sort, that it is an individual culture, and that even millionaires care about it." Californians may still find it simpler to build a handsome oil refinery or design a flywheel for a gyrostabilizer than to create a great work of art. But hope lies in their search for a cultural tradition that will impose the disciplines and restraints that are required for the creation of great art, just as engineering rules impose restraints upon the designer of the refinery or the flywheel.

With its brashness and shallowness diminishing, the West Coast may develop cultural traditions that will foreshadow future national trends. Just as the West Coast manner of speech is undialectal, a composite of all the states and thus impossible to identify as regional, so has Western culture begun to represent a homogenization of American tastes and aspirations and sensibilities. Newly arrived at the cultural fountain, Westerners have been busy seizing the heritage of the centuries from older regions of America and Europe, and attempting to adapt, convert and build empirically on this inheritance. The excitement inherent in the West prods its people in cultural matters, as it does in every other field of endeavor. Whatever shape this putty culture assumes, it will be of enduring significance in the national composite.

Sheer granite cliffs soar thousands of feet above a family of
campers exploring the Merced River in California's Yosemite
National Park. Although its main valley becomes crowded in the
tourist season, most of the 1,200-square-mile park remains wild.

Unspoiled areas
of wild grandeur

Although the society of the Pacific States is
predominantly an urban one, all three of the states
still contain large stretches of wild and magnificent
country. In these areas nature has worked on a
heroic scale: the mountains are among the highest
in the United States, the deserts are vast and
desolate, the redwood forests contain trees that
are the tallest living things on earth. Fortunately,
many of these natural wonders have been set
aside as parks or forest preserves, and people
devoted to conservation are working to protect
others. As life in the growing cities of the
West Coast—as in cities everywhere—becomes
ever more clamorous and tense, the people have
an increasing need of places where they can
see and feel the ponderous and unchanging
rhythms of nature, the round of the seasons and
the eternal return of the waves of the sea.

The Columbia River, looking deceptively placid, flows past Crown Point (right) in the 60-mile-long gorge that its massive power has gouged through the Cascade Range over the centuries. This portion of the river, which forms the principal natural gap through the mountains, eased the final leg of the journey of the pioneers who first settled Washington and Oregon, allowing them to float their covered wagons downstream on rafts. Today 23 state parks line the edge of the gorge. One of them, Rooster Rock State Park, lies below Crown Point; the point itself is also a state park and is topped by Vista House, a lookout 725 feet above the water.

Out of the serene waters of Crater Lake, in southwest Oregon, rises a tree-covered island of volcanic debris known as the Phantom Ship. The lake was formed as water filled the basin left when a volcano exploded and collapsed some 6,550 years ago.

Snow-clad Wizard Island, an extinct volcano that rose centuries
after the creation of the original basin, breaks through the surface
of Crater Lake. The lake's brilliantly clear waters, which plunge
to a depth of 1,932 feet, vary in color from indigo to turquoise.

Early-morning fog roils in slow motion, covering Crater Lake
like a sea of cotton fluff. Only comparatively recently did volcanic
activity cease. "Do not look upon this place," warned the
Klamath Indians, "for it will mean death or lasting sorrow."

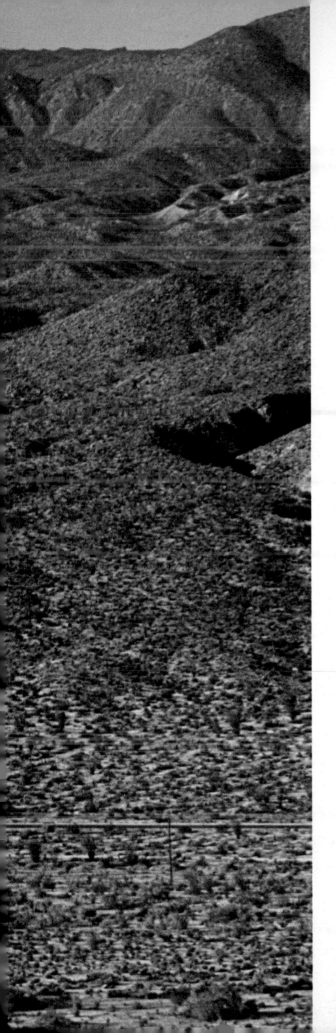

Desolate, dry hills of the Anza-Borrego Desert in Southern California, which support mainly cactus and low scrub, brood menacingly over the puny works of man—a road and a telephone line. The 488,000-acre reserve, the largest park set aside by a state, is one of California's last desert areas still untamed by man.

A rancher herds cattle and sheep toward a water hole across the high desert of eastern Oregon. The mountain barrier to the west prevents moisture-laden Pacific air from reaching this plateau land. Lack of rainfall combined with poor volcanic soil makes this desert incapable of supporting more than a few ranches.

Surrounded by ferns, fungi and mosses, Douglas firs rise from
the floor of the rain forest preserved in Washington's Olympic
National Park. Nurtured by as many as 150 inches of rain a year,
the Olympic woodland is one of the few rain forests outside
the tropics. Many of its Douglas firs are more than 200 feet tall.

Sunlight filters through towering redwoods in California's Muir Woods National Monument. These trees, which grow 300 feet tall and can live 2,000 years, covered some 1.5 million acres of California at the time Columbus found America. Most have since been felled: only 86,700 acres of them are now protected in parks.

171

Ridges of the Santa Lucia Range buttress the rough cliffs of Big Sur, as if to help the headlands withstand the force of the Pacific's rages. Big Sur is a 50-mile-long stretch of California coast south of Monterey, an area of savage winter storms and striking scenery. Although only a small section has been set aside as a park, Big Sur has remained unspoiled because of its inaccessibility—and the efforts of its residents. The people of Big Sur protested effectively when the state tried to replace the area's present two-lane road with a freeway; today they are trying to find ways to protect Big Sur's beauty despite increasing numbers of tourists and other visitors.

Suggested tours

On the following pages nine maps show sections of the West Coast that are of unusual interest. No attempt has been made to show every road or town. Instead, scenic routes, parks and other special features have been emphasized. The text accompanying each map gives a brief description of the area. Opening dates and hours, especially of the business tours, should be confirmed locally, since these vary during the year. The nine areas covered are shown in the small map below, along with a key to the symbols used.

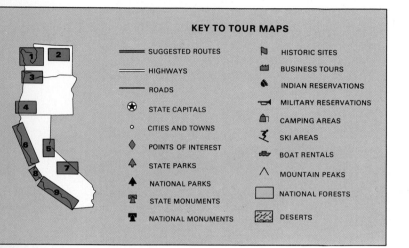

KEY TO TOUR MAPS

═══ SUGGESTED ROUTES	⚑ HISTORIC SITES
── HIGHWAYS	⌂ BUSINESS TOURS
── ROADS	🪶 INDIAN RESERVATIONS
⊛ STATE CAPITALS	📯 MILITARY RESERVATIONS
○ CITIES AND TOWNS	⌂ CAMPING AREAS
◆ POINTS OF INTEREST	🎿 SKI AREAS
⬟ STATE PARKS	⛵ BOAT RENTALS
⬟ NATIONAL PARKS	∧ MOUNTAIN PEAKS
⊤ STATE MONUMENTS	▭ NATIONAL FORESTS
⊤ NATIONAL MONUMENTS	▨ DESERTS

1. The Puget Sound area

The northwest corner of the United States has as its major attractions the waters of Puget Sound and the Pacific Ocean, the high peaks of the Cascade Range and the Olympic Mountains, and several fine cities. Among the most notable sights in Olympia, the capital of Washington, is the State Capital Group, a cluster of government buildings set in beautifully landscaped grounds.

Olympia is a good jumping-off point for a trip in almost any direction. The Olympic Peninsula offers hiking in the mountains or through the rain forests along its western rivers, as well as boating and skiing. Spots to visit along the northern shore include Port Townsend, a community with a Victorian air; the mills of Olympic Weavers, manufacturers of woolen goods, at Sequim; the Peninsula Plywood Corporation at Port Angeles; and Hurricane Ridge, a marvelous lookout point.

North of Olympia, along Puget Sound, stretch several of Washington's major cities, some of them important industrial centers with interesting tours of paper, lumber and aircraft plants. The Northwest's leading city, Seattle, was the home of the 1962 World's Fair. Today Seattle Center, as the fairgrounds are now called, still houses the 600-foot Space Needle, an amusement park, an art museum, a science center and a repertory theater. East of Puget Sound looms the Cascade Range, which includes Mount Rainier, Washington's greatest single tourist attraction. Mount Rainier National Park offers 300 miles of trails to high glaciers and meadows, a ski area, lakes and waterfalls, and many acres of virgin forest.

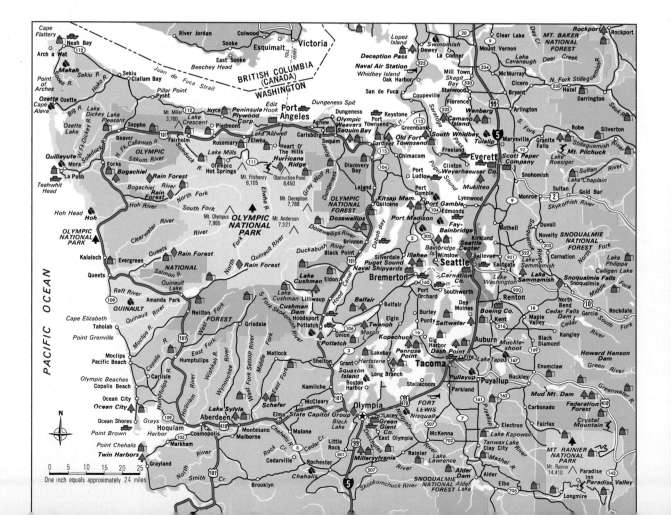

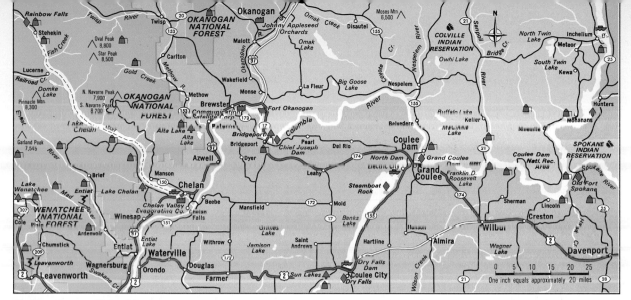

2. Northern Washington

The Columbia River Valley as it approaches the eastern slope of the Cascades presents marvels of man's industrial ingenuity as well as many natural wonders. Among the scenic attractions is fiordlike Lake Chelan, stretching 50 miles into the high, steep-sided Cascades. Access to the wild national forest interior is by ferry from the town of Chelan on Route 97. Almost as dramatic is Dry Falls, near Coulee City off Route 2. Formed when a vast ice sheet up to 4,000 feet thick diverted the Columbia from its normal bed centuries ago, the falls, now a series of dry, horseshoe-shaped cliffs, were once two and a half times higher and more than seven times wider than Niagara. Much of the hilly land north of the Columbia in

this area belongs to the Colville Indian Reservation, but it is open to the public and includes public camping grounds. Indian artifacts and relics of the pioneers can be seen at Fort Okanogan Museum, on Route 17, and at Old Fort Spokane, on Route 25. The Columbia itself is controlled in this area by dams and spillways. The Chief Joseph Dam, named after the last great chief of the Nez Percé Indians, is one of the largest hydroelectric dams in the nation. The largest is the Grand Coulee Dam, on Route 174. Both dams are open to the public, as is the Communications Satellite Corporation's earth station at Brewster, on Route 97, built as part of a commercial communications system that will someday circle the globe.

3. Oregon's Coast and the Columbia

The relentless force of water as it sculpts the land is the dominant feature of the tour routes below. The first, Route 101, winds along the varied coast, passing in turn breakers crashing on ancient cliffs, surf rolling across smooth sand beaches, forest growing to the water's edge, and small fishing villages. Few areas have such an accessible coastline—of the 400 miles of beach in Oregon, all but 23 miles are public property, including 41 state parks. At the northern end of this tour, sitting high above the mouth of the Columbia River on Chinook Point, is Fort Columbia, once a coast artillery post, today a museum

of the river's history. In it, dioramas, maps and historical relics provide a background for the second tour, through the valley cut by the river itself. The largest city in the river valley is Portland, with an extinct volcano, Mount Tabor, inside the city limits, and Mount Hood not far away. A side trip, the 170-mile Mount Hood Loop Highway, passes through the city's year-round forest playground. Up the Columbia the route divides into a water-level expressway and the Scenic Highway, which travels past lookout points high above the river, spectacular falls, and great dams with fish ladders, locks and spillways.

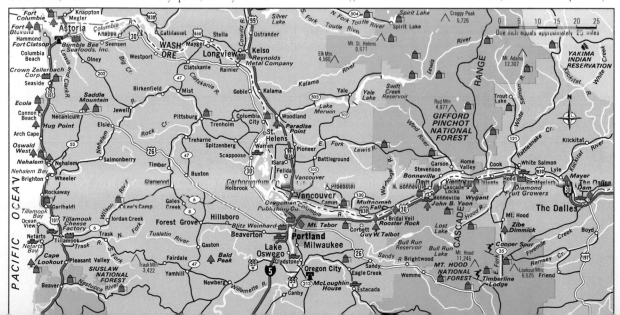

4. Southwestern Oregon

The rugged coast and mountains of southwestern Oregon have some of the finest scenery in the entire Pacific Coast area. All along the shoreline, which is followed by Route 101, lie isolated beaches, steep cliffs and rock formations that have been carved into weird shapes by the sea. Perhaps the most dramatic of these formations is Mack Arch, which soars 325 feet above the water in the shape of an immense crescent. Gold Beach, so named because gold was found there during the 1850s, is near the mouth of the wild Rogue River, whose turbulent lower reaches can be seen from the sturdy mail boats that regularly take passengers to Agness, 32 miles upstream. Farther inland,

Route 5 provides access to the upper Rogue and rocky Hellgate Canyon. Gold-rush days seem still alive in Jacksonville, on Route 238, a town with many buildings left from a century ago. In August the Oregon Shakespearean Festival company performs in the town of Ashland, near Medford, in the nation's oldest replica of an Elizabethan theater. Medford itself is a popular gateway to the Crater Lake National Park *(pages 166-167)*, via Route 62. The 35-mile Rim Drive, which opens in early July, reveals the lake's beauty, as well as the magnificent surrounding wilderness. Businesses in this area which have tours include the Medford Corporation, plywood manufacturers.

5. The Sierra Nevada

The gold-rush country and the Sierra Nevada, both included in the tour map at right, abound in reminders of California's earliest days. Among the towns that line Route 49 are many that grew from gold-rush mining camps, like Placerville, Sutter Creek and Angels Camp, the last immortalized in Mark Twain's "The Celebrated Jumping Frog of Calaveras County." The best preserved of the old camps is Columbia, today maintained as a state park; its Wells Fargo office, bank and other 19th Century buildings are unmarred by the neon signs that disfigure the main streets of other mining towns.

East of the gold-rush country rise the beautiful but forbidding peaks of the Sierra Nevada. Covering an area almost the size of the French, Italian and Swiss Alps combined, the range today is mostly national forest and park, with many campgrounds, picnic spots and recreational areas. Some of the most spectacular scenery in the range is included in Yosemite National Park *(page 163)*. Majestic Yosemite Valley, penetrated by Route 140, is perhaps unmatched anywhere, its floor a wide, meadowlike tract, its sides vertical granite walls rising 2,000 to 4,000 feet. Lake Tahoe, the nation's highest (and the world's second highest) navigable lake, is an inland sea of shimmering deep blue, and despite indiscriminate real-estate development on its shores, well worth a separate trip.

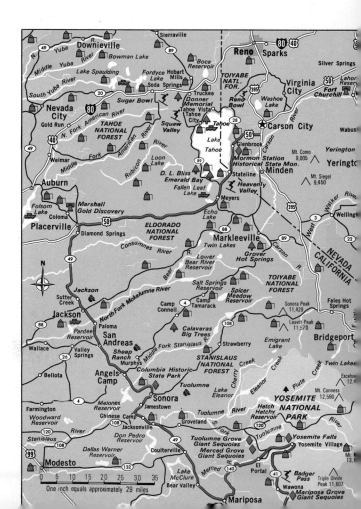

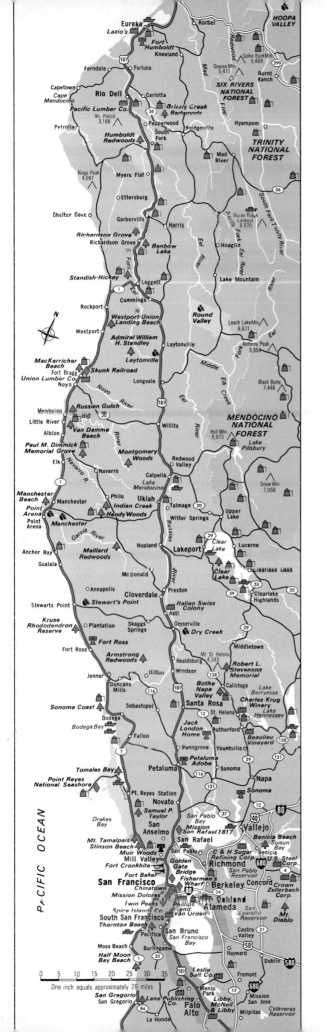

6. San Francisco and Northern California

Three very different areas are encompassed in this section of California: the fascinating city of San Francisco, the coast itself, and the wine-producing counties of Sonoma and Napa. The best way to see many sections of San Francisco is on foot, walking up and down the city's many interesting streets and through its numerous museums, art galleries and shops—although the famous San Francisco cable cars can help the visitor negotiate the city's many steep hills. Chinatown's music, smells and Oriental shops can only be experienced by walking. Here, despite the modernizing efforts of some who deplore what they call "pigtail architecture," many merchants have kept the pseudo-Oriental store fronts that attract tourists.

One of the oldest buildings in the city is the Mission Dolores, whose cornerstone was laid in 1782. Other evidences of the city's past can be found in the extensive port area, especially on Fisherman's Wharf, where descendants of Genoese and Sicilian fishermen still bring in their catch. Nearby is the Maritime Museum, which has not only ship models, figureheads and other exhibits, but also four large ships preserved from the days of sail.

At the western end of the city lies Golden Gate Park, one of the finest city parks in the world, with science museums, an art museum, lakes, meadows and many recreational areas. Not far from the park are Twin Peaks, which provide fine views of the city and surrounding hills.

North of San Francisco the coastal redwoods grow in cathedral-like groves, many of them preserved in forest monuments like Muir Woods or in parks like the Humboldt Redwoods State Park. In Fort Bragg the Union Lumber Company, the world's largest redwood mill, provides tours that allow visitors to see how efficient modern methods convert these monster trees into lumber. An interesting way to see some of the second-growth redwood and Douglas fir forests is aboard the *Skunk,* a train of the California Western Railroad, which runs the 40 miles from Fort Bragg to Willits.

Early settlement and exploration of Northern California is commemorated by several historical monuments. Fort Ross, on Route 1, was an outpost of the Russian fur traders of the 1800s. The commandant's house and two blockhouses were reconstructed in this century, but the Russian Orthodox chapel stands unchanged and is still used for occasional services. For evidence of early Spanish settlement in Northern California, one must turn back to the Bay Area. The Sonoma Mission, the northernmost in the state, houses exhibits illustrating the area's history. The Petaluma Adobe in Petaluma is a fortlike structure built by General Mariano Vallejo in the 1830s, probably to protect his 75,000-acre holdings from attack by the Russians at Fort Ross. His attractive home in Sonoma is also preserved. These fine Spanish buildings are on the edge of some of California's best wine country. The greatest concentration of wineries open to visitors is strung out along Route 29 north and south of St. Helena. The best time to tour this beautiful area of rolling hills is, of course, during the harvest in late September and early October.

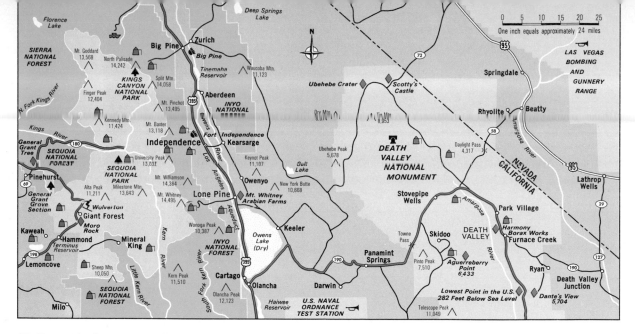

7. Sequoia forests and Death Valley

Extremes of nature dominate this area of eastern California. Death Valley, the world's lowest and hottest desert, contains some 3,000 square miles of salt flats, dry mountains, flowing dunes and colorful rock formations. Summer temperatures may reach 120° but winter temperatures are comfortable, and—as the many ghost towns attest—men have managed to live and work in the Valley. One such ghost town is Skidoo, now little more than a graveyard. Rhyolite's former grandeur is recalled by a railroad station that cost $135,000 to build in 1907. More recent is Scotty's Castle, a Moorish mansion built by a veteran prospector known as Death Valley Scotty

with money supplied by an eccentric Chicago millionaire.

Vestiges of the raw forces that helped create the forbidding Valley can be seen at Ubehabe Crater, a 2,000-foot-wide volcanic pit. Long expanses of the Valley can be seen from Dante's View on the east and Aguereberry Point on the west. A more verdant area can be found in Kings Canyon and Sequoia National Parks. Since no road traverses it, only ardent hikers or campers can see much of Kings Canyon Park, but paved roads lead to many of Sequoia's attractions, such as the General Grant Tree, among the largest in the world, and Moro Rock, which provides fine views of the surrounding country.

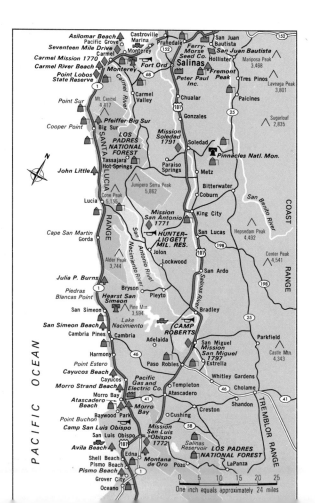

8. Big Sur and the missions

The two major attractions of this area for visitors are the magnificently wild Big Sur coast (pages 172-173) and the many mission structures built during the era when Spain ruled California. Although the entire coast is worth seeing, Point Lobos State Reserve near the artists' colony at Carmel is especially noteworthy, since it preserves one of the world's two virgin stands of Monterey cypress, wind-blown trees that cling to the cliffs overlooking the sea. South of Carmel, on Route 1, lie 100 miles of magnificent scenery, combining rugged headlands, beaches, forests and mountains. Farther inland, off Route 25, Pinnacles National Monument displays the remains of great lava flows and explosive eruptions of millions of years ago.

The chain of Spanish missions includes authentically restored San Carlos Borromeo in Carmel, where the chain's founder, Junipero Serra, is buried. The mission in the town of San Juan Bautista, which is across the plaza from the town's historic site, preserves Spanish-style buildings much as they were 150 years ago. Other things of interest in this section of California include the enormous, gaudy mansion near the town of San Simeon built by the newspaper magnate William Randolph Hearst. Business tours include one through the Ferry-Morse Seed Company's 900-acre research and seed-producing station in San Juan Bautista with its countless flower beds.

9. From San Diego to Los Angeles

San Diego and its suburbs and the vast metropolitan area of Los Angeles have enough cultural activities, sporting events, historical attractions, recreational areas and amusement possibilities to keep a visitor busy for months. Within San Diego are the multiple attractions of 1,400-acre Balboa Park (*page 71*), whose superb zoo has as wide a variety of animals as any zoo in the world. The naval base has vessels open to the public and a museum that includes an extensive model-ship collection. Homes and churches from the city's past still exist in Old San Diego, and some are open to the public. At La Jolla, a suburb of San Diego, the Scripps Institution of Oceanography's Aquarium-Museum has exhibits that explain many mysteries of the ocean and its creatures. Nearby Mission Bay Park is a recreation area of beaches, waterways and places to swim covering seven square miles. Among the more interesting business tours is one given by San Diego's Union-Tribune Publishing Company.

North of San Diego is Palomar Mountain, with the world's largest reflecting telescope, its 520 tons so well balanced that a slight push can move the entire mechanism. Closer to the coast is the large Mission San Luis Rey; better known is another Spanish mission, San Juan Capistrano, farther north near the junction of Routes 1 and 101. These two highways give access to a number of famous Southern California beaches. A coastal road that branches off Route 1 passes the Wayfarer's Chapel, designed by Lloyd Wright, son of Frank Lloyd Wright, and Marineland, which features trained dolphins and whales and a collection of other sea animals. Inland from the beaches, near Route 101, are two well-known attractions: Disneyland, which draws more adults than children, and Knott's Berry Farm, which is part farm and part Western-flavored amusement park.

Remnants of old Los Angeles, preserved from the 1800s, can be visited in El Pueblo de Los Angeles, a state historical monument. The Los Angeles County Museum in the city's Exposition Park gives a glimpse of an even older California; it contains Pleistocene animal remains found preserved in the city's famous La Brea Tar Pits. Evidence of the era of Spanish rule can be seen in the San Gabriel and San Fernando missions.

The Los Angeles County Art Museum is one of the nation's best. The finest in classical music and opera can be heard at the Music Center. Entertainment of another kind has long been the business of Hollywood, and most of the big movie lots can be visited. Universal City Studios shows visitors around its sets, sound stages and dressing rooms. Interesting business tours include the tuna-packing plant of Star-Kist Foods, Inc. and an oil refinery of the Union Oil Company of California. The Farmers' Market at Third Street and Fairfax Avenue has shops offering foods, clothing and gift items from around the world. Surrounding the metropolitan area are both forests and deserts, while within the city a variety of parks and gardens, such as Descanso Gardens with its magnificent roses and camellias, bring the outdoors close by.

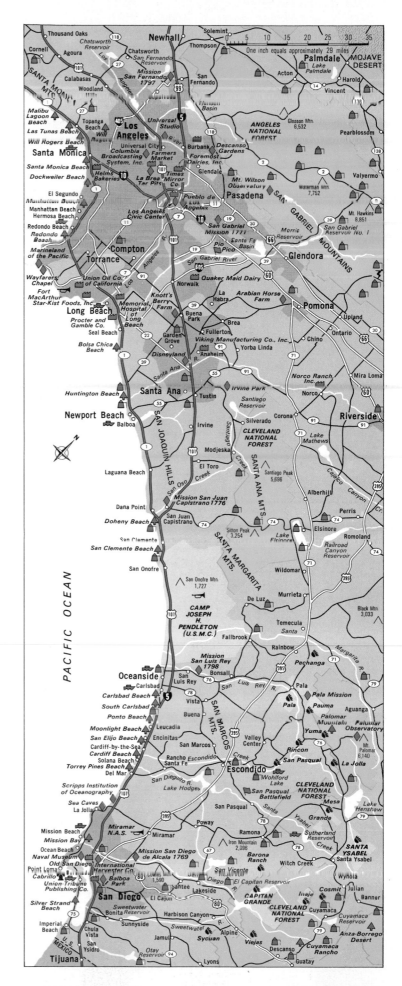

Museums and galleries

California

Bakersfield
Kern County Museum, 3801 Chester Ave. Model of late-19th Century village; Indian artifacts. Mon-Fri 8-5; Sat, Sun, Hols 1-5.

Berkeley
Robert H. Lowie Museum of Anthropology, University of California, Bancroft Way and College Ave. Archeology, ethnology, primitive art. Daily 10-5.

Cazadero
Fort Ross State Historic Park, 19005 Coast Highway No. 1. Restored 1812 fort. Daily 8-5 (summer 8-6).

La Jolla
La Jolla Museum of Art, 700 Prospect St. European and American contemporary painting, ceramics and photographs. Tues-Sun 12:30-4:30; Wed eves 7-10.

T. Wayland Vaughan Aquarium-Museum, Scripps Institution of Oceanography, 8602 La Jolla Shores Dr. Oceanography, natural history. Mon-Fri 8-6; Sat, Sun 9-6.

Lompoc
La Purisima Mission State Historical Park, Route 1. Restored Spanish mission and Indian relics. Daily 8-5 (summer 8-6).

Long Beach
Long Beach Museum of Art, 2300 E. Ocean Blvd. Southern California contemporary painting and crafts. Tues-Fri 10-5; Sat, Sun, Hols 1-5.

Los Angeles
California Museum of Science and Industry, 700 State Dr. Space show, Hall of Electricity, changing exhibits of industrial design and graphic arts. Daily 10-5.

Fisher Gallery, University of Southern California, University Park. Painting and sculpture. Mon-Fri 12-5 when university is in session.

Griffith Observatory and Planetarium, Griffith Park. Astronomy. Tues-Fri 2-10; Sat, Sun 1-10.

Los Angeles County Museum of Art, in Hancock Park off Wilshire Blvd. Excellent collections of Western, Oriental, ancient Egyptian, Greek and Roman art. Tues-Thurs 10-5; Fri 1-10; Sat, Sun 1-5.

Los Angeles County Museum, Science and History, 900 Exposition Blvd. Natural history, mineralogy; excellent collection of fish and animal fossils; American and early Californian history. Daily (except Mon) 10-5.

Municipal Art Gallery, Barnsdall Park, 1649 N. Vermont Ave. Changing shows. Tues-Fri 1-9; Sat, Sun 1-5.

Southwest Museum, Marmion Way and Museum Dr. Extensive collection of Indian artifacts. Daily (except Mon) 1-5.

University of California at Los Angeles Art Galleries, 405 Hilgard Ave. European and American graphics. Mon-Fri 12-5; Tues eves 6-10; Sun 1:30-5.

Monterey
Colton Hall, 522 Pacific St. 1849 historic house; early state history. Daily 10-5.

Old Custom House State Historical Monument, Alvarado St. Oldest government building in the state; gun collection; Spanish and Mexican artifacts. Daily 10-5.

Oakland
Oakland Art Museum, Municipal Auditorium, 10th and Fallon Sts. Nineteenth and 20th Century California art, Oriental art. Daily 10-5.

Palm Springs
Palm Springs Desert Museum, Tahquitz-McCallum Way. Geology, zoology, natural history of the desert. Tues-Sat 10-5; Sun 2-5.

Pasadena
The Pasadena Museum of Art, 46 N. Los Robles Ave. Twentieth Century art, especially German Expressionism. Tues 10-9; Wed-Sat 10-5; Sun 2-5.

Richmond
Richmond Art Center in town's Civic Center. Exhibits of painting, sculpture and decorative arts. Mon-Thurs 9-4:30, 7-9:30; Fri 9-4:30; Sun 2-5.

Sacramento
E. B. Crocker Art Gallery, 216 O St. Drawings by old masters, Korean ceramics, American glass, graphics. Daily (except Mon and Hols) 10-5.

Sutter's Fort State Historical Monument, 2701 L St. Early California history, gold-rush relics. Daily 10-5.

San Diego
Aerospace Museum, Balboa Park. Missiles and antique airplanes. Daily 10-4:30.

The Fine Arts Gallery of San Diego, Balboa Park. Superb collection of old masterpieces. Tues-Sat 10-5; Sun 1-5:30.

Museum of Man, Balboa Park. Exhibits illustrating the history of mankind. Mon-Sat 10-4:45; Sun 12-4:45.

San Diego Natural History Museum, Balboa Park. Exhibits showing the natural history of southern California; children's museum. Daily 10-4:30.

San Francisco
California Academy of Science, Golden Gate Park. Natural history, aquarium, planetarium. Daily 10-5.

California Division of Mines and Geology, Ferry Bldg. Mineralogy. Mon-Fri 8-5; first Sat of each month 10-noon.

California Palace of the Legion of Honor, Lincoln Park. One of the best U.S. collections of 18th Century French furniture and *objets d'art;* Rodin sculpture; European and American works; Egyptian and classical art. Daily 10-5.

M. H. De Young Memorial Museum, Golden Gate State Park. European and American art from ancient times to present; major masterpieces of Renaissance painting. Daily 10-5.

Josephine D. Randall Junior Museum, Roosevelt Way and 16th St. Natural history; model aircraft and railroad displays. Tues-Sat 10-5; Sun 12-5.

San Francisco Maritime Museum, Polk and Beach Sts. Ship models, maritime relics. Daily 10-5.

San Francisco Museum of Art, Veterans War Memorial, Van Ness Ave. and McAllister St. Twentieth Century painting, sculpture and graphics. Tues-Fri 10-10; Sat 10-5; Sun 1-5.

San Marino
Henry E. Huntington Library and Art Gallery, 1151 Oxford Rd. Eighteenth Century British paintings and French furnishings; Beauvais tapestries; one of the nation's best collections of Georgian art. Daily (except Mon) 1-4:30. Closed Oct.

Santa Barbara
Santa Barbara Historical Society Museum, De La Guerra and Santa Barbara Sts. Local history, including early China trade days in California. Tues-Sat 2-5.

Santa Barbara Museum of Art, 1130 State St. American and ancient art; Oriental musical instruments. Tues-Sat 11-5; Sun 12-5.

Stockton
Pioneer Museum and Haggin Art Galleries, Victory Park, Pershing Ave. Local history, minerals; 19th and 20th Century European and American art. Daily (except Mon) 1:30-5.

Tulelake
Lava Beds National Monument. Natural history. Daily 8-5 (summer 8-8).

Twentynine Palms
Joshua Tree National Monument, 74485 Palm Vista Dr. Archeology, geology, herbarium. Daily 8-5.

Oregon

Astoria
Columbia River Maritime Museum, 16th and Exchange Sts. History of Oregon shipping and fishing industries. Daily 10:30-5. Closed Mon during winter.

Fort Clatsop National Memorial, Route 101. Reconstructed fort of 1805-1806. Daily 10-5.

Eugene
University of Oregon Art Museum. Collection of Oriental art; traveling exhibits. Tues, Thurs 11-5; Wed, Fri-Sun 1-5.

University of Oregon Museum of Natural History. Indian art, artifacts; anthropology, archeology. Mon-Fri 8-5.

Portland
Oregon Historical Society, 235 S.W. Market St. Society founded in 1898 has valuable diaries, old maps, relics of early mariners. Mon-Fri 9-5; Sat 9-12.

Oregon Museum of Science and Industry, 4015 S.W. Canyon

Rd. Geology, natural science, planetarium. Mon-Fri 10-5; Sat, Sun, Hols 10-6.

Portland Art Museum, S.W. Park and Madison Sts. Northwest Indian art and contemporary Oregon art· Renaissance paintings. Tues-Thurs 12-5; Fri 12-10; Sat, Sun 12-5.

Salem
Salem Art Museum, 000 Mission St. Work of Northwest artists hung in Bush House, a museum of 1870s era. Summer: Tues-Sat 12-5; Sun 2-5. Winter: Tues-Sun 2-5.

Washington

Kelso
Cowlitz County Historical Museum, Courthouse Annex, Church and 5th Sts. Local

history, natural history, anthropology. Tues-Sat 10:30-4:30; Sun 2-5.

Olympia
State Capitol Museum, 211 W. 21 St. State history, natural history. Tues-Fri 10-4; Sat 12-5; Sun 1-5.

Port Angeles
Pioneer Memorial Museum, Olympia National Park, 600 Park Ave. Natural history, Northwest coast history. Daily 8-5 (summer 8-10).

Seattle
Charles and Emma Frye Art Museum, 704 Terry Ave. Nineteenth Century American and European painting. Mon-Sat 10-5; Sun 12-6.

Henry Art Gallery, University of Washington campus. Nineteenth Century American and

French painting, graphics. Mon-Sat 8-5; Thurs 10-10; Sun 1-5.

Museum of History and Industry, 2161 E. Hamlin St. State history, ethnology; maritime and aviation exhibits. Tues-Fri 11-5; Sat 10-5; Sun 12-5.

Seattle Art Museum, Volunteer Park. Excellent collection of Oriental art, classical and medieval works. Tues-Sat 10-5; Thurs eves 7-10; Sun 12-5.

Spokane
Eastern Washington State Historical Society, W. 2316 1st Ave. Local history, geology, Indian crafts. Tues-Sat 10-5; Sun 2-5.

Tacoma
Washington State Historical Society, 315 N. Stadium

Way. State history, natural history. Tues-Sat 9-5; Sun 2-5.

Vancouver
Covington House, 39th and Main Sts. Oldest house in the state (1845). June-Aug: Tues, Thurs 10-4; closed Sept-May.

Fort Vancouver National Monument, Fort Vancouver Park. Historic fort, fur trade items. Daily 9-4:30.

White Swan
Fort Simcoe Historical State Park and Museum. Original and restored buildings of 1850s fort. Summer: Daily 10-5. Winter: Wed-Sun 10-5.

Yakima
Yakima Valley Museum, 2105 Tieton Dr. Local history; Indian artifacts. Wed-Fri 10-4; Sun 2-5.

Local festivals and events

California
Tournament of Roses, Pasadena. Float parade preceding the Rose Bowl football game. January 1.

Chinese New Year, San Francisco. Celebration and parade. Late January or February.

National Date Festival, Indio. Fair and pageant done in Arabian Nights style, including camel races. February.

Desert Circus, Palm Springs. Ice-skating and skiing events, floats, parades, rodeos, fashion shows. March.

Camellia Festival, Sacramento. Flower show, parade of floats, folk dancing. Early March.

National Orange Show, San Bernardino. Flower show, rodeo, 4-H livestock competition, industrial and agricultural exhibits. Mid-March.

Easter Sunrise Services, Mount Davidson, San Francisco.

California Relays, Modesto. Nationally famous track-and-field meet. May.

Jumping Frog Contest, Angels Camp. May.

Ojai Music Festival, Ojai. Serious concerts with well-known musicians. May.

Boulder Creek Days, Boulder Creek. Chuck-wagon breakfast

and square dancing. June.

Shakespearean Festival, San Diego. Performances of Shakespeare's plays in the Old Globe Theatre, Balboa Park. June—August.

The Days of Kit Carson, Jackson. Antique fire-engine and fast gun-drawing contests. Late June.

Solano County Fair, Vallejo. Horse racing, horse shows, rodeo, parades. Late June—early July.

California Rodeo, Salinas. Parades, square dancing, band concerts. July.

Sonoma County Fair, Santa Rosa. Rodeo, stock shows, fireworks, horse racing. July.

Festival of Arts, Laguna Beach. Works of local artists and craftsmen. July—August.

Nisei Week in Little Tokyo, Los Angeles. Parade, judo demonstrations, flower arranging, tea ceremony. August.

Old Spanish Days Fiesta, Santa Barbara. Parade of floats, marching bands, rodeo. August.

California State Fair and Exposition, Sacramento. Horse racing, agricultural and industrial displays. Late August.

Los Angeles County Fair, Pomona. Livestock and agricultural exhibits, horse races,

rodeo, circus. Late September.

National Raisin Festival, Dinuba. Parade, sports-car rally, football game, barbecue. October.

Chinese Double Ten Parade, San Francisco. Celebrates Chinese revolution of 1911. In Chinatown. October 10.

Death Valley Festival, Death Valley. Commemorates Gold Rush. Conducted tours, campfires, community sings, breakfast parties. November.

Oregon
Portland Rose Festival, Portland. Parades, art festival, ski tournament at Mount Hood. June.

Chief Joseph Days, Joseph. Rodeo, Indian dances. July.

World Championship Timber Carnival, Albany. Log chopping, tree climbing and other lumberjack contests. July.

Oregon Shakespearean Festival, Ashland. Performances of Shakespeare's plays; troubadours, pageants, picnics. Late July—mid-September.

Astoria Regatta and Fish Festival, Astoria. Parade, barbecue, boating competition. August.

Pendleton Round-Up, Pendleton. Rodeo and pageantry of Old West. Mid-September.

Pacific International Livestock Exposition and Trade Fair, Portland. Rodeos, horse shows, exhibits. October.

Washington
Puyallup Valley Daffodil Festival, Puyallup, Tacoma and Sumner. Flower show, float parade, athletic contests. April.

Washington State Apple Blossom Festival, Wenatchee. Parades, balls, horse show, art exhibit. Late April—early May.

Lilac Festival, Spokane. Parades, concert, exhibits, flower show, torchlight parade. May.

Lummi Stomish Water Festival, Bellingham. Indian water carnival with war-canoe races. Mid-June.

Capital Lake Fair, Olympia. Carnival, midway, naval-vessel tours, flower and art shows. July.

Seattle Seafair, Seattle. Boat races, horse races, parades, sports events, salmon-fishing derby. Late July—mid-August.

Annual Loggers' Jubilee, Morton. Contests between lumberjacks, testing their on-the-job skills. August.

Stampede and Suicide Race, Omak. Riding, roping, bulldogging. Horses and riders race off cliff and across Okanogan River. August.

Western Washington Fair, Puyallup. Rodeo, carnival, animal judging. September.

Frontier Days and Southeastern Washington Fair, Walla Walla. Livestock auction, horse racing, rodeo, concerts. Early September.

Wildlife of the Pacific States

A sampling of the natural life frequently found on the West Coast is given on these pages. In each case both the object's common name and its scientific name are given. For further information, specialized books on wildlife should be consulted by the reader; a number of useful reference works are listed on page 188.

Mammals

Black-tailed jack rabbit

Ranging throughout the grasslands of the Pacific States, the black-tailed jack rabbit *(Lepus californicus)* may attain a weight of eight pounds and grow to a length of more than two feet.

California ground squirrel

A gregarious beast, the California ground squirrel *(Citellus beecheyi)* lives in large hillside colonies. It measures as much as 20 inches from nose to tip of tail, and is found in meadow and brush country from southern California to southern Washington.

Townsend's chipmunk

A relatively large rodent, Townsend's chipmunk *(Eutamias townsendii)* may grow to be nearly a foot long, including the tail. Its habitat is the humid. thick forests of the Pacific Coast states.

Mountain beaver

This creature *(Aplodontia rufa)* lives in elaborate burrows in all three of the Pacific States. It weighs only two or three pounds, grows to a length of about 18 inches and has no discernible tail.

California gray whale

A migratory animal, the California gray whale *(Eschrichtius glaucus)* spends its winters along the coast of California and its summers in the arctic, often swimming in the shallow waters close to shore. A medium-sized whale, it attains a length of 45 feet and a weight of up to 20 tons.

Coyote

Among the most intelligent of animals, the coyote (whose Latin name, *Canis latrans,* means "barking dog") runs singly or with a mate. Its familiar yap and howl are heard throughout the deserts and brushlands of the Pacific States. Its weight ranges from 20 to 50 pounds and it grows to a length of four feet.

Black bear

The smallest of Western bears, the black bear *(Ursus americanus)* weighs from 200 to 600 pounds and stands about five feet at its tallest. It is found throughout the Western mountain ranges.

Sea otter

Pursued for its fur, the 25- to 75-pound sea otter *(Enhydra lutris)* nearly became extinct in the early 1900s. Now protected by law, it is increasing in numbers.

Mountain lion (puma)

Also known as a cougar or panther, the mountain lion *(Felis concolor)* generally inhabits heavily forested areas of the West Coast. Because of its penchant for livestock, the 200-pound, seven-foot-long cat is relentlessly hunted.

California sea lion

Playful and easily tamed, the California sea lion *(Zalophus californianus)* is common along the coastline. On land it can run almost as fast as a man. The larger males may attain a weight of 600 pounds and a length of eight feet.

Olympic elk

This animal *(Cervus canadensis roosevelti),* also called the Roosevelt elk, inhabits the semiopen coastal forests of northern California, Oregon and Washington. It measures up to five and a half feet at the shoulder and weighs as much as 700 pounds. Its antlers may have a spread of five feet.

Mule deer

Among the most abundant of game animals, the mule deer *(Odocoileus hemionus)* ranges the entire Coast. Members of the species grow to a height of three and one half feet at the shoulder and weigh up to 400 pounds.

Fish and reptiles

White sturgeon

The largest stream-ascending fish in North America, the white sturgeon *(Acipenser transmontanus)* weighs up to 200 pounds. It lives in coastal and inland waters.

Pacific halibut

A member of the flounder family, the Pacific halibut *(Hippoglossus stenolepis),* which can change its colors to match its surroundings, weighs up to 50 pounds.

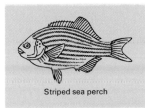

Striped sea perch

Abundant in bays, the striped sea perch *(Taeniotoca lateralis)* is found all along the West Coast.

Chinook salmon

Also called the king or Tyee salmon, the Chinook *(Oncorhynchus tschawtsha)* runs to approximately 20 pounds. Born in fresh water, the fish spends most of its adult life in the ocean, returning to its upstream birthplace to spawn.

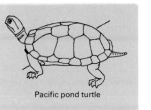

Grunion

Following a seasonal cycle, the grunion *(Leuresthes tenuis),* one of the few fish that spawns ashore, lays its eggs only after the first full or new moon in March. Its habitat is the southern California coast.

Pacific pond turtle

An aquatic reptile, the Pacific pond turtle *(Clemmys marmorata)* grows to a length of about six inches. The female leaves the water to lay eggs, which it buries in mud or sand or in open fields.

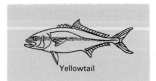

Dolly Varden trout

A fresh-water fish found from northern California to Alaska, the Dolly Varden trout *(Salvelinus malma)* attains a weight of 20 pounds and a length of 30 inches.

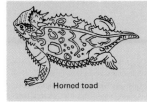

Yellowtail

A game fish in spite of its relatively small size, the 10-pound yellowtail *(Seriola dorsalis)* is most plentiful off the coast of southern California. Although the fore part of its body may vary in color, the rear is always yellow.

Horned toad

A three- to five-inch reptile whose young are born alive, the horned toad *(Phrynosoma coronatum)* is found in desert areas. The creature's skin is a mixture of yellow, gray, brown and black, the same coloration as its surroundings.

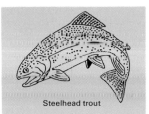

Steelhead trout

Born in fresh water, the steelhead trout *(Salmo gairdneri)* reaches maturity in the Pacific Ocean. There its rainbow of colors fades, brightening again when it returns to fresh water to breed.

Cabrilla (California kelp bass)

Ranging coastal waters from Mexico to San Francisco, the cabrilla *(Paralabrax clathratus)* rarely weighs more than five pounds, but is fished for commercially.

Pacific rattlesnake

The only poisonous snake indigenous to the Pacific States, the Pacific rattler *(Crotalus confluentus oreganus)* may be either brown, green or gray. It grows to an average length of four feet.

Birds

Sooty grouse

A forest dweller, the sooty grouse *(Dendragapus obscurus)* searches for food near streams and in the berry-rich borders between fields and woods. It ranges almost the entire West Coast, forsaking only the land east of the Cascade Range in Washington and Oregon.

Valley quail

The state bird of California, the valley quail *(Lophortyx californica vallicola)* nests on the ground, preferring the inland low-tree or shrub country where the air is dry. Its plumage is blue-gray and brown, dotted with white.

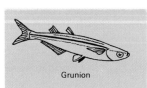

Pacific band-tailed pigeon

One of the largest members of its family, the Pacific band-tailed pigeon *(Columba fasciata fasciata)* is found along the West Coast from Washington to California.

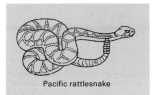

Pygmy owl

The "earless" pygmy owl *(Glaucidium gnoma)* lacks the distinctive head feathers that give other owls their catlike faces. Its habitat includes Arizona and New Mexico as well as the Pacific States.

Anna's hummingbird

Often miscalled the ruby-throated hummingbird, Anna's hummingbird *(Calypte anna)* is most commonly found in urban areas. Like most members of the hummingbird family, it can fly sideways and backward as well as forward.

Western meadow lark

The state bird of Oregon, the western meadow lark *(Sturnella neglecta)* has a distinctive black "V" on its yellow breast and patches of white on either side of its stubby tail. A permanent resident of all three of the Pacific States, it prefers to build its nest in the cover of the thick grass of meadows and fields.

Harris' woodpecker

An avian conservationist, Harris' woodpecker *(Dendrocopos villosus harrisi)* rids trees of wood borers, which are a staple of its diet. It nests in holes in dead trees in the moist coniferous forests of the Pacific Northwest.

Willow goldfinch

The state bird of Washington, the willow (or American) goldfinch *(Spinus tristis)* lives in open country from Canada to Mexican Baja California. Although it is unrelated to the canary, its coloration and song have given it the nickname of "wild canary."

Chestnut-backed chickadee

One of the few birds that nest in groves of eucalyptus trees, the chestnut-backed chickadee *(Parus rufescens)* prefers moist coastal forests, ranging from southern Alaska to central California.

Brown towhee

The brown towhee *(Pipilo fuscus)*, common in California, is often seen scratching for insects on lawns or in fields. Towhee mates, after parting to search for food, greet each other by bowing.

Hermit warbler

The hermit warbler *(Dendroica occidentalis)* summers in the mountains of California and the Northwest but winters in Mexico and Central America. It nests in thick foliage, keeping its bright-yellow head out of sight.

Nuttall's sparrow

A permanent resident of the San Francisco area, Nuttall's sparrow *(Zonotrichia leucophrys nuttalli)* is one of several varieties of white-crowned sparrow in the Western U.S. Its song varies so much from place to place that the bird is hard to identify by ear.

Flowers and trees

Oregon grape

The Oregon grape *(Berberis aquifolium)* is not a grape at all but a shrub of the barberry family. Its yellow blossoms have been designated Oregon's state flower. Its blue berries were once eaten by Indians, who also made dye from the plant's yellow inner bark.

California poppy

The state flower of California, the California poppy *(Eschscholzia californica)* puts forth its blossoms, which range in color from yellow to red-orange, from February to September. It is common along coastal bluffs and survives at altitudes of more than a mile.

Desert primrose

A shy night lover, the desert primrose *(Oenothera deltoides)* opens its white blossoms only at sundown in springtime. They remain spread during the dark hours, closing again in the morning. The plant is common to the Mojave and Colorado Deserts.

California rose bay

Despite its name, the California rose bay *(Rhododendron macrophyllum)* is the state flower of Washington. A form of rhododendron, with leathery, dark green leaves, it flourishes on the damp, shady lower slopes of the coastal mountains.

Scarlet gilia

A member of the phlox family, the scarlet gilia *(Ipomopsis aggregata arizonica)* is found in mountainous areas of southern California. Its blooms are bright red.

Baby blue-eyes

Common in California, the baby blue-eyes *(Nemophila menziesii)* puts forth its bright blue flowers from February to June.

Monkey flower

Blooms that seem to resemble simian faces are responsible for the name of this plant. The Latin name, *Mimulus lewisii,* honors explorer Meriwether Lewis.

Mountain pride

An inhabitant of the rocky upper slopes of California's mountains, the mountain pride *(Penstemon newberryi)* bears blossoms ranging from pink to rosy purple throughout the summer months.

Douglas fir

The Douglas fir *(Pseudotsuga menziesii),* designated as the state tree of Oregon, reaches a height of more than 200 feet and may live to be 1,000 years old.

Western hemlock

A northern evergreen (it even grows in Alaska), the western hemlock *(Tsuga heterophylla)* is the state tree of Washington.

Sugar pine

The largest American pine tree, the sugar pine *(Pinus lambertiana),* which grows on mountainsides from southern California to Oregon, can grow to 200 feet.

Sitka spruce

A tree that loves dampness, the Sitka spruce *(Picea sitchensis)* is common to the coastal valleys of the Northwest. It thrives in the sodden Olympic rain forest, where 200-foot specimens with trunks 10 feet thick are not unusual.

Coast redwood

The 300-foot-tall coast redwood *(Sequoia sempervirens)* is the king of trees. Its longevity is attested by its Latin name, which means "living forever."

Sierra juniper

The rugged Sierra juniper *(Juniperus occidentalis)* seems to seek out high, windy plains and rocky hills throughout the eastern sections of the Pacific States.

Port Orford cedar

The tough and close-grained wood of the Port Orford cedar *(Chamaecyparis lawsoniana)* is used to make things that last, such as ships and cedar chests.

Desert palm

The only palm tree native to the U.S. West, the desert palm *(Washingtonia filifera)* lives in the deserts and the rocky canyons of southern California.

Statistical information

Principal rivers (lengths in miles)

Columbia (British Columbia, Washington, Oregon). 1,214.

Sacramento (California): 382.

San Joaquin (California): 317.

John Day (Oregon): 281.

Klamath (Oregon, California): 263.

Deschutes (Oregon): 240.

Rogue (Oregon): 200.

Willamette (Oregon): 183.

Major ranges and mountain peaks

Blue Mountains: Averaging 6,500 feet in height, these jumbled mountains stretch 250 miles in southeast Washington and northern Oregon.

California Coast Ranges: Most of these are between 2,000 feet and 4,000 feet high and parallel the northern and central California coast for 400 miles.

Cascade Range: This string of high mountains, many dormant volcanoes, runs 700 miles south from British Columbia to northern California. Some of the higher peaks: Mount Rainier (Washington), 14,410 feet; Mount Shasta (California), 14,162 feet; Mount Adams (Washington), 12,307 feet; Mount Hood (Oregon), 11,245 feet.

Klamath Mountains: These stretch 250 miles from Oregon to California. Highest peak: Mount

Eddy (California), 9,038 feet.

Olympic Mountains: The principal peak in this western Washington range is Mount Olympus, 7,965 feet.

San Bernardino Mountains: These stretch 55 miles along the eastern edge of the Los Angeles Basin. Highest peak: Mount San Gorgonio, 11,502 feet.

San Gabriel Mountains: A 60-mile-long chain that forms the northeast boundary of the Los Angeles Basin. Principal peak: Mount San Antonio, 10,080 feet.

San Jacinto Mountains: A group of mountains that form the southeastern edge of the Los Angeles Basin. Highest peak: Mount San Jacinto, 10,805 feet.

Sierra Nevada: This 400-mile-long California range has a number of mountains exceeding 14,000 feet. Highest peak: Mount Whitney, 14,495 feet.

Bodies of water

Salt

Puget Sound (Washington): 561 square miles; maximum depth, 900 feet.

San Francisco Bay (California): 430 square miles; maximum depth, 100 feet.

Salton Sea (California): 360 square miles; maximum depth, 46 feet.

Fresh

Lake Tahoe (California and Nevada): 192 square miles; maximum depth, 1,685 feet.

Upper Klamath Lake (Oregon): 141 square miles; maximum depth, 40 feet.

Roosevelt Lake (Washington, man-made): 123 square miles; maximum depth, 375 feet.

Land areas

California: 158,693 square miles.

Oregon: 96,981 square miles.

Washington: 68,192 square miles.

Great Central Valley (California): 450 miles long; 20-50 miles wide.

Mojave Desert (California): 240 miles long; 90-160 miles wide.

Deschutes-Umatilla Plateau (Oregon): 200 miles long; up to 100 miles wide.

High Lava Plains (Oregon): 175 miles long; 25-75 miles wide.

Willamette Valley (Oregon): 125 miles long; 20-30 miles wide.

Colorado Desert (California): Highly irregular in shape; covers 3,000 square miles.

Population

By state (preliminary estimate of U.S. Census, 1965): California: 18,602,000. Washington: 2,990,000. Oregon: 1,899,000.

By city (region's 10 largest cities are listed, followed by their population and rank in the U.S. according to the 1960 Census):

Los Angeles	2,479,015	3
San Francisco	740,316	12
San Diego	573,224	18
Seattle	557,087	19
Portland	372,676	32
Oakland	367,548	33
Long Beach	344,168	35
San Jose	204,196	57
Sacramento	191,667	63
Spokane	181,608	68

Important engineering feats

San Luis Dam and Oroville Dam (California): When completed these will be third- and fourth-largest dams in the world after Fort Peck Dam in Montana and the Oahe Dam in South Dakota.

Golden Gate Bridge (California): Second-longest suspension span in the U.S. (after New York's Verrazano-Narrows Bridge), stretching 4,200 feet.

Central Valley Project (California): 500-mile complex of dams, reservoirs, canals, and so forth; one of most extensive water-conservation systems in the world.

Some U.S. superlatives

Largest county in U.S.: San Bernardino (California).

Lowest elevation in U.S.: Death Valley (California), 282 feet below sea level.

Highest spot in continental U.S.: Mount Whitney (California), 14,495 feet.

Rainiest region in continental U.S.: Western slopes of Olympic Mountains.

Deepest lake: Crater Lake (Oregon), 1,932 feet.

Largest state park: Anza-Borrego Desert (California).

Highest temperature recorded: 134° in 1913 in California.

Pronunciation glossary

Angelenos (an jell EEN os). Natives of Los Angeles.
Anza-Borrego (AHN za - bore RAY go). California desert state park.
Bodega Bay (bo DAY ga). Bay on the Pacific, north of San Francisco.
Bogachiel River (BO ga cheel). River in Washington.
Bonneville Dam (BONN a vil). Dam on Columbia River.
Carmel (car MEL). California coastal resort city.
Chaparral (SHAP a RAL). Desert shrubs.

Coquille (ko KEEL). City in Oregon.
Dungeness (DUN jen ess). Large edible crab of the Pacific Coast.
Grand Coulee Dam (COOL ee). Dam on Columbia River in Washington.
Haraszthy, Agoston (HA ross tee). Father of modern California wine industry.
Hoquiam (HO kwi um). River and city in Washington.
Juan de Fuca Strait (WAN da FEW ka). Strait between Vancouver Island and the Olympic Peninsula.

La Jolla (la HOY a). A residential section of San Diego.
Malheur (ma LURE). County and lake in Oregon.
Marin (mah RIN). California county.
Mojave (mo HAH vee). Desert, river and village in California.
Mount Rainier (ray NEAR). Mountain in Washington.
Ojai (O high). Valley and resort city in southern California.
Pico Rivera (PEE ko rih VEER a). City in Los Angeles County.
Point Reyes (RAYS). Point on California coast.
Puyallup (pew AL up). River and city in Washington.
San Joaquin (wah KEEN). County,

river, city and valley in California.
San Jose (sana ZAY). City near San Francisco.
San Juan Capistrano (WAHN cap iss TRAH no). California mission and village.
San Luis Obispo (LOO es o BISS po). California city, county and mission.
San Mateo (mah TAY o). County and city in California.
San Ysidro (ih SEE dro). Mountains in southern California.
Sequim (SKWIM). Washington city.
Snoqualmie (sno KWALM ee). Washington river, city and ski area.
Sonoma (so NO mah). County

and city in California.
Spokane (spoh CAN). River, county and city in Washington.
Tacoma (ta KO mah). City in Washington.
Tehachapi (teh HATCH a pee). City and mountain range in southern California.
The Dalles (DALS). Oregon city and Columbia River dam.
Tule (TOO lee). Kind of Central Valley fog.
Umatilla (YOU ma TIL la). County, city and river in Oregon.
Vallejo (vah LAY o). California city.
Wenatchee (win NATCH ee). Washington city and river.
Weyerhaeuser Company (WARE houzer). Largest forest-products manufacturer in the world.
Willamette (will LAM ett). River and valley in Oregon.
Yakima (YAK i mah). City, valley, county and river in Washington.
Yosemite (yoh SEM ih tee). National park located in California.

Credits and acknowledgments

Maps for front and back end papers and pages 174 through 179 by Diversified Map Corporation, St. Louis. Maps on pages 10, 13, 16, 34, 35, 63, 108, 109, 142 by Lothar Roth.

The sources for the illustrations that appear in this book are shown below. Credits for the pictures from left to right are separated by commas, from top to bottom by dashes.
Cover—Fred Lyon from Rapho Guillumette.
Front end papers—Drawings by Richard Boland.
Chapter 1: 8—Ted Streshinsky. 12—Drawings by Ben Goode. 14, 15—Drawings by Otto van Eersel. 16—Chart by Lothar Roth. 17—Drawings by Jim Flora. 19—J. R. Eyerman. 20, 21—J. R. Eyerman—drawings by Joseph Stonehill. 22, 23—Farrell Grehan, drawing by Otto van Eersel—Ted Spiegel. 24, 25—Drawing by Joseph Stonehill; J. R. Eyerman. 26, 27—Farrell Grehan, Joe Munroe from Photo Researchers—drawing by Otto van Eersel. 28, 29—Drawing by Joseph Stonehill—Jon Brenneis. 30—J. R. Eyerman—drawing by Otto van Eersel. 31—Marvin E. Newman.
Chapter 2: 32, 33—Oregon Historical Society. 36—From *San Francisco's Golden Era* by Lucius Beebe and Charles Clegg, Howell-North Books, courtesy of The Bancroft Library. 37—Drawing by Ben Goode. 38—Courtesy of The Bancroft Library. 39—Culver Pictures. 40—Courtesy of The Bancroft Library. 41—A. Curtis Collection courtesy University of Washington Library, courtesy of The New-York Historical Society. 42—Courtesy The Henry E. Huntington Library and Art Gallery. 43—Historical Collection Title Insurance and Trust Company, San Diego. 45—Wells Fargo Bank History Room. 46—Weyerhaeuser Company Photo from Oregon Historical Society. 47—Oregon Historical Society except top right University of Washington Audio-Visual Services. 48, 49—Courtesy of The Bancroft Library except right center Ted Streshinsky. 50, 51—Raymond R. Stuart—Alvin Wycoff, Historical Collections Security First National Bank. 52, 53—Historical Collection Title Insurance and Trust Company, San Diego except bottom left Historical Collections Security First National Bank.
Chapter 3: 54—Otto Hagel. 56—Drawing by Ben Goode. 57—Courtesy of Sierra Club. 58—Southern Pacific Company. 59—Map by David Greenspan. 60—Drawing by Donald Spaulding, drawing by Ben Goode. 61—Drawing by Otto van Eersel. 62—Drawing by Ben Goode. 65—Spence Air Photos. 66, 67—Garry Winogrand, Marvin E. Newman. 68 through 71—Marvin E. Newman. 72 through 75—Farrell Grehan. 76, 77—Joern Gerdts. 78, 79—Ray Atkeson.
Chapter 4: 80—Joern Gerdts. 82—Left: Bradley and Rulofson, original in possession of Mrs. Eleanora Dowdall, Oakland, California, courtesy Wine Institute; right: Muybridge of San Francisco courtesy Wine Institute. 83—Courtesy of The Bancroft Library. 84, 85—Drawings by Otto van Eersel; recipes from *Helen Brown's West Coast Cook Book* copyright 1952 by Helen Evans Brown by permission of Little, Brown and Company. 87—Drawing by Otto van Eersel. 89—Drawing by Ben Goode. 91—Joern Gerdts. 92, 93—Joern Gerdts except top right Garry Winogrand. 94, 95—Frank Denman, Marvin E. Newman. 96—Fred Lyon from Rapho Guillumette. 97—Marvin E. Newman. 98, 99—Harry Chase for the Los Angeles *Times*—Fred Lyon from Rapho Guillumette.
Chapter 5: 100 J. R. Eyerman. 102—Drawing by Otto van Eersel. 103—Culver Pictures—Brown Brothers. 104—Drawing by Lowell Hess. 105—Culver Pictures (3), NBC. 106, 107—Drawings by Donald Spaulding. 111—Jon Brenneis. 112 through 115—Joern Gerdts. 116, 117—Joe Munroe except bottom right J. R. Eyerman. 118, 119—Jon Brenneis.
Chapter 6: 120, 121—The Los Angeles *Times*. 123—Harris and Ewing. 124—Brown Brothers. 125—Horace Bristol. 129—Ted Spiegel. 130, 131—J. R. Eyerman. 132, 133—Marvin E. Newman, Ted Streshinsky—Ted Spiegel. 134—Joern Gerdts except bottom right Edmund Y. Lee. 135—Frank Denman, Joern Gerdts. 136, 137—Marvin E. Newman—Bill Ray.
Chapter 7: 138—Jon Brenneis. 140—Courtesy Museum of History and Industry, Seattle. 141—Drawing by Otto van Eersel. 147—Ted Streshinsky. 148—J. R. Eyerman—Systems Development Corporation. 149—Marvin E. Newman. 150, 151—Marvin E. Newman, Jon Brenneis—Joern Gerdts. 152, 153—Marvin E. Newman.
Chapter 8: 154—Fred Lyon from Rapho Guillumette. 156—Howard Staples. 157—Ernie Stout. 158—Left: Brown Brothers—courtesy Wells Fargo. 159—Robert Hegge—Joyce Wilson, Bill Eppridge. 161—N. R. Farbman. "Tor House" *(Cawdor and Other Poems),* Robinson Jeffers, copyright 1928 and renewed 1956 by Robinson Jeffers, reprinted from *The Selected Poetry of Robinson Jeffers* by permission of Random House, Inc. 163—Joern Gerdts. 164, 165—Ray Atkeson. 166, 167—Joern Gerdts. 168, 169—Farrell Grehan, Joern Gerdts. 170 through 173—Farrell Grehan. 182 through 185—Drawings by Rudolf Freund.
Back end papers—Drawings by Richard Boland.

The editors of this book wish to thank the following persons and institutions for their assistance: Larry Booth, Union Title Insurance and Trust Company of San Diego; Kenneth S. Buchanan, California Division of Highways, Sacramento; The Center for the Study of Democratic Institutions; The City of Portland; Commercial Fisheries, U.S. Department of the Interior; Bernard Conal, The Salk Institute for Biological Studies, San Diego; John Holley, The Portland Urban League; Sidney Horenstein, Department of Fossil Invertebrates, The American Museum of Natural History, New York; Dr. Richard M. Klein, The New York Botanical Garden; Robert D. Monroe, Chief, Special Collections Division, University of Washington Library; Museum of History and Industry, Seattle; The Oregon Historical Society; The Oregon Planning and Development Commission; Oregon State Board of Education; Oregon State Board of Higher Education; The Oregon State Highway Department, Travel Information Division; The Oregon State Marine Board; Oregon State University; Robert Pennington, Bureau of Indian Affairs, Washington, D.C.; The Portland Art Museum; Portland School District; Portland State College; Reed College; Seattle Chamber of Commerce; Seattle-First National Bank Economic Research Department; The Space and Information Systems Division of North American Aviation; Faye Stewart, Bohemia Lumber Company, Eugene; John Barr Tompkins, Head, Public Services, The Bancroft Library, University of California, Berkeley; University of Oregon; Washington State Department of Commerce and Economic Development; Washington State Historical Society, Tacoma.

Bibliography

General and historical reading

Avery, Mary W., *Washington: A History of the Evergreen State.* University of Washington Press, 1965.

Brooks, James E., ed., *The Oregon Almanac and Book of Facts, 1961-1962.* Binfords & Mort, 1961.

Caughey, John Walton, *California,* 2nd ed. Prentice-Hall, 1953.

Cleland, Robert Glass, *From Wilderness to Empire: A History of California.* Alfred A. Knopf, 1962.

Conrad, Barnaby, *San Francisco: A Profile with Pictures.* Viking Press, 1959.

Dasmann, Raymond F., *The Destruction of California.* Macmillan, 1965.

Duffus, Robert Luther, *Queen Calafia's Island.* W. W. Norton, 1965.

Federal Writers' Project, *California: A Guide to the Golden State.* Hastings House, 1939. *Oregon: End of the Trail.* Binfords & Mort, 1940. *Washington: A Guide to the Evergreen State.* Binfords & Mort, 1940.

Freeman, Otis W., and Howard H. Martin, eds., *The Pacific Northwest,* 2nd ed. John Wiley & Sons, 1954.

Highsmith, Richard M., Jr., ed., *Atlas of the Pacific Northwest,* 3rd ed. Oregon State University Press, 1962.

Holbrook, Stewart H., *Far Corner: A Personal View of the Pacific Northwest.* Macmillan, 1952.

Holbrook, Stewart H., Nard Jones and Roderick Haig-Brown, *The Pacific Northwest.* Doubleday, 1963.

Jeffers, Robinson, *Not Man Apart: Photographs of the Big Sur Coast.* Sierra Club, 1965.

Lantis, David W., Rodney Steiner and Arthur E. Karinen, *California: Land of Contrast.* Wadsworth Publishing Company, 1963.

Lavender, David, *Land of Giants.* Doubleday, 1958.

McWilliams, Carey, *California: The Great Exception.* A. A. Wyn, 1949. *Southern California Country: An Island on the Land.* Duell, Sloan & Pearce, 1946.

Morgan, Murray, *The Northwest Corner.* Viking Press, 1962. *Skid Road: An Informal Portrait of Seattle,* rev. ed. Viking Press, 1960.

Morgan, Neil, *Westward Tilt: The American West Today.* Random House, 1963.

Nadeau, Remi, *California: The New Society.* David McKay, 1963. *Los Angeles: From Mission to Modern City.* Longmans, Green, 1960.

Pomeroy, Earl, *The Pacific Slope.* Alfred A. Knopf, 1965.

Stone, Adolf, and others, eds., *California Information Almanac.* Doubleday, 1965.

Warren, Sidney, *Farthest Frontier: The Pacific Northwest.* Macmillan, 1949.

Winther, Oscar Osburn, *Great Northwest: A History.* Alfred A. Knopf, 1947.

Special topics

Andrews, Ralph W., *Glory Days of Logging.* Superior Publishing Company, 1956.

Baer, Kurt, *Architecture of the California Missions.* University of California Press, 1958.

Beebe, Lucius, and Charles Clegg, *San Francisco's Golden Era.* Howell-North Books, 1960.

Brown, Helen Evans, *Helen Brown's West Coast Cook Book.* Little, Brown, 1952.

Dana, Richard Henry, *Two Years Before the Mast.* Modern Library, 1965.

Harris, Joseph P., *California Politics,* 3rd ed. Stanford University Press, 1965.

Holbrook, Stewart H., *The Columbia.* Rinehart, 1956.

Hyde, Philip, and François Leydet, *The Last Redwoods.* Sierra Club, 1963.

Hyink, Bernard L., Seyom Brown and Ernest W. Thacker, *Politics and Government in California.* Thomas Y. Crowell, 1959.

Jonas, Frank H., *Western Politics.* University of Utah Press, 1961.

Lavender, David, *Westward Vision: The Story of the Oregon Trail.* McGraw-Hill, 1963.

Lewis, Oscar, *The Big Four.* Alfred A. Knopf, 1938.

McCoy, Esther, *Five California Architects.* Reinhold Publishing Corporation, 1960.

McCulloch, Walter F., *Woods Words.* The Oregon Historical Society, 1958.

McWilliams, Carey, *Factories in the Field.* Little, Brown, 1939. *Ill Fares the Land.* Little, Brown, 1942.

Melville, John, *Guide to California Wines,* 2nd ed. Nourse Publishing Company, 1960.

Mowry, George E., *The California Progressives.* University of California Press, 1951.

Nadeau, Remi, *City Makers.* Trans-Anglo Books, 1965. *Ghost Towns and Mining Camps of California.* Ward Ritchie Press, 1965. *The Water Seekers.* Doubleday, 1950.

Paul, Rodman Wilson, *Mining Frontiers of the Far West.* Holt, Rinehart and Winston, 1963.

Pomeroy, Earl, *In Search of the Golden West: The Tourist in Western America.* Alfred A. Knopf, 1957.

Pourade, Richard F., *The Explorers* (1960). *The Glory Years* (1964). *Gold in the Sun* (1965). *The Silver Dons* (1963). *Time of the Bells* (1961). All published by The Union-Tribune Publishing Company.

Ramsaye, Terry, *Million and One Nights: A History of the Motion Picture,* 2 vols. Simon & Schuster, 1926.

Shotwell, Louisa R., *The Harvesters.* Doubleday, 1961.

Stewart, George R., *The California Trail.* McGraw-Hill, 1962.

Thomas, Lately, *The Vanishing Evangelist.* Viking Press, 1959.

Twain, Mark, *Roughing It.* Harper, 1965.

Wolfe, Mrs. Linnie, *Son of the Wilderness; The Life of John Muir.* Alfred A. Knopf, 1945.

Nature and wildlife

Armstrong, Margaret Neilson, *Field Book of Western Wild Flowers.* G. P. Putnam's Sons, 1915.

Cahalane, Victor H., *Mammals of North America.* Macmillan, 1947.

Cannon, Ray, *How to Fish the Pacific Coast,* 2nd ed. Lane Book Company, 1964.

La Gorce, John Oliver, ed., *The Book of Fishes.* National Geographic Society, 1961.

Munz, Philip A., *California Desert Wildflowers* (1962). *A California Flora* (1963). *California Spring Wildflowers* (1961). *Shore Wildflowers of California, Oregon and Washington* (1964). All published by the University of California Press.

Peattie, Donald Culross, *A Natural History of Western Trees.* Houghton Mifflin, 1953.

Peterson, Roger Tory, *A Field Guide to Western Birds,* 2nd ed. Houghton Mifflin, 1961.

Pough, Richard H., *Audubon Western Bird Guide.* Doubleday, 1957.

Wild Animals of North America. National Geographic Society, 1960.

Guidebooks

Benét, James W., *A Guide to San Francisco and the Bay Region.* Random House, 1963.

Bryant, Beth, *The Dollar-Wise Guide to California.* Frommer-Pasmanpier Publishing Corporation, 1966.

Caen, Herb, *Herb Caen's San Francisco.* Doubleday, 1965.

California and the West. Mobil Oil Company, 1966.

Discovery Trips in Washington. Lane Publishing Company, 1956.

Fodor, Eugene, Robert C. Fisher and Barnett D. Laschever, eds., *The Pacific States.* David McKay, 1966.

Friedman, Ralph, *Oregon for the Curious.* Pars Publishing Company, 1966.

Gold Rush Country, 2nd ed. Sunset Books and *Sunset* Magazine, eds. Lane Books, 1965.

The Great Plains and the Northwest. Mobil Oil Company, 1966. (Includes Washington and Oregon.)

Hepburn, Andrew, *Complete Guide to Northern California* and *Complete Guide to Southern California.* Doubleday, 1962.

Kirk, Ruth, *Exploring Death Valley.* Stanford University Press, 1965. *Exploring the Olympic Peninsula.* University of Washington Press, 1964.

Lucia, Ellis, *Don't Call It Ore-E-gawn.* Overland West Press, 1965. *The Sea Wall.* Overland West Press, 1966.

Murphy, Bill, *The Dolphin Guide to Los Angeles and Southern California.* Doubleday, 1962.

Northern California. Sunset Books and *Sunset* Magazine, eds. Lane Book Company, 1964.

Oregon—Cool Green Vacationland. Oregon State Highway Department, Travel Information Division, 1966. (Revised every year or so.)

Robinson, John, and Alfred Calais, *California State Parks.* Lane Books, 1966.

Southern California. Sunset Books and *Sunset* Magazine, eds. Lane Book Company, 1964.

Welcome to Oregon. Oregon Welcome Committee, published yearly.

Yeager, Dorr, *National Parks in California.* Lane Books, 1965.

Zim, Herbert S., and Natt N. Dodge, *The Pacific Northwest, a Guide to the Evergreen Playground.* Golden Press, 1962.

Index

Numerals in italics indicate an illustration of the subject mentioned.

×

PRODUCTION STAFF FOR TIME INCORPORATED
John L. Hallenbeck (Vice President and Director of Production),
Robert E. Foy, Caroline Ferri and Robert E. Fraser
Text photocomposed under the direction of Albert J. Dunn and Arthur J. Dunn